T0305050

The Political Economy of Aerospace Industries

To my wife: Winifred and our family:
Adam and Rachel, Oliver and Imogen Hartley
Professor Lucy Hartley
Cecilia and Martyn, Matthew Jacob, Kathryn Olivia and
Sophie Elizabeth Ellis
And to my parents: Walter and Ivy Hartley

The Political Economy of Aerospace Industries

A Key Driver of Growth and International Competitiveness?

Keith Hartley

Emeritus Professor, Economics Department, University of York, UK

Edward Elgar

Cheltenham, UK • Northampton, MA, USA

Published by
Edward Elgar Publishing Limited
The Lypiatts
15 Lansdown Road
Cheltenham
Glos GL50 2JA
UK

Edward Elgar Publishing, Inc.
William Pratt House
9 Dewey Court
Northampton
Massachusetts 01060
USA

A catalogue record for this book
is available from the British Library

Library of Congress Control Number: 2014947034

This book is available electronically in the ElgarOnline.com
Economics Subject Collection, E-ISBN 978 1 78254 496 8

ISBN 978 1 78254 495 1

Typeset by Columns Design XML Ltd, Reading
Printed and bound in Great Britain by T.J. International Ltd, Padstow

Contents

Preface

This book is a personal story reflecting my life-time interest, fascination with, and enthusiasm for, aviation. It started with my birth in Leeds in July 1940 and the beginning of the Battle of Britain. Leeds was fortunate to avoid heavy bombing in World War II. My recollection of the war years was one of black-out curtains, sirens and air raid shelters. I also recollect what must have been D-Day with large numbers of aircraft flying over Leeds at night en route to France. My father served for a period in the RAF and he started my enthusiasm for aircraft when he gave me a black-painted model of a Spitfire. He furthered my interest by taking me to a Battle of Britain air display at RAF Church Fenton near Leeds. This was my first encounter with World War II fighters and bombers and the new Meteor and Vampire jets. Later, I returned the favour by taking my three children to regular Battle of Britain air displays at RAF Finningley, near Doncaster, which was a Vulcan bomber base.

At secondary school in Leeds, my interest in aviation continued and was reflected in diary entries. Looking back, I see that I was obsessed with recording crashes of RAF aircraft and whether the pilot ejected successfully. At the time, little did I realise that the high rate of Meteor aircraft crashes partly reflected technical problems with the aircraft and the limitations of its ejector seat. The 1950s was also a 'golden age' for British aviation and the UK aircraft industry. This was the period of major change and innovation in military and civil aircraft. Military types included the Hunter, Swift, Canberra and the V-bombers. Civil types included the Comet, Brabazon, Princess, Viscount and Britannia. It was also my first experience of flight. The annual family holiday was taken at Blackpool and I saved sufficient to afford a pleasure flight in a de Havilland Rapide which flew around Blackpool Tower.

My first encounter with economics came when I arrived at Leeds Central High School. My form master persuaded me to study A-level economics with an example based on inheritance tax. The example interested me but I was not persuaded by his argument that the state had a right to all an individual's assets on death. By the time I left school, I had decided on a career in teaching and spent a year as an unqualified teacher at Hunslet Carr School. Later, I studied economics at Hull

University. On graduation in 1962, I was offered an opportunity to study for a PhD: when asked whether I had a topic for my PhD, I had no hesitation in selecting 'The Economics of the Aircraft Industry'. Shortly after starting my PhD, I met my future wife and we were married in 1966.

My PhD allowed me to visit many of the UK's major aircraft firms and meet some of the industry's leading personnel, including Sir Sydney Camm of Hurricane fame. Little did I realise it at the time, but the early 1960s marked the end of many famous company names. The names of Avro, Blackburn, Bristol, de Havilland, Gloster, Handley Page, Hawker, Supermarine and Vickers all disappeared in a major industry re-structuring.

After leaving Hull, I arrived in 1964 at the new University of York where initially I taught Industry and Labour economics. These were exciting times under the academic leadership of Alan Peacock and Jack Wiseman with Lord Eric James as Vice Chancellor. Coincidentally, the Heslington site of the new University had previously been the head-quarters of 4 Group RAF Bomber Command. Work on my PhD continued and I had opted to submit my thesis by publication so avoiding the tedium of writing a lengthy thesis which would never be read by anyone! I accumulated sufficient publications for the PhD which was awarded in 1974: Professor Berrick Saul was my external who later became Vice Chancellor at York. Interestingly, at the start of my PhD, one famous economics professor originally forecast that there 'was not a PhD in the aircraft industry' – further proof that economists are not very good at forecasting! The year 1974 also added to my academic experience when, together with the family, I spent a semester at the University of Illinois.

In 1977, I was awarded a NATO Research Fellowship which allowed me to visit the major US defence establishments. These included the Pentagon, McDonnell at St Louis, General Dynamics at Fort Worth, Lockheed, Northrop and Rand in Los Angeles and Boeing in Seattle. A family trip to the USA made it even more enjoyable. The Fellowship also allowed me to visit European aircraft firms and led to a book on NATO Arms Co-operation (Allen and Unwin, 1982).

By this time, my academic career had shifted towards the relatively new discipline of defence economics. In 1982, I was appointed the first Director of York's new Institute for Research in the Social Sciences (IRISS), and in 1990 I created a Centre for Defence Economics which remained in existence until my retirement from the University in 2007.

Why write a book on the Political Economy of Aerospace Industries? This book reflects my interest in the industry and in the view that the economic analysis of the industry is important to understanding its performance and role in an economy. The emphasis on Political Economy reflects the continuing influence of government on the fortunes of the industry.

Many have contributed to this book, some unknowingly. These include Ron Barback, Derek Braddon, Neil Davies, Keith Hayward, David Kirkpatrick, David Moden, Alan Peacock, Philip Pugh, Todd Sandler, Ron Smith, Graham Trevarthen, Stuart Wilson and Jack Wiseman. My graduate students have helped and they include Ian Jackson, Peter MacDonald, Ben Solomon, Selami Sezgin, Tony Turner and Vasilis Zervos. Further contributions resulted from my role as adviser and consultant to such organisations as the UN, EC, EDA, UK House of Commons Defence Committee, UK Ministry of Defence, QinetiQ, DSTL and other UK Government Departments. I learned much from being Chair of the Finance Group of the Aerospace and Innovation Growth Team. I have also been consultant to a number of aerospace companies including BAe, Lockheed Martin and Saab.

The greatest contribution has been from my wife who has had to tolerate my obsession with aviation (as well as fly fishing and football). Wisely, none of my children chose to become economists. My son was attracted by the legal profession and both daughters have become academics: Lucy as a Professor of English at the University of Michigan, USA and Cecilia as Senior Lecturer in Human Resources at Manchester Metropolitan University. I remain under the illusion that the best is yet to come!

Keith Hartley
April 2014

1.   Introduction: an important industry?

INTRODUCTION

Aerospace is often claimed to be an important industry. Is it important and, if so, why is it important? This chapter addresses these questions. It considers whether there is an economic case for government support for the industry or whether some of the arguments are spurious and examples of special pleading. The task of the economist is to identify myths and special pleading and subject them to rigorous and critical economic analysis and assess the supporting evidence. The chapter presents a preliminary review of these arguments, many of which are addressed in more detail elsewhere in the book. A starting point requires a definition of the industry.

DEFINITION

Government official statistics provide definitions of the industry. For example, the official European statistics (Eurostat) defines the industry as the manufacture of air and spacecraft and related machinery. This classification includes the manufacture of aeroplanes for the transport of goods or passengers for use by defence forces, for sport or for other purposes; the manufacture of helicopters, gliders and dirigibles. It also includes the manufacture of parts and accessories for the aircraft of this class, including engines and their parts, major assemblies (e.g. fuselages; wings; doors; landing gear; fuel tanks), propellers and helicopter rotor blades as well as aircraft seats. Further sectors included are the manufacture of ground flying trainers, spacecraft, launch vehicles, satellites and intercontinental ballistic missiles (ICBM) as well as the overhaul and conversion of aircraft or aircraft engines. There are some interesting exclusions comprising the manufacture of telecommunications equipment for satellites, the manufacture of aircraft instruments, the manufacture of air navigation systems and the manufacture of lighting equipment for aircraft (Eurostat, 2012). The advantage of using official statistics is their international comparability. Also, the official statistics comprise information from enterprises whose main activity is the manufacture of aerospace products. Other data from industry trade associations use different definitions of the industry, including firms whose main activity might be classified elsewhere.

For our purposes, a broad working definition will be used. The aerospace industry comprises all those firms involved in the research, design, development, manufacture, repair, maintenance and disposal of aerospace products. These comprise military and civil aircraft and helicopters, business and pleasure aircraft, missiles and space systems. Also included are the firms supplying parts and components including aero-engines, avionics equipment, flight simulators for pilot training and ejector seats for combat aircraft. Examples include combat aircraft such as the American F-22 Raptor and the F-35 Lightning; Airbus A380 and Boeing 747 airliners; Bombardier and Embraer regional jet airliners; Tomahawk cruise missiles; space rockets such as the European Ariane series and their associated satellites. Elsewhere, firms specialise in supplying aero-engines (e.g. Pratt and Whitney (USA) and Rolls-Royce (UK)); major parts and components (e.g. wings; centre fuselages); seats and interiors for civil aircraft; undercarriages; and avionics equipment, including cockpit displays.

Major firms or prime contractors and systems integrators focus on R&D and manufacture. These activities embrace the design, development and testing of an aircraft, helicopter or missile followed by its manufacture. Manufacture comprises final assembly using a range of parts and components which are 'bought-in' from specialist suppliers of equipment (e.g. aero-engines) and a range of other suppliers and subcontractors which form an extensive supply chain. Similar organisational arrangements apply for the manufacture of motor cars which focus on final assembly.

Aerospace involves two alternative forms of industrial organisation. First, the typical industrial model in the USA, Europe and other nations involves prime contracting firms undertaking R&D, design, testing and manufacture. Second, some industries separate design and production. In such cases, there are separate and specialist design bureaux which specialise in the design, development and testing of an aircraft with separate and specialist production plants manufacturing the final design (e.g. Russia). These alternative forms of industrial organisation represent efforts to minimise ˎa firm's transaction costs (the costs of doing business). The first organisational form has operated in competitive markets and its survival and predominance suggests its superiority. Next, questions arise about whether aerospace is an important industry and why?

AN ECONOMIC CASE FOR THE AEROSPACE INDUSTRY: MARKET FAILURE

In private enterprise economies, any industry and its component firms survive on the basis of market forces and the profitability of its firms. But left to themselves, private markets might fail to work properly in the sense of failing to fully and accurately reflect consumer preferences. Such market failure provides a basis for government intervention to 'correct' these failures and 'improve' the operation of markets. Is there evidence of market failure in aerospace markets?

Private markets can fail to work properly because of market imperfections and externalities. Imperfections comprise monopoly, oligopoly (a few large firms in the industry) and entry barriers preventing new entrants to a market. Externalities arise where there are benefits and costs which are 'external' to the market. Examples of harmful externalities include pollution, aircraft noise and traffic congestion. Beneficial externalities include research and development which provides benefits to other firms in an economy (spill-overs) and flood controls which provide protection to large numbers of households. Some of the medical treatment for injured soldiers in Afghanistan and Iraq has been beneficial to the treatment of civilian personnel (a beneficial spin-off). Aerospace examples include the application of military aircraft technology to civil aircraft, including the jet engine, radar and composite materials.

A special class of externality comprises 'public goods' which have some distinctive features. These goods differ from normal private goods in that they are characterised by 'non-rivalry' and 'non-excludability'. Non-rivalry means that one person's consumption of the good is not at the expense of anyone else's consumption of the good and non-excludability means that once the good is provided, people cannot be excluded from its consumption. Defence is a classic example of a public good. For example, once a city is provided with air defence, one person's consumption of its air defence is not at the expense of anyone else's consumption; nor can any citizen be excluded from the protection provided by air defence (Hartley, 2011; Tisdell and Hartley, 2008).

Where market failures are identified, government has to decide whether to intervene to 'correct' such failures. At the outset, government needs to determine whether the market failure is substantial enough to merit state intervention, bearing in mind that intervention is not costless. The form and extent of state intervention will depend on the precise causes of market failure. For example, where market failure results from monopoly and entry barriers, state intervention to correct such failure can embrace a variety of policy solutions. The options include competition policy (e.g. breaking-up a monopoly or allowing foreign imports) to state regulation (e.g. of prices or profitability) or state ownership of a private monopoly. Some of these policy measures have been applied to the world's aerospace industries. For example, a number of the world's aerospace industries (e.g. USSR; Indonesia) have been acquired by government whilst others have remained under private ownership (e.g. USA; UK) although state ownership has not always been the solution to a private monopoly problem. In some cases, state ownership has reflected a government desire to control wartime profitability to prevent excessive wartime profits being earned by aircraft firms. Or, state ownership has reflected a government desire to own and control an important and military strategic industry. This suggests that there are other arguments for an aerospace industry. One view is that aerospace is a strategic industry.

A STRATEGIC INDUSTRY?

Aerospace is a strategic industry in two senses. First, it is a militarily strategic industry and second, it is an economically strategic industry.

In the *military–strategic* sphere, aerospace products are a central component of national defence. Combat aircraft, helicopters and missiles provide both defensive and offensive air power. Transport aircraft and helicopters provide a capability to carry military personnel and equipment to various locations in the world. The question then arises as to whether a nation relies on the import of foreign aerospace equipment or whether it depends on a domestic source of supply. A national aerospace industry has a variety of military and economic benefits. These include independence, security of supply and re-supply, especially during conflicts, together with the ability to obtain equipment specially designed for the operational requirements of national air forces and the ability to be an informed buyer. There are also claimed to be additional wider economic benefits in the form of jobs, exports and advanced technology, including technical spin-offs to the civilian economy. These benefits need to be assessed critically identifying special pleading, myths, emotion and nationalism. When evaluating these claims, economists need to consider their underlying economic logic and the available empirical evidence. A key economic question concerns the alternative use value of resources. Would the resources allocated to the aerospace industry make a greater contribution to jobs, exports and technology and ultimately national economic welfare if they were used elsewhere in the economy?

Aerospace is also viewed as an *economically strategic industry*. These are industries which are regarded as more important than others in national economic development (i.e. leading industries). Examples include civil aircraft, biotechnology, computers and telecommunications (Siebert, 1997). These economically strategic industries have some distinguishing economic characteristics. They are high technology and R&D-intensive industries with technical spill-overs (external economies) to the rest of the economy; they are decreasing cost industries reflecting scale and learning economies; and they are imperfectly competitive based on national monopolies and oligopolies (a few large firms) associated with monopoly profits. These economically strategic industries are seen as dominant in international trade: hence, the argument that governments should intervene and support such industries with the aim of enabling a nation to obtain a share of the monopoly profits.

Identifying a potential role for governments in strategic industries creates two problems. First, there is a belief that strategic industries can be identified by governments and that government should promote them. The alternative view is that properly functioning private markets will identify strategic and leading industries unless there are significant market failures. Here, possible market failures include externalities (e.g. technical spill-overs) and the short-termism of capital markets 'failing' to fund strategic industries (an argument which needs to be evaluated critically: see Chapter 10). Second, national governments will become involved in strategic rivalry supporting their 'national champions'. For example, in civil aircraft markets, foreign governments may retaliate by creating a new and rival civil aircraft industry (e.g. the original formation of Airbus). Governments will also become involved in international trade disputes (e.g. over subsidies). The outcome is highly complex 'game-playing' involving governments and their 'national champions'. It is not clear that the eventual outcomes are efficiency improving: they might well reduce efficiency through distorting international trade!

Civil aircraft is regarded as an economically strategic industry which has received extensive government support. European examples of state support include the funding of R&D, the finance of uneconomically low production rates, the provision of long-term financial support, state ownership, the provision of favourable export finance and government requirements for national airlines to buy from the national aerospace industry. Overall, governments have changed market outcomes in the civil aircraft market.

Airbus is a good example of the new international trade theory based on imperfect competition, advanced technology, scale economies and the notion that governments can create a nation's comparative advantage. The entry of Airbus into the world jet airliner market prevented Boeing achieving a monopoly position enabling Airbus to obtain a share of these monopoly profits. But, the creation of Airbus as a world class firm was not costless (especially for French and German taxpayers). There also arose a policy conflict between the USA and Europe with Boeing accusing Europe of government subsidies for Airbus and Europe accusing Boeing of receiving support from military procurement. These conflicting claims were assessed by the World Trade Organization (WTO) which found that Boeing had received between $3–4 billion of US subsidies and that Airbus had received $18 billion in subsidies; but it did not view European repayable launch investment as a subsidy.

Airbus is also an example of the traditional *infant industry* case for state support of new entrants. Where there are significant scale and learning economies, it is often argued that state support is needed to allow an infant industry to enter a market and get started. It is claimed that new entrants need to be supported until they become as efficient as established foreign rivals and are able to compete on equal terms with their more experienced foreign suppliers. State support can take the form of subsidies, tariffs or preferential purchasing. Of course, the challenge for policy-makers is to determine when the infant industry has become established and is able to compete with its foreign rivals by achieving scale and learning economies. Otherwise, state support becomes permanent and enables a protected industry to remain sheltered and less efficient than its foreign rivals.

AN IMPORTANT INDUSTRY?

The analysis outlined above focusing on market failure and strategic industries provides a basis for answering the question of whether aerospace is an important industry and why it is important.

Typically, there are claims and assertions that aerospace is an important industry. Such claims focus on aerospace as a high technology and leading industry for national economic development. They point to its importance for jobs, technology, spill-overs and exports. Some of these arguments fail to address the opportunity cost question concerning the alternative use value of a nation's resources allocated to the aerospace industry. Most economic activity creates jobs so to claim that aerospace is important for jobs is not a convincing argument in this form: it has to be shown that aerospace is better in the employment field than alternative uses of resources. Typically, there are other industries which provide more jobs (e.g. construction): the number of jobs provided by an industry will be determined by its production technology and by wage rates. Labour-intensive production and low wage rates will create larger numbers of jobs. However, the jobs argument for aerospace might be better presented in terms of the quality of jobs (skills) rather than their quantity (numbers). Here, it has to be shown that aerospace provides proportionately more high quality jobs than many other industries. Examples include scientists, technologists, engineers and skilled production workers, including the numbers and proportions with university degrees (see Chapters 8 and 10; Hayward, 1994).

A similar analysis applies to the technology, spin-off and export arguments for the importance of the aerospace industry. Other industries also contribute technology and exports benefits (e.g. computers; motor cars; pharmaceuticals). Does aerospace make a greater contribution than these other industries? This becomes an empirical question. The technology argument merits further exploration. Certainly, aerospace involves advanced technology and it has demonstrated its ability to solve complex technical problems reflected in the creation and development of manned flight embracing combat aircraft, civil jet airliners, space exploration and manned landings on the Moon. The new technology has been reflected in new products which have emerged over the past 110 years (see Chapter 2). Technical progress has been both evolutionary and revolutionary (e.g. the jet engine was a revolutionary technical change).

In addition to new advanced technology, some of the technology has 'spilled-over' into other fields. Examples of such 'spill-overs' include the application of military jet engines to civil aircraft; the development of radar; the application of composite materials from military aircraft to civil airliners; the application of aircraft technology to racing cars and motor cars; the use of jet engines on ships; and the application of helicopter rotor blade technology to wind turbines. Whilst these and other examples are impressive, they fail to address the key issue of the market value of such 'spill-overs'. A listing of *numbers* of examples is no substitute for *market values*. Nor does the technology spill-over argument identify the technology transfer mechanisms. These might include staff mobility and the relationship between prime contractors and their supply chains. Nevertheless, technical spill-overs form a beneficial externality and hence a possible source of market failure.

It is possible that aerospace markets are more likely to be characterised by major market failures than other industries and markets. Two possibilities come to mind. First, technology and R&D markets are likely to fail due to the costs of establishing property rights in valuable ideas and their 'spin-offs'. Second, governments dominate the demand side of defence markets and such dominance is a likely source of market failure (see Chapters 3, 6 and 9).

The strategic industry analysis provides a basis for identifying the importance of the aerospace industry. Aerospace is distinctive in that it is strategic in both the military and economic spheres. It is an important supplier of aerospace equipment for a nation's armed forces and it is an R&D-intensive and decreasing cost industry with beneficial externalities through technical spill-overs. Governments are central to understanding the industry, its behaviour and performance.

CONCLUSION

Aerospace is an advanced, high technology industry with an impressive record of innovation and developing and producing high technology products. These are believed to be a source of international competitiveness for modern developed economies which need to re-allocate resources from labour-intensive industries to areas where they are more competitive (creating new comparative advantages in international trade).

Aerospace is one such area which provides an R&D-intensive and knowledge-intensive manufacturing industry capable of providing the next generation of highly paid jobs able to sustain and raise living standards. The rhetoric is impressive and the identification of aerospace as a strategic industry provides a basis for identifying the industry as important. But these are only qualitative arguments which are valuable as a first stage in identifying aerospace as an important industry. However, a convincing case showing the industry's importance requires supporting empirical evidence. How does aerospace compare with other industries and the alternative use of its resources? Understanding of the issues requires a brief overview of the history of the industry's development and its current position in the world market.

REFERENCES

Eurostat (2012). *Statistical Database: Classifications, NACE 30.3*, European Commission, Luxembourg.

Hartley, K. (2011). *The Economics of Defence Policy*, Routledge, London.
Hayward, K. (1994). *The World Aerospace Industry*, Duckworth and RUSI, London.
Siebert, H. (ed.) (1997). *Towards a New Global Framework for High-Technology Competition*, JCB Mohr, Tubingen.
Tisdell, C. and Hartley, K. (2008). *Microeconomic Policy: A New Perspective*, Edward Elgar Publishing, Cheltenham, UK and Northampton, MA, USA.

2. An overview of the world aerospace industry

INTRODUCTION

This chapter provides a broad overview of the world's aerospace industries. It comprises two parts. Part I presents a brief history. This shows the industry's transformation from an infant industry to an advanced technology industry. It shows a sector shifting from a private venture industry to one with substantial dependence on government funding.

Part II presents some descriptive statistics of the world's major aerospace industries and firms. These provide some of the 'stylised facts' to be analysed in this book.

I. A BRIEF HISTORY

THE EARLY PIONEERS AND WORLD WAR I (1903–1918)

The aircraft industry is an example of the emergence and rapid development of a new industry. It did not exist in 1900, but by 2014 it had transformed from an aircraft industry to an aerospace industry. Governments have been central to the development and transformation of the industry through their military demands and state funding of both military and civil aircraft.

In private enterprise economies, an industry emerges and develops on the basis of private markets which comprise privately-owned companies and large numbers of private consumers (purchasers). These market arrangements can be classified as private provision and private finance. A contrasting situation comprises state-owned firms and government as a major customer representing state provision and state finance. This distinction between private and state provision and finance provides a basis for understanding the development of the aircraft and aerospace industry.

The early pioneers of manned flight were mostly privately financed inventors using patents and prizes from competitions to capture any return on their investments. Other sources of funds included the pioneer's main business activity, mail business, sponsorship by wealthy individuals, air shows and passenger rides. The Wright Brothers (USA) made the first manned and powered flight in December 1903 when they flew 120 feet in 12 seconds. The first British manned powered flight was made in 1908 (by Cody, a US citizen, followed by Brabazon in 1909 as the first British citizen).

Early aviation pioneers included Bleriot (France), Fokker and Zeppelin (Germany), Boeing, Glenn Curtiss and Glenn Martin (USA) and Sikorsky (Russia; later USA). British pioneers included Farman, Dunne, de Havilland, A.V. Roe, Handley Page, the Short Brothers and Thomas Sopwith. Some of the pioneers established their own named aircraft companies. Interestingly, hardly any of the early pioneering aircraft companies have survived (exceptions include Boeing and Sikorsky).

The early period was also dominated by the 'race to be first.' For example, the race for the first flight; the race for the longest flight; the race for the first to fly across the English channel (Bleriot, France, 1909); the first non-stop transatlantic flight (Alcock and Brown, UK, 1919); the first solo non-stop transatlantic flight (Lindbergh, USA, 1927); the first flight across the Pacific (Kingsford-Smith and Ulm, Australia, 1928); the first woman to fly across the Atlantic (Amelia Earhart, USA, 1932); and another woman, Amy Johnson (UK), achieved a series of long-distance records in the 1930s.

Even at this early stage, some inventors were sponsored by military customers (e.g. the Wright Brothers in 1908 obtained a contract from the US Army). In 1912, the UK created a state-owned enterprise in the form of the Royal Aircraft Factory which became involved in the early British aircraft design and production for the Royal Flying Corps.[1] This Factory was originally planned to design experimental aircraft and was not meant to be involved in aircraft production. However, it became responsible for the design of most British military aircraft in the early years of World War I. The Factory produced some of its aircraft designs but the majority of production was undertaken by private British companies, some of

---

[1] The Royal Aircraft Factory was originally the Army Balloon Factory which became interested in powered flight. Its aircraft were designated with an 'E' to identify them as Experimental (e.g. SE is Scout Experimental; BE is Bleriot Experimental; FE is Farman Experimental; and RE is Reconnaissance Experimental). In 1918, its name was changed to the Royal Aircraft Establishment (RAE) to avoid confusion with the newly formed Royal Air Force (RAF).

which had not previously built aircraft. Critics of the Royal Aircraft Factory claimed that private British aircraft companies offered superior designs and that the Factory should not be involved in production work.

World War I led to a major increase in demand for both quantity and quality of aircraft for military roles. For example, in 1914, each of France, Germany and Great Britain operated 113 to 232 front line combat aircraft; by 1918, these numbers had increased to 2,390 for Germany, 3,300 for Britain and 4,511 aircraft for France (Angelucci, 1981, p29). Fighter aircraft speeds increased from around 60mph in 1914 to over 120mph in 1918 and aircraft were also capable of flying further and higher. The aircraft industries in the major combatant nations, namely, Austria, France, Germany, Italy, Russia, Great Britain and later the USA, expanded rapidly (see Table 2.1). There were ever-increasing demands for speed and power which resulted in major technical advances. For example, there were new aircraft construction techniques, new materials, new and more powerful engines and new aircraft designs each with implications for the skilled labour requirements for the new aircraft industry (Angelucci, 1981). World War I also led to the development of specialist bomber aircraft, especially in the UK (e.g. Handley Page four engine heavy bomber capable of flying from England to Berlin: APR, 2013).

Table 2.1   Aircraft production during World War I

Country	Total aircraft production
France	67,987
Great Britain	58,144
Germany	48,537
Italy	20,000
USA	15,000

Note: Five leading nations only.

Source: Angelucci, 1981, p29.

THE INTER-WAR PERIOD (1918–1938)

Peace, following the end of World War I, resulted in the cancellations of military orders and little prospect of any new significant military orders (there were large stocks of surplus aircraft). This led to exits from the industry and some mergers and efforts to diversify into other industries and markets. Diversification examples included entry into motor vehicles, metal working and even turning hangars into pig-rearing and mushroom-growing (Hayward, 1989, p12). Some pioneer firms attempted to enter the civil aviation market.

Civil aircraft was an infant industry in the 1920s and early 1930s but during this period civil aviation became the determining factor in the development of the aeroplane (Angelucci, 1981, p109). In the USA, the growing demand for air travel with its large domestic market supported a number of rival firms and airlines with manufacturers achieving profitability levels which encouraged investment in large-scale production. The USA was one of the few countries where air travel could compete with rail travel over long distances. Competition between US airlines promoted innovation in civil aircraft. One result was the introduction of the Douglas DC-3 (1936 which was a derivative of the DC-2) which revolutionised air transport with its speed and range.[2]

In contrast to the USA, the UK government supported civil aircraft development through subsidising the new Imperial Airways which was required to use British aircraft; but it was also tasked with developing air routes to the Empire which represented a UK-specific requirement. Generally, governments supported civil aircraft development through the award of government airmail contracts.

During this period, it became apparent that the newly developing aircraft industry was closely dependent on government. Aircraft had emerged as a new weapon of major military importance; military demands determined the industry's future; and the industry was important to a nation's military capability. Eventually, governments realised that policies were needed to support both military and civil aircraft developments. Air Ministries recognised the need to retain design capacity: they provided sufficient work to support major design teams by allocating contracts to selected firms with the aim of promoting competition in design. To increase their prospects of survival, firms tended to specialise in specific product areas such as fighters, flying boats, bombers and naval aircraft. In the UK, this led to companies such as Bristol, Gloster and Hawker specialising in fighter aircraft, to Blackburn and Shorts specialising in flying boats and Fairey specialising in bombers.

In the UK, government support for a select group of firms (the ring or family) was criticised for its 'featherbedding' of the industry; for its

---

[2] Over 600 civil versions were produced and some 13,000 units of the military version (known as the Dakota).

continued support of existing firms rather than promoting rationalisation to create larger firms able to compete with the US rivals; for its failure to promote mass production; and for the Air Ministry's conservatism in design requirements (e.g. Empire policing in the 1920s did not require high speed aircraft).

Government policy towards the aircraft industry revealed the classic choice between private and state enterprise. Some nations such as the UK and USA preferred to retain private ownership of aircraft industries, using state finance and state funding to support the industry. In the 1920s, the Italian aircraft industry survived by exporting aircraft (e.g. to Russia). France adopted an alternative policy when in the 1930s, it nationalised its airframe sector creating six state-owned aircraft manufacturing companies. The aim of French nationalisation was to reorganise the aircraft industry and improve its efficiency and total output. In the event, the companies failed to rationalise and modernise and the focus remained on allocating production amongst different companies with small-scale orders and a failure to achieve economies of scale. Similarly, the Soviet Union created a state-owned aircraft industry which emphasised the setting of world records and focused on heavy bombers. It also created a different organisation with specialist design bureau and separate and specialist production plants.

The Japanese aircraft industry in this period comprised firms such as Kawasaki Aircraft Industries, Mitsubishi (manufacturers of the Zero fighter for the navy) and Nakajima aircraft companies. The army and navy each had its own aviation design establishments (e.g. the Japanese Naval Air Arsenal designed and manufactured its own aircraft). By 1938, the aircraft industry was dominated by the armed forces in the form of the army and navy each exerting tight control over the industry.

Innovation in this period was promoted by competitive air races (the Schneider Trophy in Europe and the National Air Races in North America), long-distance competitions and the pursuit of world records. Competitions led to technical progress in the development of aircraft, engines and materials. The search for higher speeds led to the development of new engines and new airframes. Monoplanes replaced biplanes; aluminium replaced wood and fabric; propellers became more efficient; undercarriages were retractable; and cockpits were enclosed. Innovation was also promoted by imaginative designers willing to launch advanced types of aircraft mostly as private ventures (Hurricane; Spitfire; Wellington in the UK).[3]

---

[3] Some industry rationalisation occurred in the inter-war years. In the UK in 1935, Hawker acquired Armstrong Siddeley, A.V. Roe and Gloster to form the

During this period, Germany showed how its aircraft industry survived the penalties of World War I. The Armistice of 1918 and the Treaty of Versailles in 1919 required the complete abolition of the German air force and a ban on the design, financing and construction of any military aircraft. Only private industry was allowed to build aircraft which had to be civil aircraft of limited size and performance. The German aircraft industry responded to these constraints by developing civil aviation and operating overseas subsidiaries. Initially, Germany's new air force – the Luftwaffe – was developed secretly through pilot training schemes in the Soviet Union, by using gliders to train pilots and by using bombers and military transports as commercial aircraft.

The structure and organisation of the aircraft industry was also changing as firms sought new methods of economising on their trans-action costs (the costs of doing business). There were incentives to horizontal and vertical integration. Firms merged or acquired rivals (horizontal integration); some aircraft firms became involved in aero-engine work and others merged with airlines (vertical integration). For example, the American Boeing company created its own airline and then merged with Pratt and Whitney to form the United Aircraft and Trans-portation Corporation (UATC in 1929). UATC owned the Boeing Air-plane Company of Seattle, the Chance Vought Corporation, Hamilton (a propeller company) and Pratt and Whitney (aero-engines). It later acquired Sikorsky and more airlines. However, in 1934 following the Air Mail scandal, the US government concluded that such vertically owned firms were anti-competitive and new anti-trust laws prevented airframe or engine companies from owning airlines. As a result, UATC was broken into three companies, namely, Boeing, the United Aircraft Corporation (now United Technologies Corporation) and United Airlines.[4]

In Europe, rearmament in the 1930s resulted in increased military demands for both quantity and quality leading to further innovation in military aviation and increases in speed. Additional production capacity was financed by the state, with expansion achieved through a combin-ation of capacity increases by existing firms, by including second tier

---

Hawker Siddeley Group. Vickers bought Supermarine (1928) and de Havilland was closely associated with Airspeed which it bought in 1940. Few UK airframe firms were vertically integrated with an aero-engine division (e.g. Bristol; de Havilland).

[4] Boeing acquired the manufacturing interests west of the Mississippi; United Aircraft Corporation acquired the manufacturing interests east of the Mississippi (Pratt and Whitney; Vought, Hamilton Standard, Sikorsky) and United Airlines acquired the airline business of the group.

firms and by contracting-out aircraft and engine production to other suitable manufacturing firms, mainly in the motor industry. The UK further increased production capacity through its shadow factory scheme. However, the UK industry and the Air Ministry had much to learn about large-scale production. War demands for volume production exposed the limitations of the UK aircraft industry with its tradition of small-scale production based on a chief designer with no experience of 'designing for production.' In contrast, by the end of the War, US firms resembled the major car plants with moving production lines and larger research, design and development organisations (Barnett, 1986).

WORLD WAR II (1939–1945)

World War II led to major technical changes affecting aviation. There were new demands for combat aircraft capable of flying faster and further. In 1939, typical speeds of fighter aircraft were some 350mph; by 1945, piston-engine fighters were achieving speeds of some 450mph. However, World War II led to the development of the jet engine which represented a revolutionary change in technology affecting both military and civil aviation. Germany became the first nation in the world to build and operate in service a jet fighter aircraft (Messerschmitt, Me262, April, 1944: speed of 520mph) and the first rocket-powered aircraft (Me163, 1944: speed of 596mph). The UK followed with the Gloster Meteor jet fighter, which first flew in 1943 and entered service in July 1944 (speed of 415mph). It was powered by the Whittle jet engine which was later developed by Rolls-Royce into the Derwent series (Hayward, 1989, p35).

There were other revolutionary technical changes comprising the atomic bomb (delivered by a B-29 aircraft) and the first generation of cruise missiles and ballistic rockets (German V-1 and V-2 weapons). New heavy bombers emerged in both the UK and USA leading to strategic bombing; radar and electronic warfare were developed; and the aircraft carrier and carrier-borne aircraft became major weapons of naval warfare.

Mass production was the industrial feature of World War II. For example, German production of its Me109 fighter aircraft totalled some 35,000 units whilst the British Supermarine Spitfire total output was some 20,350 units. Such large-scale output enabled aircraft plants to achieve economies of scale and learning and to replicate the mass production methods of the motor car industry. Table 2.2 shows examples of military aircraft production by nation in 1944 (the year of peak production). Compared with World War I, the 1944 output of US military aircraft considerably exceeded the total output of aircraft produced by France throughout World War I.

Table 2.2   Military aircraft production in 1944

Nation	Military aircraft output, 1944
USA	96,318
Germany	39,800
USSR	30,000
UK	29,220
Japan	28,180

Source: Angelucci (1981).

World War II also resulted in international specialisation of aircraft production. During the War, the UK concentrated on the production of fighters and bombers and relied on the USA for the supply of military transports: a decision which gave the US aircraft industry a competitive advantage in civil airliners at the end of the War. For example, the total output of the US C-47 military transport (Douglas Dakota) reached some 13,000 units. By 1942, however, the UK was considering the task of re-creating its civil aircraft industry. The Brabazon Committee recommended various civil aircraft projects, including bomber conversions, to enable the UK to re-enter the civil aircraft market. The War also destroyed Britain's European and Japanese rivals in aircraft markets.

POST-WAR ADJUSTMENT AND THE COLD WAR (1945–1990)

The end of the War led to the inevitable reduction in demand for military aircraft. But, unlike 1918, the emergence of the jet engine created demands for new generations of jet-powered combat aircraft and nations whose aircraft industries had been destroyed in the War aimed to re-enter the industry. There were further differences from 1918 which stimulated the demand for aircraft. Civil aviation markets developed, especially for jet airliners; and the Cold War led to an arms race between the USA and

USSR.[5] By 1950, the Korean War led to increased demands for military aircraft and a period of rearmament.

Technical change affected the economics of the industry. Aircraft were becoming technically more complex, taking longer to develop and becoming costlier, leading to fewer being bought so making it more difficult to achieve volume production in small domestic markets (e.g. Europe). Solutions to rising unit costs comprised international collaboration and importing foreign aircraft (e.g. from the USA).

Technical change also meant substitution effects. Missiles, cruise missiles and rockets replaced fighter and bomber aircraft. Missiles became more complex requiring more electronics inputs on combat aircraft. This led to a rapid development of the defence electronics industry with some aircraft firms acquiring defence electronics businesses (another example of vertical integration). Speeds continued to increase with military aircraft achieving supersonic flight (1947) with the Lockheed SR-71 Blackbird reaching speeds of 2,193mph (first flight: 1964). Civil jet airliners also achieved supersonic flight with the Russian Tupolev Tu-144 (first flight: 1968 and 16 built) and the Anglo-French Concorde (first flight: 1969 and 20 built).

After World War II, the jet airliner emerged as a competitive form of transport which revolutionised commercial air travel. The British de Havilland Comet first flew in 1949 and entered service in 1952; but it suffered from technical failures which meant that the de Havilland company faced possible bankruptcy. The company was rescued by the government through cash assistance and an RAF order for modified Comets as military transports. In the meantime, the American Boeing company developed a rival jet airliner, namely, the Boeing 707 which first flew in 1954 and entered service in 1958. Other US aircraft companies also entered the jet airliner market with the Douglas DC-8 (first flight: 1958) and the Convair 880/990 series. At this stage, the world large civil jet airliner market was dominated by a small number of large US aircraft firms (forming an oligopoly) using private finance to fund new civil aircraft projects.

There was, however, a new entrant to the civil aircraft industry, namely, Airbus Industrie. This was formed in 1970 and was originally a European collaboration jointly owned by the French and German governments and Hawker Siddeley Aviation (UK). Airbus Industrie was formed to compete with the US civil aircraft firms with collaboration providing

---

[5]   In the UK, firms were also retained in the aircraft industry through the award of government development contracts, some of which were for duplicate projects to provide 'insurance' against project failures.

the basis for longer production runs allowing European firms to compete with their US rivals.[6] Interestingly, Airbus as a new entrant had, by the late 1990s, achieved a duopoly position with Boeing in the world market for large civil jet airliners. Inevitably, controversy arose over the financing of Airbus airliners. Boeing accused Airbus of receiving illegal subsidies in the form of launch aid. In reply, Airbus accused Boeing of also receiving subsidies through military and research contracts and state and local subsidies. The WTO reviewed these claims and in 2012 confirmed the illegality of subsidies to Boeing and the legality of repayable loans (launch aid) to Airbus.

Economic factors affected the size, structure and organisation of aircraft industries. Rising unit costs of military aircraft resulted in industrial re-structuring reflected in mergers, capacity reductions and exits from the industry. Rising costs led to smaller production numbers. The increasing importance of electronics led to some aircraft firms acquiring electronics companies (vertical integration) and the search for new markets led some companies to diversify into other markets (e.g. motor cars; civil aircraft; helicopters). Supersonic flight required new materials and new labour skills for design, development and production. Similarly, the search for weight reductions for both military and civil aircraft led to the use of new materials and a requirement for new labour skills. Rising unit costs of combat aircraft also led to the development of multi-role combat aircraft capable of performing a variety of military roles so replacing several aircraft.

At the end of World War II the UK aircraft industry was a world-leader based on its pioneering work on the jet engine; but its position was overtaken by the USA and USSR aircraft industries (Hamilton-Paterson, 2010). After 1945, the US industry introduced a variety of technical innovations reflected in its jet fighter and bomber aircraft and in its experimental programmes. The USSR aircraft industry demonstrated similar technical innovation in its combat aircraft which achieved large-scale production of a small number of types (e.g. MiG fighter aircraft).

The industries of continental Europe were destroyed during World War II. Germany, Italy and Japan are also examples of the challenges of re-entering the industry. The French aircraft industry rapidly re-emerged,

---

[6] Originally, Airbus was a joint France, Germany and UK government initiative but the UK government withdrew and was replaced by Hawker Siddeley Aviation. CASA (Spain) joined in 1971 and the shares of each partner were France (Aerospatiale) and Germany (Deutsche Airbus), 37.9%, Hawker Siddeley, 20% and Spain (CASA), 4.2%. Originally, Airbus was a subsidiary of EADS but in 2014, EADS was renamed as Airbus.

based on a mix of state and private industry with the privately owned firm of Dassault dominating the industry and world military aircraft export markets (e.g. Mirage jet fighters). West Germany re-entered the aircraft industry through the licensed production of US combat aircraft (F-104), followed by involvement in European collaborative projects (e.g. Alpha Jet; Tornado; Typhoon). Italy re-entered the industry through the national development of jet trainers and light combat aircraft, licensed production of US aircraft and helicopters, and involvement in joint ventures with Brazil, Europe and the USA (AMX; Tornado; Typhoon; Agusta-Bell). Japan's re-entry was based on extensive licensed production of a range of US military aircraft and helicopters with some limited development of domestic combat aircraft (Mitsubishi F-1) and a regional jet airliner. Japan also achieved a space programme involving launchers and satellites. Sweden is interesting in its maintenance of an independent and privately owned aircraft industry which through the Saab company developed a range of advanced combat aircraft (Saab Lansen; Draken; Viggen; Gripen) and regional airliners. Saab was also involved in the motor car industry (the aircraft-car industry model of diversification) but the car business was purchased by General Motors in 2000 and the motor car company was declared bankrupt in 2011.

Economic factors also affected government policy on the aircraft industry, especially in Europe where international collaboration became an important element of policy. From 1959, there were joint European ventures involving France, Italy, West Germany and the UK with later additions of Spain, the Netherlands and other nations. European collaborations involved military aircraft, helicopters and missiles, civil aircraft (e.g. Concorde; Airbus) and space systems. These collaborations ranged from bilateral to multilateral (e.g. 4-nation Typhoon; seven-nation A400M airlifter; 20 member states of European Space Agency (ESA): Hartley, 2012).

Technical progress was taking the industry into space and the emergence of the aerospace industry. The Cold War led to a space race between the USA and USSR both seeking supremacy in space exploration (1957–1975). The rockets used in this race were based on the World War II German rocket programme (von Braun). The space race was reflected in satellites, humans in space and the manned Moon landings (USA: 1969). The Saturn V rocket used for the moon landings was manufactured by Boeing, North American and Douglas and the lunar module was built by Grumman (contract awarded in 1962). The USA introduced its Space Shuttle as a reusable launch system which operated between 1981 and 2011. Originally, its prime contractor was the North American company which was acquired by Rockwell and then by Boeing. Its main engine was supplied by Pratt and Whitney Rocketdyne.

THE PERIOD 1990 ONWARDS

The end of the Cold War arms race was followed by a disarmament race as nations sought a 'peace dividend' (UNIDIR, 1993). But wars were not ended and from 1990 there were conflicts in the Middle East, the former Yugoslavia and Kosovo and examples of ethnic cleansing. A new threat emerged in the form of terrorism and the terrorist attacks on the USA of 9/11 where jet airliners were used as 'flying bombs' to destroy the World Trade Center and parts of the Pentagon. Wars in Afghanistan and Iraq maintained the demand for military aircraft, helicopters and missiles. There was a new emphasis on cruise missiles and the emergence of unmanned air systems, including aerial drones, all of which raises questions about the long-term future of manned combat aircraft.

The end of the Cold War space race was followed by international co-operation in space in the form of the International Space Station (ISS, launched in 1998). This is an international joint venture between Russia, the USA, Canada, Japan and 11 members of the ESA. However, the end of the Cold War led to a dramatic decline in the former USSR aerospace industry. During the Cold War, the Soviet aviation industry produced annually some 100 civil aircraft; by 2005, the entire Russian civil aircraft industry was producing 10 aircraft per year with some firms producing as few as one to two civil aircraft per year: their products were not competitive compared with Western jet airliners (EC, 2009). In 2006, the Russian aerospace industry was consolidated into three state-owned joint stock companies. The United Aircraft Corporation (UAC) is responsible for all military and civil fixed wing aircraft; Russian Helicopters assumed responsibility for military and civil helicopters; and United Engines specialises in aero-engines.

The world civil jet airliner market was dominated by duopoly with Airbus and Boeing comprising the market for large jet airliners and Bombardier (Canada) and Embraer (Brazil) were forming the market for regional jet airliners. But the market is changing. The search for larger jet airliners led to the introduction of the world's largest passenger airliner, namely, the Airbus A380 (up to 853 passengers) which created a rival to Boeing's monopoly of the large aircraft market (Boeing 747). New rivals were also entering the regional jet airliner market, including China and Japan.

Indeed, a number of nations emerged as new entrants to the aerospace industry. China is developing its military aircraft, missile, civil aircraft and space capabilities (e.g. Comac AR121 regional jet airliner and C919 narrowbody airliner). In 1999, China split its Aviation Industries of China (AVIC) which formed the entire national aviation industry into two groups, namely, China Aviation Industry Corporation 1 (AVIC 1) and China Aviation Industry Corporation 2 (AVIC 2). The creation of two groups was designed to promote competition although this move occurred when the world trend was towards greater industrial consolidation. Later, in 2008, AVIC 1 and AVIC 2 were merged into China Aviation Industry Corporation (AVIC) which comprised 10 business segments and 200 subsidiaries.

Japan is developing a regional jet airliner (Mitsubishi Regional Jet) and Russia is re-entering the world civil aircraft market with its regional jet airliner (Sukhoi Superjet 100). India and South Korea are also developing national aerospace industries. India has already acquired a major space capability including launchers and satellites. South Korea has developed capabilities in military trainer aircraft, helicopters and space satellites and is seeking to enter the regional turboprop airliner market.

The current world aerospace industry is radically different from the industries of 1914 and 1940. Technology has changed and there are fewer but larger firms. The future aerospace company of 2065 will be different from today's firms (see Chapter 14). The next section provides a statistical overview of the current size of the world's aerospace industries and its major firms.

II. A STATISTICAL OVERVIEW

Ideally, a statistical overview of the world's aerospace industries requires data on output, employment, productivity, exports and imports for both industries and firms (see Chapter 7). However, there are inevitable data problems. Such data are not always available for all nations with an aerospace industry; definitions of the industry vary (e.g. the inclusion of suppliers; inclusion of security and 'other products'); there are different definitions of key variables (e.g. employment; exports); and data collection is of mixed reliability. Nonetheless, there are some reliable data sources such as government national industrial statistics, Eurostat, studies for the European Commission, some industry Trade Associations, the Stockholm International Peace Research Institute (SIPRI), company annual reports and some trade magazines (e.g. Flight International). This section presents a review of available data. Generally, there are reliable data for Canada, USA, France, UK and the European Union.

Table 2.3 presents data for the world's aerospace *industries*. In terms of size, there are major aerospace industries in the USA, China, Russia, France and the UK; but size is not an indicator of technical capability and international competitiveness. Nonetheless, these data invite the question of what determines the size of a nation's aerospace industry.

Table 2.3   The world's aerospace industries, 2012

Nation	Sales (US$ billion)	Employment (numbers)
Brazil	7.8	23,368
Canada	43.4	170,000
Finland	2.1	8,000
France	50.0	162,000
Germany	39.8	100,700
Italy	12.2	36,300
Netherlands	3.0	16,000
Poland	0.6	16,000
Spain	9.4	36,160
Sweden	(1.5)	(13,900)
UK	37.9	100,658
Europe	*178.5*	*498,200*
China	2.7	400,000
India	(3.1)	(32,659)
Indonesia	(n/a)	3,700
Japan	16.8	32,000
Russia	19.2	406,000
South Africa	(0.3+)	(4,580)
South Korea	(1.4)	(2,928)
USA	220.1	620,500

Notes:
1. Nations and trade associations use different definitions of their aerospace industry.
2. Employment numbers vary depending on the definition of the aerospace industry and whether employment is direct employment only (excluding suppliers or indirect employment) and includes other multiplier effects.
3. Data were not always available for 2012 so data from the period 2008–2011 is reported, using the latest available data. Nor are employment and sales data necessarily for the same year. The total for Europe is based on 20 European nations, including 17 EU states.
4. (…) shows where sales and employment data are based on the nation's major aerospace firms: see Table 2.4. (n/a) is not available.

Sources: Industry trade associations; ADIA (2012); Treball (2013).

What is the relationship between size and 'success' reflected in such market performance indicators as exports, international competitiveness, productivity and profitability? These questions will be addressed elsewhere in this book.

Further insights into the world's aerospace industries are available from data on the world's major aerospace *firms.* These are shown in Table 2.4. Again, the data need to be analysed. Economists focus on the determinants of firm size and whether size determines success or vice versa. The data in Table 2.4 show the scale advantages of US aerospace firms over their rivals in Europe and the rest of the world. EADS/Airbus is an exception with a size similar to Boeing as the largest US aerospace firm. Such differences in firm size, especially in Europe, show the opportunities for mergers to create larger firms able to compete with their US rivals. However, caution is required since the data in Table 2.4 are for aerospace sales only. Some companies have a range of non-aerospace business and are considerably larger than indicated by their aerospace sales only. For example, BAE Systems has a large defence business outside of aerospace. In 2010, BAE Systems was ranked second in the world's top 100 arms companies with Lockheed Martin ranked first, Boeing third and EADS ranked seventh (SIPRI, 2011; see Chapter 8).

Table 2.4   Major aerospace firms

Company	Aerospace Sales, 2012 ($ billion)	Total Employment, 2013
USA		
Boeing	81.7	169,147
Lockheed Martin	47.2	115,000
General Dynamics	31.5	96,000
United Technologies	29.1	212,400
Northrop Grumman	28.1	68,100
Raytheon	24.4	67,800
General Electric	20.0	305,000
Europe		
EADS/Airbus (F,G,S)	74.8	143,358
Finmeccanica (It)	20.2	66,271
Safran (F)	15.9	66,200
Rolls-Royce (UK)	13.7	55,200
BAE Systems (UK)	8.7	84,600
Thales (F)	5.8	65,000
Dassault Aviation (F)	5.2	18,016
Saab (Sw)	1.5	13,900

Company	Aerospace Sales, 2012 ($ billion)	Total Employment, 2013
Rest of world		
United Aircraft Corporation (R)	4.8	100,000
Bombardier (C)	8.6	35,000
Embraer (B)	6.2	18,669
Mitsubishi Heavy Industries (J)	5.5	63,500
Israel Aerospace Industries (Is)	3.4	16,000
Hindustan Aeronautics (In)	3.1	32,659
Korea Aerospace Industries (SK)	1.4	2,928
Denel (SA)	0.3	4,219
AVIC (China)	2.7	400,000

Notes:
1. Companies ranked by value of aerospace sales from Flight Top 100. For each nation, only the major firms are shown: other firms are listed in the Flight list of the Top 100 aerospace firms but not shown in the table.
2. Employment data for the Flight Top 100 were not published in 2013. Data for 2013 are reported for all company or group employment (comprising both aerospace and non-aerospace employment): hence, the employment figures are not comparable with the aerospace sales data.
3. Countries are B is Brazil; C is Canada; F is France; G is Germany; In is India; Is is Israel; It is Italy; J is Japan; R is Russia; S is Spain; SA is South Africa; SK is South Korea; Sw is Sweden.
4. AVIC is Aviation Industry Corporation of China which represents the entire aviation industry of China.

Sources: Flight (2013); UAC (2013).

CONCLUSION

In its relatively short history starting in 1903, the aircraft industry has transformed to an aerospace industry reflecting its entry into the space market. The industry has changed from one where technology was based on privately funded independent inventors to one dependent on large-scale development teams employing highly qualified scientists and engineers often financed by governments, especially in military markets. The industry of 2014 is radically different from the industry of 1903 to 1913. It comprises a smaller number of larger firms with a mixture of private and state ownership. Questions arise as to what the industry might look like in the future, say, in 2065 (some 50 years ahead)?

A statistical overview identified industries and firms of varying size. These size differences need to be explained and assessed. Here, a starting point involves an analysis of aerospace markets and the economics of the industry. Next, the standard 'toolkit' of industrial economists is applied, namely, the industry structure, conduct and performance model.

REFERENCES

ADIA (2012). *Key Facts and Figures 2012*, Aerospace and Defence Industries Association of Europe, Brussels.

Angelucci, E. (ed.) (1981). *World Encyclopedia of Military Aircraft*, Janes Publishing Company, London.

APR (2013). *Air Power Review: Special Edition, Royal Air Force, Celebrating 75 Years*, Centre for Air Power, Shrivenham, Spring.

Barnett, C. (1986). *The Audit of War: The Illusions and Reality of Britain as a Great Nation*, Macmillan, London.

Flight (2013). Top 100: Special Report, *Flight International*, Quadrant House, Surrey, vol 184, 5408, 24–30 September, p34.

Hamilton-Paterson, J. (2010). *Empire of the Clouds: When Britain's Aircraft Ruled the World*, Faber and Faber, London.

Hartley, K. (2012). *White Elephants? The Political Economy of Multi-National Defence Projects*, New Directions: The Foundation for European Reform, Brussels, October.

Hayward, K. (1989). *The British Aircraft Industry*, Manchester University Press, Manchester.

SIPRI (2011). *SIPRI Yearbook 2011*, Stockholm International Peace Research Institute, Stockholm, Sweden.

Treball, B. (2013). *Spain's Aerospace Industry*, Ajuntement di Barcelona, Barcelonactiva.

UAC (2013). *Annual Report of Joint Stock Company United Aircraft Corporation for 2012*, Moscow.

UNIDIR (1993). *The Economic Aspects of Disarmament: Disarmament as an Investment Process*, United Nations Institute for Disarmament Research, Geneva.

3. Aerospace markets

INTRODUCTION

At first sight, aerospace markets are like all other markets in comprising buyers and sellers of aerospace products, namely aircraft, helicopters, missiles and space systems. But once the buyers are identified, some distinguishing features emerge. This chapter shows that aerospace markets are 'different' from other private commercial markets and have some distinguishing and important economic features resulting from the importance and role of government. It starts with a definition of aerospace markets followed by their distinguishing features. Military and civil aerospace markets are analysed and attention is given to the newly developing space market.

THE MARKET

Military Markets

Aerospace is not a single market but comprises many sub-markets. There are *military* and *civil* markets for aircraft, helicopters, missiles and space systems. Military markets are varied with markets for combat aircraft, trainer aircraft, military transports and specialised aircraft (e.g. air tankers; radar, surveillance and communications aircraft). There are also military markets for various types of missiles, including surface-to-air missiles for air defence, air-to-air missiles launched from aircraft and cruise missiles launched from aircraft, warships, submarines and land. Space has a military role with military markets for rocket launchers and satellites for communications and surveillance.

Buyers in military markets are different from buyers in, say, markets for motor cars where there are large numbers of private consumers. In contrast, military markets are dominated by governments as buyers. Governments buy military aerospace products for their armed forces and they are the only buyer for their nation's armed forces. For example, only the US government buys military aerospace equipment for the US Armed

Forces (i.e. Army; Navy; Marine Corps; Air Force). As a result, government is either a large buyer or, for some equipment, it might be the only buyer (e.g. air tankers; communications satellites). A sole buyer is known as a monopsony. Either as a large or sole buyer, government acquires buying power which it can use to determine the size, structure, conduct, ownership and performance of its national aerospace industry.

Military aerospace equipment is costly. Unit production costs range from $11 million for a primary trainer aircraft to $130 million for a modern combat aircraft to $665 million for an electronic platform aircraft (e.g. for airborne early warning). Military helicopters are also costly. Unit costs for an anti-submarine helicopter are some $37 million whilst an attack helicopter might cost $44 million per copy. Similarly, unit production costs are some $8.5 million for a cruise missile, $9.3 million for an unmanned reconnaissance vehicle and almost $75 million for a ballistic missile (2012 prices: Pugh, 2007).

Industry forms the supply side of both military and civil aerospace markets. Industries comprise groups of firms supplying aerospace products where the firms are either privately-owned or state-owned. Within each *national* aerospace industry, the number of firms in the market determines the extent of competition. However, if the market is defined to be the *world market*, the number of firms and the extent of competition are much greater. On the supply side, some firms specialise in specific aerospace products: for example, firms specialise in military and civil helicopters; some specialise in civil regional jet airliners; some specialise in military missiles. The number of firms in any national or world market determines the extent and type of competition. Larger numbers of firms means more competitive markets with an emphasis on price competition. Fewer firms means greater emphasis on non-price competition (e.g. innovation and new types of aircraft: see Chapters 2, 6 and 7).

Within each national aerospace industry, there are few major firms and in many national industries, only one major firm. For example, the US military aerospace market is dominated by such firms as Lockheed Martin, Boeing, Northrop Grumman, General Dynamics and Raytheon (all privately-owned). BAE Systems dominates the UK military aerospace market and Finemeccanica is Italy's major military aerospace firm. Interestingly, the world civil aerospace market is dominated by duopolies (two firms). Airbus and Boeing form a duopoly in the world market for large jet airliners, whilst Bombardier and Embraer form a duopoly in the world regional jet airliner market and ATR (Europe) and Bombardier (Canada) form a duopoly in the turboprop market.

Civil Markets

Civil aerospace markets also comprise a variety of sub-markets. There are markets for regional airliners (turboprops and jets), medium- and long-range jet airliners, jumbo jets (e.g. Airbus A380; Boeing 747), business aircraft, helicopters, private aircraft (pleasure; sports) and micro-lights. There is also a new and emerging market in civil space travel. These markets differ from their military counterparts in that none of them are dominated by a major or single buyer and that governments are not dominant buyers. Typically, civil markets are characterised by large numbers of privately-owned and state-owned airlines where some airlines are 'national carriers'. Business aircraft are usually bought by large firms or leasing companies whilst private aircraft and microlights are bought by individual households.

Jet airliners are not cheap. Development costs were almost $15 billion for the Airbus A380 airliner and these are fixed costs which have to be recovered over the production of the aircraft. Unit purchase prices vary from $37 to $50 million for regional jet airliners; from $75 to $88 million for Boeing 737 and Airbus A320 airliners; to $350 to $390 million for Boeing 747 and Airbus A380 jumbo jets (2012 prices). The high costs for the development and production of civil aircraft raises questions as to whether private firms and private capital markets can fund such projects. Often governments are involved in funding the development of civil aircraft and engines. They are also involved in other aspects of civil aerospace markets.

THE IMPORTANCE OF GOVERNMENT

Governments are central to understanding military and civil aerospace markets. In *military aerospace* markets, governments dominate demand and their procurement choices determine the size of national aerospace industries. Rearmament and conflict lead to increased demands for military aerospace equipment resulting in an expansion of the industry reflected in increased output and employment. In contrast, peace and disarmament result in reductions in military demands leading to job losses, plant closures and exits from the industry.

Governments also influence industry structure by specifying entry conditions and determining firm size. For example, government can allow foreign firms to bid for national defence contracts (or prevent foreign bidders); it can allow new entrants from outside the traditional defence industry to bid for defence contracts; and it can prevent exit by 'bailing-out' key defence firms faced with bankruptcy. It can determine firm size by using its buying power to require firms to merge as a condition of receiving contracts and it can prevent mergers which are viewed as 'anti-competitive'. Government can also influence the form of competition and industry performance. It can specify whether competitions should be based on price or non-price factors (e.g. equipment performance; delivery dates) and it influences industry performance by determining the profitability of non-competitive defence contracts and by restricting exports (e.g. restricting the types of equipment which can be exported and to which nations). Finally, governments determine owner-ship of the industry. They can use their buying power to determine the size, structure, conduct and performance of a *privately-owned* industry or they can attempt the comprehensive control of all industry variables, including costs, profits and pricing through *state-ownership* (national-isation).

Governments also determine *civil aerospace* markets through their control of property rights in the form of airspace and landing rights. Foreign airlines require access to a nation in the form of landing and over-flying rights. International airlines are a part of mutually beneficial international trade and exchange whereby overseas passengers contribute to a nation's market transactions. But such trade requires access to a nation which for international air travel is via a major airport (e.g. located near a capital city). Major airports are usually natural monopolies where the market will only support one firm (some airports are also hub networks). Airports can be government or privately-owned with govern-ment often regulating airports to control their monopoly power. Govern-ment also enforces its property rights over airspace through international agreements with the ultimate sanction of using military force to police its airspace. Government is also involved in maintaining the safety of air travel through requirements for training aircrew and ensuring the reliabil-ity of aircraft.

Access to airports requires landing and take-off rights which are known as airport 'slots' where such slots are allocated to airlines by a government or an airport. Typically, at the world's major international airports (e.g. London; New York; Paris), a single airline or alliance dominates most flights and controls most slots and such slot concentra-tion has adverse impacts on new entry, competition and prices (Starkie, 2006). Slots are valuable resources and can affect market structure: for example, unrestricted market trading in slots might reinforce an airline's dominant position whilst slots provide incentives to acquire an airline for access to its slots.

International air travel involves governments in international collective action which can promote beneficial international trade. Nations will trade their national landing and over-flying rights in exchange for equivalent rights to access the airspace of other nations. But some nations might be unwilling to accept such international transactions and will impose restrictions on over-flying rights and on landing rights at their major airports (leading to retaliation by other nations excluded from access: 'tit-for-tat' policies). Examples have arisen where a nation has enforced its property rights over its airspace by the shooting down of intruding airliners (with consequences such as trade sanctions and compensation payments). International collective action on international air travel was reflected in the 1944 Convention on International Civil Aviation (Chicago Convention of 1944) which created the International Civil Aviation Organisation (ICAO) of the United Nations. The ICAO established the rules of sovereignty over airspace and international air travel. However, Open Skies Agreements radically changed the international air travel market. These Agreements are bilateral and multilateral agreements between nations aimed at creating free market competition between airlines and fares determined by competition (e.g. USA–EU Open Skies Agreement, 2007).

Industry responded to government international collective action by creating in 1945 the International Air Transport Association (IATA). This was the industry trade association for the international airlines. Originally, it was the price-setting body for the international airlines (a cartel). Price-setting by IATA airlines was allowed by governments and reflected in bilateral government agreements. However, deregulation of airlines and the emergence of 'low-cost' carriers led to the end of IATA's price-setting role.

Governments further influence civil aerospace markets on the demand side of the market and through the funding of new civil aircraft and engine projects. As with military markets, governments are involved with the demand for civil aircraft. They might own the national state airline (national champions and flag carriers) which might be required to buy its aircraft from the national aerospace industry; or governments might provide tax-subsidy incentives for national privately-owned airlines to buy nationally. Other demand-side measures include government funding support for national airlines to maintain a reserve of capacity for mobilisation in national emergencies; the use of civil air transport by the military (e.g. government contractor flights); the requirement that government personnel use national airlines for international travel (e.g. Fly American Act); and government purchasing military versions of civil aircraft (e.g. USAF purchasing military versions of Boeing airliners).

Developing a new civil aircraft or engine is costly. Private firms and capital markets can provide some funding for such projects but often capital markets might 'fail' to provide sufficient funds for the start of a new project. In such cases, governments can provide state funds for new civil aircraft projects (e.g. Concorde; A380: see Chapter 10). Funding might be provided for research and development, for production and for exports and it might be for the aircraft, the engine or for a major component. State funds might comprise grants, subsidies and loans where loans are subject to various repayment conditions (e.g. related to sales). State funding can be of two general types, namely, direct or indirect. Direct funding is *project-specific* providing funds for a specific aircraft or engine. Indirect funding is not project-specific and often takes the form of *regional or locational funds*. Examples include grants or tax incentives for new plant and equipment or for research and development or financial assistance to firms for worker training and retraining. The issue of state funding for large jet airliners was the subject of a World Trade Organization case between Airbus and Boeing which raised economic issues about whether private capital markets are a major source of market failure in the financing of civil aircraft projects (see Chapters 2 and 10).

SPACE MARKETS: FAMILIAR PROBLEMS IN A NEW DOMAIN?

The Economics of Space Markets: Market Failure Analysis

Space is a relatively new and developing market. It has both military and civil sectors. Military demands are for satellites providing communications and surveillance. Civil demands are for space exploration (basic research) and various satellite systems. Governments fund military demands and space exploration whilst civil commercial space activities are funded by the private sector. The newly developing market in space tourism and commercial space travel is likely to be privately funded. Private funding has been used to develop the first generation of commercial space ships (e.g. SpaceShipOne; Virgin Galactic with reported fares of $200,000 per seat). Here, it can be argued that it is not the responsibility of government to fund the developing space tourism market; but, instead, the government's role should be restricted to creating an appropriate regulatory framework. This raises the wider question of whether there is a role for government in the newly developing space market.

Economists justify state intervention in private markets where there are major market failures (Tisdell and Hartley, 2008). These failures result from market imperfections (e.g. monopoly; entry barriers); externalities (both beneficial and harmful such as beneficial technological spill-overs and harmful pollution); and where there are public goods characterised by non-rivalry, non-excludability and free riding (e.g. defence). For some of these reasons, markets may not exist: these are missing markets such as markets for risk and futures trading and where transaction costs mean that it is too costly to create a market. Space markets have three distinguishing economic characteristics concerned with common property, strategic industries and governments.

First, space is a common property resource lacking any private markets with property rights. Unlike civil aerospace markets, nations do not have sovereignty over 'their outer space'. Similar characteristics apply to other common property, such as the high seas (international waters) which is reflected in the over-exploitation of such common property leading, for example, to 'over-fishing' and depletion of valuable fish resources. In space, over-exploitation is reflected in the growing problem of space debris and the excess demand for access to limited space orbits for satellites. In fact, space debris threatens the availability of valuable orbits. One solution to the over-exploitation problem is collective action resulting in international agreements to regulate the use of common property (e.g. EU common fishing policy for its territorial waters; international agreements on whale fishing: Sandler and Hartley, 2001).

Property rights in space are governed by the Outer Space Treaty (1967) which established international space law and forbids governments from claiming sovereignty and property rights over the Moon and other planets. This Treaty prohibits nuclear weapons in outer space (but not conventional weapons in outer space).

In space, there are international regulations governing the orbit and frequency at which telecommunications satellites can operate (i.e. the limited amount of orbit space is allocated by the International Telecommunications Union Radiocommunications Bureau); but there is a lack of an adequate international co-ordinated surveillance system for a comprehensive tracking, management and removal of all space debris (UNIDIR, 2009, p45). As an alternative to international collective action, property rights can be assigned to a specific group (e.g. fishermen). Other examples of common property include the world environment (problems of global warming), rivers and water, some types of information and research, access to common pastures and road use. As a result, where property rights are not well defined, markets may be inefficient: hence the case for some form of state intervention (where there are different forms of intervention).[1]

Space is common property where a market does not exist so we cannot expect markets to allocate resources efficiently if a market does not exist. Common property means that the resource is owned by no one and may be used by anyone. However, unlike common property resources on earth, access to space is not costless and entry costs form a barrier to entry. Entry into the space market requires a rocket launcher and its associated launch facilities capable of carrying a payload into space. There is an adequate market in launchers so that nations without a rocket launcher and its facilities are able to hire such capability. The space industry supplies the launchers and satellites for gaining access to space. Two types of launchers have been developed, namely, the one-off shot of a rocket launcher and the re-useable Space Shuttle.

Second, space industries have the features of an economically strategic industry. These are high technology oligopoly industries (e.g. large civil jet airliners) where international trade is characterised by substantial rents and where government support for its national industry enables it to obtain a share of such rents. The industries are R&D-intensive with technology spill-overs and decreasing costs (Krugman, 1989; Tisdell and Hartley, 2008, pp177–178). R&D is costly, risky and long-term. For example, the European lander Huygens took over 20 years from initial conception to landing on Saturn's Moon Titan (HCP 66, 2007).

Third, as with other aerospace markets, governments are central to understanding space markets being involved in both demand and supply sides of the market. They are major buyers of space systems, especially of launchers (for military use and space exploration); they provide funds for space R&D; they are major buyers of aerospace systems (military aircraft, helicopters and missiles; funds for civil aircraft development) where aerospace firms are also involved in space markets so providing opportunities for cross-funding between these sectors. Governments also determine entry into the space industry and market. For example, government allows the establishment of launch sites in a country; it imposes licensing requirements for launches and for undertaking any activity in space; it requires third party liability insurance during launches and while the satellite is in operation; and in some cases, government covers the insurance costs and risks of launch vehicles. Also,

---

[1] For example, with global warming, if the world community seeks a 'perfect' international agreement, no treaty might be agreed. A practical imperfect treaty might be better than none at all.

in some nations, space firms are state-owned. However, there are some private market opportunities with the private funding of satellites and the emerging space tourism markets. Nonetheless, the extensive involvement of government in the space market raises the possibility of government failure in this market. Public choice analysis provides an alternative approach to understanding the political economy of space markets.

A Public Choice Analysis

Space markets can be analysed as political markets where such markets are dominated by agents in the political market, namely, voters, political parties, governments, bureaucracies and producer groups. Groups will pursue their self-interest with voters seeking maximum satisfaction from their votes; political parties will be vote-maximisers; governments will seek re-election; bureaucracies will be budget-maximisers; and producer groups will be income and profit maximisers (rent-seekers). The behaviour of these agents will affect public choices in space markets. In fact, a principal–agent analysis can be applied to space policy. This analysis shows that resource allocation problems arise because of the difficulties which arise in writing and monitoring contracts aimed at inducing agents to act in the best interests of the principal. Voters (as principals) are likely to be ill-informed about space so they will let their elected representatives (as agents) make choices on space policy. In turn, governments will be advised and influenced by their bureaucracies with a special interest in space (e.g. a space agency). Such bureaucracies will aim to maximise their budgets. To do so, they will over-estimate the demand for public sector space programmes and under-estimate its costs resulting in economically inefficient outcomes. Such behaviour will be supported with arguments about the technology and spin-off benefits from space activities. It will be claimed that space is high technology, that all technology is 'good' and more is desirable and that high technology will ensure a nation's future international competitiveness with no reference to the opportunity costs of space activities. These arguments are likely to be supported by producer groups which will benefit from the award of public sector contracts (especially from cost-based contracts).

Economists have the task of subjecting these claims to critical scrutiny separating myths, emotion and special pleading from sound economic analysis and supporting evidence. Attention needs to be given to whether the resources used in public sector space activities would yield greater social benefits if they were used elsewhere in the economy. For example, would the resources used in public sector space activities create more jobs, more technology and greater spin-offs if they were used in, say, university research or elsewhere in the aerospace or motor vehicle or information technology industries?

Questions also need to be asked about the precise causes of market failure in the space sector. Are space markets failing and if so, why? For example, are private capital markets failing to provide the necessary funds for space exploration because of the high development costs, lengthy development periods, substantial technical and commercial risks and long-term returns from developing launcher rockets? Private capital market failure is likely to be reinforced because of the common property features of space markets (missing markets) plus any beneficial externalities associated with technology spin-offs. These factors might explain why private capital markets are unwilling (and unable) to provide risk finance at 'reasonable cost' for space *exploration*. But this does not necessarily constitute a market failure since the capital market is taking the view that there are more profitable alternative uses for its scarce funds. Indeed, private capital markets fund some space activities such as telecommunications satellites. Space exploration is different and can be viewed as basic research where typically private markets will 'underinvest' in basic research: hence, providing a case for state intervention. However, this is not a convincing case for state support of space exploration. There are a variety of other industries and sectors which are involved in basic research (e.g. universities) and governments have to make difficult choices in allocating scarce funds between these alternatives.

In making its choices, governments will be influenced by agents in the political market (the space–industrial–political complex). They will be similarly influenced by such agents in other public sector activities such as education, health, defence and construction. These agents have the potential to affect public choices (decisions) in ways which can lead to substantial economic inefficiencies. There are incentives to use market failure analysis to support the arguments of both bureaucracies and producer groups seeking budgets and contract awards. For example, it will be claimed that space exploration leads to substantial beneficial externalities through technology spin-offs (or spill-overs) but that these are difficult to measure. Critics might reply that the difficulties of measurement reflect the fact that there is nothing to be measured!

The message is clear. Claims about market failure and the benefits of space exploration need to be subject to critical analysis based on sound economic theory with supporting evidence. Private markets can fail but public choice models show that governments can also fail. Public choice analysis shows the potential inefficiencies of political markets which need to be recognised in any economic evaluation of space policy (see Chapter 9).

CONCLUSION

Whilst government is central to understanding aerospace markets and industries, they cannot ignore the basic economics of the industry. What are cost trends; how important is the scale of output for international competitiveness; and are there any distinctive features of the industry's cost curves? Chapter 4 addresses these questions.

REFERENCES

HCP 66 (2007). *UK Civil Space Policy*, House of Commons, Select Committee on Science and Technology, Seventh Report, TSO, London, July.

Krugman, P. (1989). Industrial organization and international trade, in Schmalensee, R. and Willig, R. (eds), *The Handbook of Industrial Organization*, Elsevier, New York.

Pugh, P.G. (2007). *Source Book of Defence Equipment Costs*, Dandy Books, London.

Sandler, T. and Hartley, K. (2001). The economics of alliances: The lessons for collective action, *Journal of Economic Literature*, XXIX, 3, 869–896.

Starkie, D. (2006). *Slot Concentration at Network Hubs*, IATA, Montreal, Canada.

Tisdell, C. and Hartley, K. (2008). *Microeconomic Policy*, Edward Elgar Publishing, Cheltenham, UK and Northampton, MA, USA.

UNIDIR (2009). At the crossroads: the necessity for rules of the road for space, Karl, A. *Disarmament Forum*, United Nations Institute for Disarmament Research, Geneva.

4. The economics of the aerospace industry

INTRODUCTION

Costs are central to economics and a determinant of industry structure. This chapter outlines various cost concepts used in the aerospace industry. These include acquisition and life-cycle costs, cost growth and cost escalation. Aerospace is also regarded as a decreasing cost industry where learning economies are a major influence on unit production costs. Typically, decreasing cost industries are monopolies.

AIRCRAFT LIFE-CYCLE COSTS

The typical life-cycle for an aircraft involves four stages, comprising development, production, operational service and disposal. *Development* involves basic research, concept analysis, design, development and the flight testing of prototypes. During development, the prototype aircraft are tested, modified and re-tested until the required performance and reliability are achieved. For military aircraft, the end result of development is the acceptance of the aircraft for operational service. For civil aircraft, the equivalent is the award of a certificate of airworthiness (CoA) by the national aviation agency confirming that the aircraft is safe to use for commercial operations. Such certificates are issued by, for example, the US Federal Aviation Administration (FAA) and the European Aviation Safety Agency (EASA which certified the Airbus A380 airliner).

Development is costly; it takes considerable time; and it involves highly skilled scientists, engineers and technologists. Development costs are fixed costs which are incurred regardless of the number of aircraft produced (i.e. non-recurring costs). The larger the output of an aircraft, the more can such fixed costs be spread over a larger output so reducing unit development costs. For military aircraft, nations with a large home market, such as the USA, are able to spread development costs over long production runs, which provide an international competitive advantage.

Nations with a small home military market (e.g. European nations) have to spread their development costs over a smaller output. However, small nations can adjust by being more efficient in the development stage and by exporting which enables them to amortise their development costs over export sales. Nations can also reduce the burden of development costs by collaboration with other nations (e.g. four nation Typhoon); but international collaboration leads to inefficiencies reflecting bureaucracy and work-sharing requirements (see Chapters 12 and 13).

Development costs are also a challenge for civil aircraft manufacturers. Private firms have to finance their development costs and aim to recover them over future sales, which might be over many years. Typically, privately-owned civil aircraft firms have to make a future market assessment before starting a new project to assess their prospects of recovering development costs and achieving a profit on their investment. A requirement for starting a new, costly civil aircraft project will be initial orders from major airlines (e.g. orders for, say, 100–200 aircraft) with a 'break-even' point for recovery of development costs in the region of some 500–1,000 aircraft (depending on the type of airliner and its development costs). For example, the Airbus A380 airliner was originally expected to break-even at an output of 270 units, but this estimate was revised to 420 units with alternative estimates indicating break-even by 2015. A crude rule of thumb suggests that to achieve profitability, a modern medium–large jet airliner requires sales of over 1,000 units (e.g. Boeing jet airliner series: 707; 727; 737; 747; 777; etc.).

Production involves the manufacture and final assembly of the aircraft comprising its fuselage including cockpit, wings and tail plane. Final assembly will add the engines, avionics and undercarriage to the aircraft plus any additional components required by the customer (e.g. seats and interior cabins for civil passenger airliners). For a combat aircraft such as Typhoon, some 40 per cent of unit production costs are allocated to the airframe, 40 per cent for equipment and 20 per cent for the engines. Production is also a skill-intensive activity requiring engineers, project managers and other skilled labour.

There is a relationship between development costs and unit production costs with development costs varying in proportion to unit production costs. The ratio of development cost to unit production cost varies between different types of aircraft and missile as shown in Table 4.1. For example, the total development cost for a fighter strike aircraft with unit production costs of $100 million is some $10 billion.

Table 4.1   Ratio of development cost to unit production cost

Type of equipment	Ratio of development cost to unit production cost (R)
Fighter/strike aircraft	100
Helicopters	120
Large fixed wing aircraft	40
Air-to-surface guided weapons	6,500
Area defence: surface-to-air missiles	500

Notes:
1. For fighter/strike aircraft, ratio rises to 200 if a new engine is included.
2. Helicopter ratio may vary with complexity of helicopter: higher for advanced attack helicopters and lower for cargo/utility types.
3. Large fixed wing aircraft comprise transport, tankers, electronic platforms and large bombers.
4. Air-to-surface guided weapons exclude anti-tank weapons.
5. Area defence missiles: values are much higher for point defence missiles.
6. Values are approximate and are in the same currency and at the same price date. They are for a new design; lower values apply to designs which are variants of an established type.

Source: Pugh (2007).

Acquisition costs are defined as the total of development and production costs. The ratios in Table 4.1 can be used to provide broad estimates of the total acquisition costs for military aircraft. Acquisition costs are estimated:

$$AC = (R+Q) \times UPC \qquad (4.1)$$

Where:

AC is acquisition cost comprising development and production costs;
R is the ratio of development to unit production cost (see Table 4.1);
Q is total output;
UPC is unit production cost.

Using this formula, the total acquisition costs of a fighter/strike aircraft with a unit production cost of $100 million and a total output of 500 units will be some $60 billion.

After manufacture, the aircraft is delivered to the customer and will enter *operational service*. Military customers will operate the aircraft in its military combat or support role during which it will have to be maintained and repaired and there might be 'mid-life' updates designed to modify the aircraft and keep it up-to-date. Civilian customers in the form of airlines will also require that their airliners be serviced, repaired and modified (e.g. fitting of new cabin interiors). For airliners, a major requirement is the maintenance and repair of aircraft engines. For both military and civilian customers, some of the repair and maintenance work is undertaken 'in-house' and some is 'contracted-out' to the original manufacturer.

At the end of its operational life for its initial user, an aircraft might be retained, sold to other users or scrapped. Older military aircraft might be placed in storage for a period where the storage or 'mothballing' option involves costs of storage and maintenance. Stored military aircraft provide spares for operational aircraft or they form a reserve to be used in conflict. Alternatively, older military aircraft might be sold to overseas air forces. Older civil airliners might also be stored or sold to other airlines (e.g. for charter trade) or converted to freight aircraft. Finally, at the end of their useful lives, military and civil aircraft will be sold for their scrap values.

Aircraft life-cycles are lengthy. For a modern combat aircraft, development might require some 10–20 years; production might require a similar period of 10–20 years; and operational service might last for 30–50 years. There are overlaps between each of the stages. For example, production will start before the completion of development; development continues during production; and operational service starts relatively early in the production phase and continues well beyond the end of production.

For a modern combat aircraft, a typical time-scale for production might be 8–12 months of development flying after the first flight of the first development aircraft. This will demonstrate proof of concept prior to a decision on the start of production. After 12 months, there will be a decision on production investment and the setting-up of production tooling which will take a further 18 months. Manufacturing will start by month 30, with a further four years needed to produce sufficient numbers of aircraft to form an operational squadron (i.e. a total of some 78 months from the first flight to in-service). In the case of Typhoon, the first production contract was awarded in 1998, four years after the first flight of the aircraft with a UK in-service date some five years later (the difference between the typical 78 months and Typhoon's 9 years might indicate the inefficiencies of collaboration). Table 4.2 shows examples of life-cycles for UK and US combat aircraft.

Table 4.2   Examples of military aircraft life-cycles

Stage	Boeing B-52	Canberra	Typhoon
Initial contract	1946	January 1946	1984
First flight	April 1952	May 1949	March 1994
First delivery	February 1955	May 1951	June 2003
End of production	1962	1960	2015
Retirement	2045	June 2006	2030 (2055/60)
Operational life	90 years	55 years	27 (52–57)years

Notes:
1. Initial contract is either the first start on the project concept or a formal contract for an aircraft. First delivery is date of entry into service.
2. Future retirement dates are as estimated in 2014. Typhoon end of production is estimated and for the UK only (i.e. excluding exports). Typhoon official retirement is declared to be 2030; figures in brackets show author's alternative estimates.
3. B-52 is a US heavy bomber. Canberra is a UK light–medium bomber built by English Electric. Typhoon is a multi-role combat aircraft and is a four nation collaborative programme (Germany; Italy; Spain; UK).

Total life-cycle costs consist of all aspects of an aircraft's costs over its life-cycle comprising development, production, operational service, mid-life updates and disposal. In the 1980s, development and production accounted for less than 20 per cent of the life-cycle costs of combat aircraft with maintenance accounting for 50 per cent of costs and operations, updates and fuel accounting for the remaining 37 per cent of life-cycle costs (Pugh, 1986, p124). Over time, the share of acquisition costs in life-cycle costs has increased. For a modern combat aircraft, development and production costs are 40 per cent to 50 per cent of life-cycle costs with operations and support costs forming the remaining 50 per cent of costs (Woodford, 1999). On UK Typhoons, acquisition costs form 61 per cent of life-cycle costs (based on actual and estimated costs: NAO, 2011). The shift to the military use of UAVs is likely to change the share of acquisition and operations costs in total life-cycle costs raising the share of acquisition costs and lowering operations and support costs.

There is a further aspect of costs related to cost increases. The start of a new aircraft project is based on estimates of development and unit production costs, of delivery dates and of market sales. Typically, actual costs exceed the initial estimates; delivery dates are subject to slippages; and it is not unknown for market sales estimates to be optimistic. Within life-cycle costs, there are major cost increases during the development phase of the project. *Cost growth* is the tendency of the costs of a specific project to increase as it moves from the concept stage through development to production. Such cost growth can reflect optimistic estimates (optimism bias), design changes, unexpected problems which require additional resources and inflation in input prices of labour and materials. There is a considerable literature on cost growth in defence projects. For example, a sample of UK and US defence projects showed cost growth of 12 per cent to 26 per cent and average delays of 21–24 months. UK estimates of defence inflation show that defence inflation was higher than the GDP deflator (a measure of inflation in the UK economy) in five out of seven years between 2005 and 2012 (with quality and quantity held constant: DASA, 2013). There is less published data for civil aerospace projects. However, for the Airbus A380 development costs increased by some 25 per cent (current prices) with delays on first delivery of two years and five months together with post-delivery problems with wing cracks. Similarly, first deliveries of the Boeing 787 Dreamliner were delayed by three years and five months followed by the grounding of the fleet in January 2013.

There is a further dimension to cost increases. Cost growth refers to cost increases for a specific project. In contrast, *cost escalation* describes the tendency for costs to increase for successive generations of defence equipment. Not only are aerospace projects costly in absolute terms but the long-run historical trend has been for unit costs to rise for each new generation of equipment: aerospace projects are costly and becoming costlier.

LONG-RUN COST TRENDS

Norman Augustine claimed:

> that the unit cost of certain high technology hardware is increasing at an exponential rate with time. From the days of the Wright Brother's airplane to the era of modern high-performance fighter aircraft, the costs of an individual airplane has unwaveringly grown by a factor of four every ten years. This rate of growth seems to be an inherent characteristic of such systems, with the unit cost being most closely correlated with the passage of time rather than with changes in manoeuvrability, speed, weight, or other technical parameters. The same inexorable trend can be shown to apply to commercial aircraft, helicopters and even ships and tanks, although in the last two somewhat less technologically sophisticated instances, the rate of growth is a factor of two every ten years. (Augustine, 1987, p140)

Augustine formulated this trend line into a Law. In the year 2054, the entire US defence budget will purchase just one aircraft. This aircraft will have to be shared by the Air Force and the Navy 3.5 days each per week except for a leap year, when it will be made available to the Marines for the extra day (Augustine, 1987, p143). On this basis, Augustine's Law has major implications for cost-estimating and for the future size of a nation's Armed Forces. In relation to cost-estimating the Law can be used as an estimating and predictive technique: a trend line can be used to predict the future costs of major defence systems. Such an approach might be a cost-effective solution to obtaining first estimates of the likely future costs of new defence projects, but it has severe limitations. First, correlations do not imply causation. Second, trends are vulnerable to sudden changes as expressed in the following view: a trend is a trend, but the question is will it bend; will it alter its course from some unforeseen force and come to a premature end!

The Law also has implications for the future size of all Armed Forces, namely, a long-run trend of declining numbers of front-line equipment. The result will be smaller air forces, armies and navies based on any reasonable forecast of future defence budgets, leading eventually to a single tank army, a one ship navy and Starship Enterprise for the air force.

Augustine's Law can be represented:

$$AUC = f(t) \tag{4.2}$$

Where AUC is average unit cost in current prices, (t) is time measured by year of initial operation, and the relationship is positive with an exponential trend.

For tactical military aircraft, unit costs increase by a factor of four every ten years. This relationship was observed by Augustine over the period 1910 to the mid-1980s. The trend of increasing costs with time has been broadly the same for commercial aircraft as for military aircraft. For example, a modern airliner of the 1980s costs five times the market value of the entire airline industry as it existed in 1938; and the passenger's seats in a 1980s jet airliner cost more than the entire airliner of the late 1940s (Augustine, 1987, p145).

Augustine also formulated a related Law for project delays (the Law of Unmitigated Optimism). He suggested that 'Any task can be completed in only one-third more time than is currently estimated' (Augustine, 1987, p204). A survey of US defence projects found that these systems were delivered in one-third more time than had been estimated.

There have been few independent UK studies of historical cost trends for major defence projects. The exceptions are Kirkpatrick and Pugh. Kirkpatrick (1995) reported that the unit production cost of UK combat aircraft (excluding strategic bombers) had risen since 1945 at a compound annual growth rate of 11.5 per cent (corrected for inflation and production quantity). This implied that for successive generations of equipment, the real unit cost of tactical combat aircraft increased by a factor of about 2.5 every decade (e.g. unit costs from Meteor to Tornado). Such increases in unit costs reflect the military search for technical superiority over rival forces (the technological arms race). Policy efforts to counteract the rising cost trends include increased exports, improvements in manufacturing technology and organisation, international collaboration and government procurement reforms. However, whilst such policies offer useful savings, they cannot appreciably offset the growth rates in the unit costs of defence equipment (Kirkpatrick, 1995, p279). Inevitably, these cost trends will mean that the UK (and other similar-sized nations) will be unable to afford a viable force of combat aircraft to replace the current Typhoon combat aircraft. The result will be either the abandonment of costly forces and an independent military capability and/or the creation of an economically efficient military alliance providing joint forces. However, such an alliance cannot avoid the problem of rising unit costs and its implications for procurement choices.

Kirkpatrick returned to the theme of cost trends and their consequences. He started from the proposition that 'better weapons win victories' and confirms that the unit production costs of tactical combat aircraft have risen by about 10 per cent per year in real terms. Overall, a replacement weapon system has about the same level of effectiveness against an improved threat as its predecessor had against the original threat but at a higher unit cost for the replacement system (Kirkpatrick, 2004). Also, there is a trend towards an increasing role for fixed costs. For European aircraft projects which entered service during the Cold War, the ratio of development to total production costs was usually in the range of 10 per cent to 20 per cent but recent examples have suggested a ratio of 30 per cent to 50 per cent (Kirkpatrick, 2004, p268). The increased importance of fixed costs within projects means that the production of modern weapons will become concentrated in the richer nations able to afford the up-front costs with a corresponding concentration of production in a smaller number of larger prime contractors.

A UK Ministry of Defence study of cost escalation recognises defence equipment as a 'tournament good' where to maintain military superiority, the equipment needs to be technically advanced and superior to that of its potential enemies. For a sample of UK defence projects over the period 1955 to 2011, unit cost escalation averaged 6 per cent per year for combat aircraft compared with a similar figure for main battle tanks and an average of 4.3 per cent for naval frigates (Davies et al., 2012).

The end of the Cold War was expected to reduce military competition leading to reduced unit cost escalation. The reality was different. The end of the Cold War appears to have made no difference to unit cost escalation. Over the last 150 years or more, unit cost escalation has been remarkably insensitive to changes in the world geo-political situation (Pugh, 2007, p26). This analysis has major implications for the future of the UK aerospace industry where radical change is unavoidable. It seems that unit cost escalation is robust and will remain with us (and with all other nations, allies and rivals) and that policy-makers need to recognise its implications for force size and structure, industrial capabilities, international collaboration and procurement reforms.

Evidence on unit costs and cost escalation for European and US defence equipment is shown in Table 4.3. They confirm that military aerospace and other defence projects are costly and that unit cost trends are rising.

AEROSPACE AS A DECREASING COST INDUSTRY

Aerospace has three major determinants for a decreasing cost industry. First, it has large fixed *development* costs which mean that its unit total costs decline with greater output. Second, a larger scale of output results in economies of scale leading to lower unit *production* costs resulting from variations in all factor inputs. Scale economies reflect fixed production costs (known as indivisibilities), increased specialisation and greater mechanisation. Third, learning economies lead to decreasing unit production costs. Learning economies are a distinctive feature of aerospace industries.

LEARNING ECONOMIES

Learning is one of the major sources of productivity improvements in the aerospace industry and hence on the economics of aircraft manufacture and its international competitiveness. Learning effects are reflected in the overall industry productivity performance. However, industry data do not show the productivity changes occurring at the *product level* which is

Table 4.3   Unit costs and escalation

Equipment	Unit Production Cost ($ millions, 2012 prices)	Cost trends (annual rate of increase: %)
AIR SYSTEMS		
Combat aircraft	134	4
Bomber aircraft	583–4,856	10
Advanced trainer aircraft	33	4
Primary trainer aircraft	12	7
Transport/tanker aircraft	78–388	4
Electronic platform aircraft	126–700	2
Reconnaissance UAV	10	6
Cruise missile	9	8
Attack helicopter	47	5
Anti-submarine helicopter	40–126	6
Utility helicopter	4–31	4
SEA SYSTEMS		
Aircraft carrier	2,136–10,682 (Ac)	3
Air defence warship	1,240 (Ac)	2
Nuclear-powered submarine (SSN)	2,525 (Ac)	1
LAND SYSTEMS		
Main battle tank	8	1
Infantry fighting vehicle	8	4
Multiple rocket launcher	9	5

Notes:
1. Ac is acquisition cost, namely, total cost comprising development and production divided by number of units purchased. For all other projects, unit costs are unit production costs excluding development costs.
2. Data are in constant prices based on the UK GDP deflator and exchange rates and normalised for quantity by using unit costs.
3. Figures are rounded.

Source: Pugh (2007).

where learning economies are evident. Typically, aerospace output comprises a heterogeneous set of military and civil aircraft, helicopters, missiles, engines, equipment and space systems with different learning effects for each product. For example, in the 1980s and early 1990s, labour learning curves varied from 78 per cent to 80 per cent for aircraft,

80 per cent to 93 per cent for helicopters, 85 per cent to 94 per cent for aero-engines, 90 per cent to 95 per cent for missiles and 80 per cent to 90 per cent for avionics (Sandler and Hartley, 1995, pp124–125). Learning curves also provide a useful technique in cost-estimating relationships.

Labour learning curves have been widely used in the aerospace industry where an 80 per cent learning curve was typical, showing that direct labour inputs declined by 20 per cent for each doubling of the cumulative output of an aircraft. For example, if the first unit of production requires, say, 1,000 hours of direct labour, unit number two will require 800 hours; unit number four requires 640 hours; unit eight needs 512 hours (80 per cent of unit four) and unit sixteen requires 410 hours (where each labour input refers to a doubling of cumulative output). An example of an 80 per cent labour learning curve is shown in Figure 4.1. Learning curves also apply to other types of defence equipment and civil products (e.g. electrical appliances; machine tools: Hartley and Sandler, 2001). Learning curves are usually expressed as:

$$y = aX^{-b} \qquad\qquad (4.3)$$

Where:

y = number of direct labour hours per unit produced,
X = cumulative output of a given type of aircraft,
a = the direct labour hours required for the first unit,
b = slope of learning curve usually defined in relation to a doubling of *cumulative* output.[1]

Learning curves have been known variously as progress curves, experience curves and improvement curves. Their cost per unit may be either the average cost for a given number of units or the cost of a specific unit known, respectively, as the *cumulative average* learning curve or the *unit* learning curve.

One of the earliest references to learning curves in the aircraft industry was made by T.P. Wright in 1936. Wright examined the effect of quantity production on cost focusing on the contribution of labour, tooling, materials and overheads to cost reductions as quantity increased. On labour inputs, Wright identified improvements in the proficiency of workers with practice and repetition (learning-by-doing), especially in

---

[1] Cumulative output is total output over the life of the aircraft. For example, 100 units per year produced over 10 years results in a cumulative output of 1,000 units. In contrast, economies of scale refer to annual output levels.

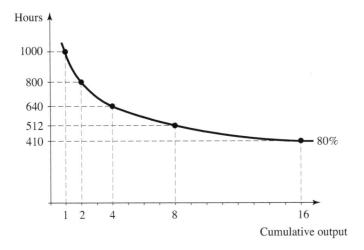

Figure 4.1   80% labour learning curve

assembly operations as well as other types of work. He suggested an 80 per cent curve for average labour cost in relation to quantity: such a curve becomes a straight line when plotted on log-log graph paper (the linear progress curve hypothesis: Wright, 1936).[2]

Examples of Cost–Quantity Relationships

Learning economies are reflected in cost–quantity relationships. Data were obtained on such relationships for two samples of UK aircraft. First, for a sample of a World War II propeller-driven fighter and bomber aircraft; and second, for a sample of 1945–1960 jet-powered fighter and bomber aircraft. Table 4.4 presents data on cost–quantity relationships for World War II aircraft.

---

[2]   An example of learning during World War II was reported for the German Messerschmitt Me 109 fighter aircraft. The construction time for each Me 109 had fallen by 53% by 1942 compared with its pre-war levels; and it fell by a further 15% in 1943: hence, by 1943, construction time was some 40% of its pre-war level (Isby, 2012).

Table 4.4   Cost–quantity relationships for UK World War II aircraft

Aircraft	Quantity (units)	Date of contract	Unit price (£000s)	Percentage reduction (%)
Spitfire				
Mks1&V	First 1,490	1941	4.7	
	Next 996	1941	4.4	6
Mosquito				
MkII	1–50	1943	13.6	
	251–336	1943	9.1	33
MkVI	1–20	1944	18.4	
	501–800	1944	8.6	53
MkXVI	1–52	1945	10.4	
	129–215	1945	9.1	12
Halifax (HP)				
Mk1	1–20	1942	41.0	
	21–200	1942	30.0	27
Halifax (EE)				
Mk2	1–25	1942	37.2	
	401–450	1942	20.2	46
Lancaster				
	1–252	1943	22.9	
	1,313–1,993	1943	17.0	26

Notes:
1. Halifax (HP) represents Halifax aircraft manufactured by Handley Page; Halifax (EE) represents aircraft manufactured by English Electric.
2. Quantity shows number of aircraft ordered in a specific contract. For example, Lancaster was ordered in various batches starting with a batch of 252 aircraft ending in 1943 with a batch from 1,313 to 1,993 units.
3. Date of contract refers to year in which contract was agreed.
4. Unit price is unit production price of the airframe shown in £000s for the year of the contract: hence, Lancaster is shown in 1943 prices. Contract details are broadly similar, but some differ in their definition of unit prices where unit prices include a profit margin.
5. Percentage reduction is percentage reduction in unit price over the contracts shown. For example, unit price of Lancaster in 1943 fell by 26 per cent between the two contracts shown in the table.
6. Data selected for contracts shown in the same year, for the same type of aircraft and for different quantities. Not all contract data showed unit prices for lots of varying sizes within one contract. The sample was selected to show unit prices for different lots: for example, lots of 1–25; then 26–50; 51–100; and 101–200 units all as part of the same contract within one year.

Source: DSTL (2010).

There are three features of the data for UK World War II aircraft. First, Table 4.4 confirms substantial reductions in unit prices with increased quantities. The Spitfire is an exception where the price reductions are relatively minor in relation to the scale of output. Second, production quantities are substantial reflecting war-time orders (e.g. for some 2,000 units). Third, the unit price of the Lancaster is lower than its rival Halifax; and the unit price of Halifaxes built by English Electric is below that for the same aircraft built by Handley Page which was the original developer of the aircraft. Finally, unit prices reflect unit production costs plus a profit margin. Typically, profit margins are a percentage of unit production costs. For the sample in Table 4.4, typical profit margins were some 3.5 per cent of unit production costs ranging from 2 per cent to 3 per cent, to a maximum of 5 per cent.

Table 4.5 shows similar data for post-1945 UK jet-powered combat aircraft. Compared with World War II aircraft, there are some significant differences. In real terms, unit prices of combat aircraft rose considerably between World War II aircraft and the post-1945 sample.[3] Following the end of the War, production quantities are generally smaller and there are some interesting price differences between competing aircraft. For example, the Vampire is cheaper than the Meteor and the Vulcan is considerably cheaper than the Victor which raises questions about whether UK procurement policy achieved best 'value for money' with its purchases of the Meteor and Victor. Also, the percentage reductions in unit prices are generally substantial with the notable exceptions for the English Electric Canberra and Lightning. Profitability also varied between aircraft types with typical profit margins of 6 per cent on unit production costs within a range from 3 per cent to 9.8 per cent. Overall, profit margins were higher on post-1945 UK military aircraft.

There are also examples of cost–quantity relationships for civil airliners. For example, on the Lockheed Tri-Star jet airliner, unit number one required some 1.1 million man hours compared with an input of 226 thousand man hours for unit number 112 (Benkard, 2000). Similarly, on the Boeing 787 airliner, unit production costs declined by 60 per cent from the first production aircraft to the 100th aircraft (Flight, 2013a, p47).

---

[3] For example, in constant 2014 prices and £000s, the unit price of the Spitfire was £24.2; the Meteor was £60.2; the Lightning was £536.1. Similarly, the unit price of the Mosquito was £49.7 compared with the Canberra at £252.2; the Lancaster was £92.9 compared with the Vulcan at £988.6 (all in £000s, 2014 prices, based on the RPI).

Table 4.5   Cost–quantity relationships for UK jet-powered combat aircraft, 1945–1960

Aircraft	Quantity (units)	Date of contract	Unit price (£000s)	Percentage reduction (%)
Meteor				
Mk1	1–20	1946	27.8	
	101–400	1946	11.2	60
Vampire				
	1–5	1946	29.0	
	101–120	1946	6.1	79
Attacker				
	1–15	1951	37.5	
	45–61	1951	22.7	40
Hunter				
Mks 1 & 4	1–46	1955	66.0	
	47–146	1955	42.0	36
Javelin				
	1–20	1957	125.0	
	101–200	1957	66.0	47
Lightning				
Mks 1 & 2	50xMk1	1959	199.0	
	42xMk2	1959	167.8	15
Canberra				
BMk6	1–20	1954	72.5	
	21–37	1954	66.6	8
Vulcan				
Mk1	1–25	1954	365.0	
	26–62	1954	261.0	28
Victor				
Mk1	1–5	1956	750.0	
	6–25	1956	462.5	38

Notes:
1. Fighter aircraft are Gloster Meteor, de Havilland Vampire, Supermarine Attacker, Hawker Hunter, Gloster Javelin and English Electric Lightning.
2. Bomber aircraft are English Electric Canberra, Avro Vulcan and Handley Page Victor.
3. Remaining details as in Table 4.4.

MODIFICATIONS TO LEARNING CURVES

With learning curves, complications arise in separating learning economies from economies of scale. Learning curves apply to each type of
aircraft and reflect reductions in direct labour hours due to improved
operator speed through greater experience acquired from repetition. But
other factors affecting learning include improved management, improvements in tools and tool co-ordination, greater efficiency in the production
of sub-assemblies and greater efficiency in parts-supply systems
(reflected in the supply chain: Asher, 1956). However, problems arise in
identifying learning curves since they capture a range of dynamic
influences on unit costs including economies of scale and scope, process
improvement and new technology. A further qualification is needed.
Typically, learning arises in labour operations in airframe production: its
impact on aircraft unit production costs will depend on the importance of
labour in total unit production costs (i.e. comprising airframes, engines
and avionics). Also, as a cost-estimating technique, learning curves are
subject to controversy over the relevant slope of the curve and whether
learning is continuous (the linear progress curve hypothesis: Asher,
1956).

Dis-continuities in learning curves arise from major modifications in
the aircraft type and from breaks in production. Major changes to the
type of aircraft require learning to re-start and return to its pre-
modification levels. Similarly, production breaks, depending on their
length, lead to the loss of experience or forgetting and the need for
learning to re-start once production resumes (some experienced labour
might quit the firm to be replaced by inexperienced staff). For example, a
break of one year in Typhoon production is equivalent to returning to unit
one in production (i.e. learning has to restart). Also, following the loss of
experienced labour, it might take 4–5 months for new labour to become
experienced (equal to 90 units) with some estimates suggesting that this
period might be as long as one year for production staff and two years for
engineers. An example is shown in Figure 4.2.

Comparisons have been made between UK and US aerospace learning
curves. During the 1950s and 1960s some stylised facts emerged on
learning curves. By the end of the 1960s, the typical UK aerospace
industry learning curve for airframes was 80 per cent with UK learning
curves tending to 'flatten-out' around 100 units of output (reflecting the
small scale of UK production). However, in the early 1980s, the view
was that UK industry learning performance at the top of the learning
curve (i.e. at the start stage) was better than the US; but the US

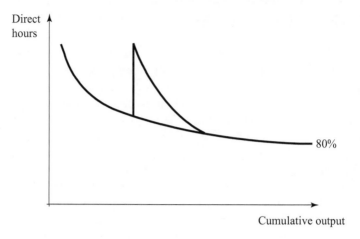

Figure 4.2   Learning modifications and production breaks

out-performed the UK beyond 100 units reflecting the advantages of long US production runs. In contrast, the typical 1950s/1960s US learning curve was 75 per cent for airframes and showed continuous learning (up to 5,000 units on the Phantom), reflecting the larger scale of US output. Modern learning curves are different.

Whilst learning remains important in the economics of aircraft manufacture, there have been some significant changes since the 1960s. These include changes in manufacturing techniques, new materials and business practices (e.g. lean methods; supply chain changes). Greater precision in modern aircraft manufacture requires more capital-intensive methods which results in fewer opportunities for labour learning. But the major change has been in the volume of production. The UK airframe sector, through its participation in the civil Airbus programmes, is now achieving US scales of production. For example, in the 1950s and 1960s, only 8 out of 36 different UK transport aircraft types reached sales of more than 100 units. In contrast, by June 2014, the Airbus A320 family had achieved US scales of production with an output of 6,132 units and total orders of 10,504 units.

High sales volume allows UK aerospace firms at both the prime and supplier levels to undertake major investments in new production techniques, methods, tooling and specialised equipment. Examples include:

1.   The move away from fabricated structures with high parts counts to structural solutions using machined components;

2.   Investments in computer-aided design tools and techniques, high speed CNC machines and automated assembly methods (including automated riveting). Some of these changes in production techniques have led to machines and technology (capital) replacing labour with fewer opportunities for labour learning;

3.   Investment in new plant and equipment (e.g. Airbus UK at Broughton);

4.   The development of next generation composite manufacturing processes in the form of Resin Transfer Moulding and Resin Transfer Infusion.

Various proposals have been made to allow aerospace firms to achieve learning economies. These include collaborative projects, greater exports and joint aircraft programmes where two or more services *within* a nation participate in the development and procurement of a single aircraft design (e.g. US F-35 aircraft). Not all such proposals have been successful.

In theory, proposals for joint programmes between different services within a nation compared with a set of single service programmes should lead to savings by removing duplicate R&D and achieving scale and learning economies in production. However, studies show that joint aircraft programmes have encountered higher rates of cost growth than single aircraft programmes and have not saved overall life-cycle costs and should be avoided (Lorell et al., 2013).

CONCLUSION

For UK civil and military airframe manufacture, learning curves continue to be relevant and they show two features. First, *continuous learning* reflecting longer production runs of each type of aircraft, compared with the 1950s/1960s experience of UK learning curves 'flattening out' at some 100 units. On the Typhoon combat aircraft, a 90 per cent continuous learning curve is typical for combined labour and other operations. This is similar to the typical US fighter production cost improvement curve with an 87 per cent slope (Lorell et al., 2013, p12).

Second, *step changes showing substantial productivity improvements between different generations of aircraft*. This means that whilst each aircraft type demonstrates learning, there have also been substantial downward shifts in cost curves between generations of aircraft. For example, for UK civil aircraft, between the 1960s and 1970s generation and today's types, step changes in productivity well in excess of 50 per cent have been achieved. Similarly, the Typhoon learning curve is located substantially below that for the previous generation Tornado combat aircraft. These productivity gains reflect the adoption of lean manufacturing practices, with improved design for manufacture, better tooling methods and investment in modern machine tools, all of which applies over and above the normal learning curve.

Similar downward shifts in learning curves have been reported by Dassault Aviation on its Falcon 5X business jet. Dassault estimated that the assembly process for the 5X will require around 20 per cent fewer man-hours than for previous programmes. This productivity improvement reflects advances in production technology, embracing digital technologies in manufacturing and a greater use of automated assembly, including robots used on the assembly line (Flight, 2013b, p48).

Overall, new technology in design and manufacture will result in a reduced importance of labour inputs and hence of learning in aerospace manufacturing. Increasingly, new materials and automation means the substitution of machinery for labour and hence fewer opportunities for traditional labour learning. The next chapter considers the wider aspects of technical progress in the aerospace industry.

REFERENCES

Asher, H. (1956). *Cost–Quantity Relationships in the Airframe Industry*, Rand Corporation, Santa Monica, California.

Augustine, N. (1987). *Augustine's Laws*, Penguin Books, Harmondsworth, England.

Benkard, C.L. (2000). Learning and Forgetting: The Dynamics of Aircraft Production, *American Economic Review*, 90, 4, 1034–1054.

DASA (2013). *Defence Inflation Estimates: Statistical Note*, Ministry of Defence, TSO, London, January.

Davies, N., Eager, A., Maier, M. and Penfold, L. (2012). *Intergenerational Equipment Cost Escalation*, Defence Economic Research Paper, DASA, Ministry of Defence, London.

DSTL (2010). *Historical Cost Data of RAF Aircraft 1935–65*, MoD using DSTL version, Ministry of Defence, Defence Science and Technology Laboratory, London.

Flight (2013a). Paris: 787 Programme, *Flight International*, 11–17 June, vol 184, 5394, Surrey.

Flight (2013b). Falcon 5X: Nesting Grounds, *Flight International*, 29 October to 4 November, vol 184, 5413, Surrey.

Hartley, K. and Sandler, T. (eds) (2001). *The Economics of Defence*, International Library of Critical Writings in Economics, 128, Edward Elgar Publishing, Cheltenham, UK and Northampton, MA, USA.

HM Treasury (2000). *Productivity in the UK*, HM Treasury, London, November.

Isby, D. (2012). *The Decisive Duel: Spitfire vs 109*, Little, Brown, London.

Kirkpatrick, D. (1995). Rising unit costs of defence equipment: The reasons and results, *Defence and Peace Economics*, 6, 4, 263–288.

Kirkpatrick, D. (2004). Trends in the costs of weapons systems and the consequences, *Defence and Peace Economics*, 15, 3, 259–273.

Lorell, M.A. et al. (2013). *Do Joint Fighter Programs Save Money?* Rand, Santa Monica, California.

NAO (2011). *Management of the Typhoon Project*, National Audit Office, HCP 755, TSO, London, March.

Pugh, P. (1986). *The Cost of Seapower*, Conway, London.

Pugh, P. (2007). *Source Book of Defence Equipment Costs*, Dandy Books, London.

Sandler, T. and Hartley, K. (1995). *The Economics of Defense*, Cambridge University Press, Cambridge.

Woodford, S. (1999). *Recent Combat Aircraft Life Cycle Costing*, Defence Evaluation Research Agency, ADA388024, Farnborough, Hants.

Wright, T.P. (1936). Factors affecting the cost of airplanes, *Journal of the Aeronautical Sciences*, 3, February.

5.   The economics of technical progress

INTRODUCTION

Technical progress has been a distinguishing feature of the aerospace industry. The industry is now generally regarded as an advanced and high technology industry and one which is believed to be important for economic growth. Since its creation in 1903, it has produced aircraft which fly faster, further and higher, carrying greater loads more safely. Its technology has not only been reflected in its outputs or products but also in its development and manufacturing techniques.

For economists, technical progress in the aerospace industry is a form of non-price competition which raises a number of questions. How is technical progress measured and what are its determinants? Who funds new technology? Is government a key driver; or are conflicts a major determinant? How important is the size of firm and whether markets are competitive or monopolistic? Why do aerospace firms compete on the basis of technology (non-price forms) rather than relying on price competition? Does aerospace technology 'spin-off' and 'spill-over' to other sectors of the economy? And are aerospace industries a source of economic growth as claimed by some governments?

MEASURING TECHNICAL PROGRESS

There is no single and simple indicator measuring technical progress in the aerospace industry (or any other industry). Instead, there are a variety of performance measures which provide indicators of technical progress. These include the speed of aircraft, its range, the altitude it can reach and its carrying capacity. A distinction can be made between military and civil aircraft. For military aircraft, speed, range, altitude and weapons carrying ability affect its combat and military effectiveness. For civil aircraft, there is a greater focus on the number of passengers carried, the range of the aircraft, their economics and their safety. Technical progress in civil aircraft also contributes to the expansion of national and world market opportunities for beneficial trade and exchange.

Data on the maximum speeds of fighter and bomber aircraft over time are shown in Table 5.1. Speeds have increased over time, but they are not

Table 5.1 Military aircraft speeds

Fighter Aircraft	Speed (mph)	Bomber Aircraft	Speed (mph)
Henri Farman (Fr: 1914)	65	Farman F40 (Fr: 1914)	84
Sopwith (UK: 1918)	121	Caproni (It: 1918)	78
Hawker Fury (UK: 1931)	207	Airco DH4 (UK:1917)	143
Spitfire Mk1 (UK: 1938)	355	Douglas B-18 (US: 1937)	226
Spitfire Mk XIV (UK: 1944)	448	Junkers Ju-88A (Ger: 1938)	280
Me 109 K-4 (Ger: 1944)	452	Vickers Wellington (UK: 1938)	235
North American Mustang (US: 1944)	437	Lancaster (UK: 1942)	287
Me163(rocket) (Ger: 1944)	596	Boeing B-17E (US: 1942)	317
F-86 Sabre (US: 1950)	675	Boeing B-29A (US:1944)	358
Lockheed F104A (US: 1956)	1,532	Canberra B2 (UK: 1950)	570
Lockheed SR-71 (US: 1966)	2,200+	Avro Vulcan (UK: 1956)	640
McD F-15 Eagle (US: 1974)	1,678	Boeing B-52G (US: 1958)	660
F-22 Raptor (US: 2005)	1,500	F-111 (US: 1967)	1,450

Notes:
1. Fr is France; Ger is Germany; It is Italy; McD is McDonnell Douglas.
2. Aircraft from Me163 and after are jet-powered.
3. Dates are for first entry into service.

The political economy of aerospace industries

the only indicator of technical progress.[1] For fighter aircraft, other indicators include altitude, range, weapons carrying capacity and mission-effectiveness. Similarly, for bomber aircraft, other indicators include range and bomb-load.

Civil passenger-carrying aircraft have also shown substantial technical progress over time. Some examples are shown in Table 5.2. There is a clear trend of speed increasing over time.[2] Two aircraft were significant indicators of revolutionary technical change, namely, the Comet as the world's first jet airliner and Concorde as the first supersonic passenger-carrying aircraft. Other performance indicators, namely, passenger numbers and range, have also increased over time. Civil passenger-carrying aircraft are also much safer (e.g. measured by numbers of airline passenger fatalities per year).

Table 5.2   Civil aircraft speeds, passengers and range

Aircraft	Date	Speed (mph)	Passengers (number of seats)	Range (mls)
DC-3 Dakota	1936	207	21–32	1,425
Lockheed Constellation	1945	377	62–95	5,400
DH Comet 1	1952	460	36–44	1,500
Tu-104	1956	590	50–100	1,430
Boeing 707	1958	607	110	2,800
Boeing 747	1970	594	539	5,300
Concorde	1976	1,354	92–120	3,900
Airbus A380	2007	634	853	9,500

Notes:
1. DC-3 (Douglas), Constellation and Boeing airliners are all US aircraft; Tu-104 is Tupolev (USSR); DH is de Havilland; Concorde is Anglo-French; and Airbus is European.
2. Date is for first introduction into service and performance data refer to early variants.

---

[1]   For fighter aircraft, the Spearman rank correlation coefficient between dates (year) and speed was +0.92 and the corresponding correlation coefficient for bomber aircraft was +0.98. Both coefficients were positive and were statistically significant.

[2]   The Spearman rank correlation coefficient between date and speed for civil aircraft and date and passenger numbers were each +0.95 which was statistically significant. The rank correlation coefficient between date and range was +0.61 which was not significant at the 5% level.

Some of the major technical changes have been reflected in qualitative indicators of technical progress (i.e. notable firsts). For example, the achievement of the first manned flight represented a major technical change and the introduction of the jet engine formed a revolutionary technical change. Similarly, technical progress was further reflected in the development of radar and avionics, manned space flight, the manned Moon landings and in the development of missiles, cruise missiles and inter-continental ballistic missiles. Some of these developments have attracted widespread public interest. Other major technical changes have been less conspicuous such as new design, development and production techniques. For example, the aerospace industry pioneered the application of new materials and computer-aided design technology and its development and production processes are skill-intensive requiring scientists, technologists, engineers, project managers and skilled production workers (high salary and high wage jobs). The ability to combine and integrate the various skills and technologies provides the aerospace industry with distinctive systems integration capabilities. It is then argued that these skills and capabilities are precisely those needed if advanced industrial countries are to compete with low wage and newly developing nations. It is further claimed that the aerospace industry provides the next generation of highly paid jobs needed to raise living standards in advanced industrial economies (e.g. fast food outlets only provide part-time and low wage jobs). But technical progress comes with a price tag: it is not free.

THE PRICE OF TECHNICAL PROGRESS

Technical progress is costly. Table 5.3 presents examples of the historical rising trend for the unit costs of UK combat aircraft. Over the 10 year period 1936 to 1946, real unit costs of fighter aircraft increased by a factor of 1.9, followed by an increase of 8.5 times over the next 13 years from 1946 to 1959 and a rise by a factor of almost 8 times between 1959 and 2003. Questions arise as to whether these real terms increases in unit costs for combat aircraft reflected the threats from wars (rearmament, World War II and the Cold War) and revolutionary technical change following the introduction of jet aircraft? The data on relative unit costs for similar aircraft also raise questions about the cost-effectiveness of some procurement choices. For example, the Lancaster's unit costs were considerably below those for the Stirling and Halifax; similarly, the Meteor was considerably more expensive than the Vampire; and the Valiant jet bomber was the costliest of the V-bombers. However, the relative cost differences are only suggestive rather than conclusive: they need to be standardised for output levels and for relative performance before definitive conclusions can be reached.

Table 5.3   Historical cost trends for UK combat aircraft, 1936–2012

FIGHTER AIRCRAFT			BOMBER AIRCRAFT		
Aircraft	Original price (£000s)	Constant 2012 prices (£000s)	Aircraft	Original price (£000s)	Constant 2012 prices (£000s)
Swordfish	5.5 (12/36)	247.1	Hampden	10.9 (8/38)	472.9
Gladiator	3.1 (11/37)	130.8	Wellington	15.3 (4/40)	579.6
Hurricane	4.0 (9/39)	174.1	Stirling	24.0 (10/42)	818.7
Spitfire	5.1 (6/40)	189.7	Halifax	30.0 (6/42)	1007.5
Typhoon	10.5 (3/43)	351.2	Lancaster	18.4 (6/43)	617.9
Meteor	13.9 (3/46)	457.8	Mosquito	9.1 (8/43)	307.0
Vampire	6.1 (2/46)	199.7	Canberra	54.0 (6/51)	1434.9
Venom	20.1 (1/53)	473.6	Valiant Mk1	385.0 (9/55)	8547.0
Hunter Mk1	53.5 (1/55)	1190.0	Vulcan Mk1	365.0 (12/54)	8418.9
Javelin	77.0 (1/57)	1566.3	Vulcan Mk2	358.0 (1/58)	6983.9
Lightning Mk1	199.0 (4/59)	3923.4	Victor Mk1	235.5 (5/55)	5335.1
Typhoon	23160.0 (6/03)	30888.5	Tornado	2573.1 (6/79)	11175.9

Notes:
1. Data are for *airframe* unit production costs including a profit allowance. Other component costs are excluded. The DSTL data does not include Tornado and Typhoon: these were based on author's estimates with airframe costs at 33 per cent and 40 per cent of unit production costs, respectively.
2. Most data exclude costs of jigs, tools and flight testing.
3. Data are for the contract for the year shown. For example, contracts for Spitfire and Hurricane are shown at the start of World War II; subsequent contracts resulted in lower unit prices as output increased. For example, unit costs for Spitfire MkVIII in October 1944 were £4,958 (at 3,000 units); see also data for Vulcan Mk1 and Mk2. Jet bomber projects ranked by date of service entry.
4. Constant prices based on UK Retail Prices Index for 1936–2012. Current prices are for the contract year shown for each aircraft: for example, unit prices for Spitfire are at June 1940.

Source: DSTL (2010); Davies et al. (2012).

The unit prices of civil aircraft have shown a similar rising trend. For example, the Douglas DC-3 aircraft in 1935 had a unit price of $61,775 in 1935 prices (excluding engines) which converts to a unit price of $1.04 million in 2012 prices (based on US consumer prices). This aircraft had a speed of 207mph, it carried 21–32 passengers with a range of 1,425 miles. In contrast, the Airbus A380 airliner had a list price of $403.9 million in 2012; it had a speed of 587mph; and it carried a maximum of 853 passengers with a range of 9,500 miles.[3] The price difference in real terms between the DC-3 and the A380 was a factor of 388. However, the A380 was vastly superior in terms of speed, range and passenger capacity which might be taken as indicators of technical progress between 1935 and 2012.

WHO PAYS FOR TECHNICAL PROGRESS?

Technical progress in the aerospace industry is not a free gift. Someone has to pay and the broad options are the public or private sector or a combination of both. Historically, the industry developed on the basis of individual inventors and entrepreneurs who pioneered manned flight (see Chapter 2). These early pioneers with some aerodynamic knowledge designed and tested their ideas often at great risk to themselves (e.g. the early pioneering aircraft were unsafe and often crashed). Their inventions were funded privately from individual savings and assets or from private sponsorship. Later, income was obtained from public sponsorship, especially from military sources and from income resulting from success in competitions and revenue from passengers carried on pleasure trips. Examples of the early aviation pioneers included the Wright Brothers (USA), Louis Bleriot (France), Fokker (Netherlands) and Sikorsky (Russia).

The Wright Brothers were inventors, builders and flyers. Their bicycle business which manufactured, repaired and sold bicycles provided funds for their growing interest in flight. They pioneered developments in aircraft controls, propellers and engines. Initially, secrecy was used to protect their inventions from copying by rivals. Eventually, they were awarded a patent for their flying machines which provided protection for their valuable ideas and a return on their investments. Later, revenue was generated from various sources such as the award of a US Army contract,

---

[3] List prices for airliners are subject to discounting. Discounts of 20% to 60%, with an average of 45%, are common, with discounts offered to the early buyers of a new aircraft type or to airlines buying large quantities.

the creation of an aircraft manufacturing business (the Wright Company established in 1909), the establishment of a flying school, competitions for prize money and fares from air cargo flights. After a temporary merger with Martin, the Wright Company merged with Curtiss to form the Curtiss–Wright Corporation which manufactured aircraft, engines and propellers (1929). By 1945, Curtiss–Wright was the largest US aircraft firm. However, during World War II, the company had failed to invest in the R&D required for advanced aircraft design and it failed to adjust to the design and production of jet aircraft: it sold its aircraft division to North American Aviation in 1948. By 2013, Curtiss–Wright was a diversified engineering and precision manufacturing firm supplying specialist components with markets in defence, commercial aerospace, power generation and energy.

Louis Bleriot was a French aviation pioneer. He established a profitable business manufacturing car headlamps, the funds from which were used to finance his experimental work on aircraft. He won prize money for the first air crossing of the English Channel and then created an aircraft manufacturing business named Bleriot Aeronautique. The successful crossing of the English Channel led to orders for Bleriot aircraft and further funds were raised from flying schools established in France and Britain. In 1936, the Bleriot company and all other privately-owned French aircraft companies were nationalised by the French government.

In its formative years, the aircraft industry was based on private finance with individual inventors and entrepreneurs forming owner-managed enterprises. Aircraft research and development was based on private venture initiatives. World War I changed the pure private market model with the state becoming closely involved in funding technical progress and the expansion of the industry (Chapter 2). However, following the end of the War, individuals as inventors and entrepreneurs remained dominant although they were often part of larger shareholder-owned firms. Examples of prominent aircraft designers and engineers in the post-1918 period included R.J. Mitchell (Spitfire and the Supermarine company); Sydney Camm (Hurricane and Hawker company); Geoffrey de Havilland who developed the innovative Mosquito fighter bomber (initially developed on a private venture basis); Willy Messerschmitt who was a prominent designer of World War II fighter aircraft; and Donald Douglas and James McDonnell who were prominent designers and owners of US aircraft companies. These designers were leaders of design teams of aeronautical engineers and draughtsmen reflecting a long-run trend towards aircraft development work requiring larger design teams with increasingly skilled labour requirements. The age of the individual inventor entrepreneur with an owner-managed and controlled firm has been replaced by larger and highly skilled design and development teams which are now parts of large corporations which are either privately-owned by shareholders or state-owned enterprises.

Within military aerospace markets, technical progress is determined by governments with their procurement requirements. Conflict is a major cause of technical progress with its demands for new and more advanced aerospace equipment (e.g. faster fighter aircraft; stealthy bomber aircraft and missiles: see Table 5.1). Disarmament following conflict leads to reduced demands for military aerospace equipment and less urgency for new technology. In military markets, privately-owned firms will be unwilling and unable to fund the costly R&D programmes for modern combat aircraft, helicopters and missiles. Such programmes require products which initially have a single buyer, namely, a government where there are no other buyers. As a result, the firm is dependent on the government order where governments can change and be replaced with a new government which might cancel the project. Privately-owned firms will be unwilling and unable to provide the scale of funding for developing and producing a specialised military project which is designed solely for the national government with no alternative buyers. Firms will be concerned that their costly investments in highly specialised development and production skills and facilities will never be recovered (this is known as the 'hold-up' problem). In these circumstances, governments provide the funds needed for their procurement requirements (see Chapter 11).

Technical progress in civil aircraft is also dependent on government both directly and indirectly. In capitalist economies, government might fund completely the costs of new developments in civil aircraft (e.g. Concorde) or might contribute towards the costs of such projects with considerable funding from private sources. For business and 'pleasure' aircraft, all the costs and risks of development and production will be borne by the private sector with funds from company profits, private capital markets and from major suppliers. In non-capitalist economies, governments will provide all the funding needed for developing a new civil aircraft. Whatever the type of economy, the size and terms of state funding for civil aircraft development will affect technical progress leading to greater technical progress than would occur in completely private markets (see Chapter 10).

Governments also affect technical progress in civil aircraft markets indirectly through 'spin-offs' from military aerospace markets. Some of the new technologies required for military aerospace markets might 'spin-off' and be used on new civil aircraft (e.g. jet engine).

TECHNOLOGY 'SPIN-OFFS'

Technology spin-offs have been known by various names including technology spill-overs,[4] technology externalities, diffusion of technology and technology transfer. They involve the commercial application of technology (knowledge) from an original application to some other application either within the same firm or the same industry or some completely different industry within a nation or to other nations in the world economy.

There is no shortage of examples of spin-offs involving the aerospace industry. Technical advances for military aircraft have been transferred and applied to civil aircraft. Examples include radar, the jet engine, flight control systems and composite materials. The advanced technology on the Eurofighter Typhoon has created world leaders in carbon fibres, sensor fusion, glass fibre cables for data transmission, as well as flight control systems and modular avionics. Some of these technologies and new materials have been applied to Airbus and Boeing jet airliners (Hartley, 2008). The US space agency NASA has identified an impressive list of spin-offs from the US space programme. These include LEDS (light-emitting diodes), by-pass operations, and a range of applications in health and medicine, transportation, public safety, weather forecasting and computer technology. Some technologies have been applied to markets outside the aerospace industry. For example, aerospace technology has been applied to motor cars, including Formula 1 racing cars (e.g. lightweight materials; anti-skid braking; GPS) and helicopter blade technology has been applied to the turbine blades used for wind farms. Jet engine technology has led to the development of new materials able to withstand high temperatures and jet engines have been used for marine propulsion. Space activities in the form of satellites have led to satellite imaging and satellite navigation which have resulted in productivity improvements in agriculture and the development of satellite television and mobile phones.

Whilst the examples of technology spin-offs from aerospace are impressive, they only provide qualitative evidence: they need to be evaluated critically. A key question for economists concerns the *market value* of aerospace technology spin-offs. Here, there are major estimation problems in identifying genuine causal relationships between the original

---

[4] Some writers distinguish between spin-offs where technology remains with the aerospace industry and spill-overs where technology is applied to other industries outside the aerospace industry.

technology and its applications and distinguishing these from exaggerated claims from special interest groups with an interest in achieving government support for the industry. Critics of any market valuation claim that technology spin-offs are difficult to measure; but it might be that the difficulties of measurement reflect the fact that there is 'nothing to be measured!' Further estimation problems arise from the long lead times involved in advanced technology aerospace projects where today's technology might only find other applications at some date well into the future. There are also counter-factual problems: what would have happened in the absence of the aerospace technology (e.g. would similar technologies have been developed by, say, the motor car industry and at what cost?). Finally, there is the task of placing a market value on spin-offs which are basically non-market outcomes with no market prices. One of the few published studies to estimate the market value of aerospace technology spin-offs was undertaken to measure the economic impacts of the planned buy of US F-35 combat aircraft by the Netherlands. Technology spin-offs and spill-overs were estimated at $1.22 billion from an expected value of $9.2 billion for development and production representing some 13 per cent of the value of the F-35 contract for the Dutch economy (2004 prices: De Vijver and Vos, 2006).

More problems arise in any economic and critical evaluation of aerospace technology spin-offs involving their transmission mechanism and whether there is a genuine market failure. Critics question the mechanism whereby aerospace technology spin-offs are transmitted to other sectors of an economy. A study of Typhoon identified various transmission mechanisms, including labour turnover where skills are transferred either within a company or to other firms (e.g. motor car industry); through staff on Typhoon acting as consultants (e.g. to Formula 1 racing car industry); through the supply chain with advanced technology flowing to small-medium size companies in the supply chain; and through links with universities. Of course, it might be that technology is transferred from other industries to the aerospace industry (inward flows of technology rather than outward flows from aerospace to other industries).

Genuine market failure is used to justify state intervention in private markets. With technology spin-offs, the key question is whether there are market failures in R&D markets. At the outset, it has to be recognised that research and development are highly risky and uncertain activities. Private firms undertaking R&D will seek to protect their costly investments through patents but patents might be costly and have a limited life. Aerospace R&D is high risk with long-term rather than immediate returns and technical spin-offs to other sectors of the economy. Economic

theory suggests that competitive markets will under-invest in research
due to its risks and uncertainties and the costs of establishing complete
property rights in marketable ideas. Under-investment in research also
arises from increasing returns in the use of information reflecting
beneficial externalities in the form of technology spin-offs and decreasing
marginal costs in the dissemination of information. Market failure in
aerospace is most likely to arise in civil aircraft markets where further
questions arise about the operation of private capital markets. Are private
capital markets able and willing to provide funds for the development
costs of large civil aircraft or are there genuine capital market failures
preventing such funds being available at the launch stage of a new civil
aircraft project? The economic case for subsidising civil aircraft development is assessed in Chapter 10.

Military markets are different. Government provides the necessary
funding for military aerospace R&D and the issue here is whether the
state negotiates contracts with provision for firms to pay for any
commercial exploitation of state-funded R&D. Alternatively, technology
transfer from a firm's military division to its civil business (and elsewhere in the economy) might be achieved without any payment to the
state for the transfer of commercially valuable technology.

Even where technology transfer is regarded as a beneficial external
economy and a source of market failure, it does not follow that
government support for a specific military or civil aerospace project is
the most appropriate and efficient policy solution. Failure in R&D
markets might be 'corrected' by state intervention in other activities such
as changes to patent laws and protection of inventions and innovations or
the 'correction' of failures in private capital markets. Nor does it follow
that an aerospace project is the most efficient solution to correcting
market failure. Other industries and projects might offer greater technology spin-offs; nor can it be guaranteed that an aerospace project or
any other project will lead to valuable spin-offs. For example, if a new
combat aircraft leads to technology spin-offs, these should be viewed as
unexpected windfall gains. No one can predict that a specific project will
lead to guaranteed spin-offs; and with combat aircraft, their end-purpose
is to contribute to national defence with any spin-offs regarded as
accidental by-products of the procurement.

FIRM SIZE, MARKET STRUCTURE AND THE FORM OF COMPETITION

In the early and formative years of the aircraft industry, technical progress was determined by inventor entrepreneurs acting as owner-controlled and owner-managed firms operating in private competitive markets. Individuals survived by marketing their ideas through sales to various customers including governments, private consumers, demonstration flights and success at competitions. At this stage in the industry's development, technical progress was based on small firms operating in private competitive markets. Fast forward to 2014 and firm size, market structure and ownership are completely different. Today, technical progress in the aerospace industry is determined by large firms competing in monopoly or oligopoly markets where firms are owned by private shareholders or by governments or by a combination of the two.

Economic theory provides predictions about the impact on technical progress of firm size and market structure. A starting point is the case for large firms. This argues that only large firms are able to undertake and fund the costly R&D necessary for technical progress and to finance the application of new ideas into commercial products. For example, only large firms can afford to purchase highly specialised laboratory equipment and to hire teams of costly scientists, technologists and engineers. Large firms can also spread risks over several projects; they have access to internal funds to finance costly and risky R&D; and they are able to transfer technology between different divisions of the company. However, there is an opposing argument in favour of small firms, namely, that large organisations are bureaucratic and discourage creative thinking and entrepreneurship. In contrast, small firms encourage innovative inventors and enable them to achieve a return on their investment in new and marketable ideas. Empirical evidence found that the majority of major inventions resulted from small private inventors rather than the R&D divisions of large firms. Here, a distinction is needed between invention and innovation where large firms might be required to undertake the development work needed to convert original ideas into marketable products or processes.

There is a further argument based on the importance of market structure for technical progress. Some economists take the view that the competition of the competitive model is not the 'best' market structure for technical progress. The costs of development mean that it can only be undertaken by large firms and not by the small firms of the competitive model. Moreover, firms need some market power with a substantial share of the market to provide an incentive to undertake costly R&D. The costs of establishing property rights in new ideas are central to the debate. In the competitive model, competition is based on prices. New ideas are likely to be copied by rivals who have not borne any of the costs of development and will obtain a share of the pioneer's profits and the benefits will be passed to consumers through lower prices. As a result, competitive markets will tend to 'under-invest' in invention and research: an innovating competitive firm will find its new ideas promptly copied. There are, of course, mechanisms for protecting new ideas, namely, patents, high penalties for illegal copying and private policing arrangements, all of which involve costs. Imitators will also need time to copy an innovation (e.g. reverse engineering takes time). Or, inventors can be rewarded through competitions for prize money or through government procurement contracts. Alternatively, where research has value to large numbers of firms in an economy (basic research) it is likely to be funded by governments (e.g. in universities).

Monopoly markets are the complete contrast to competitive markets. It has been claimed that monopoly is more likely to promote technical progress. Here, it is argued that large firms with monopoly power can afford to undertake costly R&D and then use their monopoly power to obtain a return on their R&D investments. In such market structures, a successful innovation creates a *temporary* monopoly allowing the successful innovator to capture a return on its invention; but such inventions are never permanent since new firms will always discover new and better products (Schumpeter's creative destruction).

There is an alternative market structure which is believed to promote technical progress, namely oligopoly which comprises a small number of relatively large firms. In such markets, firms compete on a non-price basis rather than through price competition. Non-price competition includes technical innovation, advertising and product differentiation, each of which has different time dimensions in terms of the speed with which they can be changed. For example, prices and advertising can be changed quickly; product characteristics take longer to change; and in the long run, R&D allows firms to introduce completely new products. In oligopoly markets, firms are large so that they have the *capacity* for costly R&D and the existence of small numbers of firms means that each oligopolist has market power which provides an *opportunity* to achieve a return on its R&D investments. The absence of price competition means that the returns from costly R&D will accrue to the innovator and to a few rivals who might imitate but the benefits will not be passed immediately onto consumers through lower prices.

Casual empiricism supports the advocates of large oligopolistic firms promoting technical progress. It appears that much industrial R&D is undertaken by large firms and that the research-intensive industries are oligopolistic. Examples include aerospace, chemicals, energy, motor vehicles and pharmaceuticals. Within civil aerospace markets, there are duopolies (two large firms) in both the large civil jet and regional jet airliner markets (Airbus and Boeing; Bombardier and Embraer). But both markets are threatened with new entrants as regional jet airliner firms seek to develop larger airliners and new firms enter the regional jet airliner market. Such markets are also characterised by similar products with aerospace companies supplying similar aircraft with some differentiation. Airbus and Boeing offer similar airliners with their Airbus A320 and Boeing 737 'families'. Over the period 1970 to 2007, Boeing had a world monopoly of the 'jumbo jet' market with its 747 series but its monopoly ended with the entry into service in 2007 of the Airbus A380 airliner. More recently, both Airbus and Boeing competed with new but similar large jet airliners in the form of the Airbus A350 XWB (extra wide body) and Boeing 787 Dreamliner models with each claiming to be superior to its rival in certain respects (e.g. fuel economy; numbers of passengers; range) with price discounts available for early and large orders. The oligopoly model seems to 'fit the facts' of the world civil aircraft market. It also corresponds to the facts of the world military aircraft market but the monopoly model appears more relevant for some *national* military aircraft markets (e.g. France; Italy; Sweden; UK).

Oligopoly firms have a further distinguishing feature, namely, their decision-making is interrelated and interdependent. This provides opportunities for applying game theory which focuses on decision-making by oligopoly firms in relation to prices or output or other choices about R&D spending, advertising, product differentiation, entry and location.[5] Decisions about these variables lead to payoffs in the form of firm profitability which will depend on the reactions of their rivals. For example, in aerospace there will be gains for the first firm to develop a new airliner (first mover advantage), but its gain will be dependent on the time required by a rival firm to develop a competitive airliner. There are also gains from an established firm pursuing policies designed to deter new entrants from entering the market (strategic entry deterrence). Here, the rivalry between Airbus and Boeing resembles a repeated game rather

---

[5] John Nash won the Nobel Prize in Economics for his work on game theory. His life was portrayed in the film *A Beautiful Mind* starring Russell Crowe.

than a single game with firms learning about their rivals reactions such that aggressive behaviour by one firm leads to hostile reactions from its rivals.

In military markets, strategic behaviour embraces rival firms and government procurement agencies. For example, in bidding for major government defence contracts, large firms and the procurement agency will play games of bluff, chicken and 'tit for tat'. Faced with the prospect of foreign firms winning a defence contract, domestic rivals will focus on the jobs, technology and balance of payments impacts of importing. Inevitably, firms can, and will, react to their rivals in many different ways which makes oligopoly theory difficult, challenging and characterised by uncertainty. It can generate many possible outcomes ranging from collusion to aggressive price wars which shows the complexity of interdependence in oligopoly markets (Lipczynski et al., 2009; see also Chapter 7).

AEROSPACE INDUSTRIES AND GROWTH

The aerospace industry is often viewed by governments as a major source of economic growth. It is claimed to be a source of high technology and a provider of highly skilled and high wage jobs which enable advanced and developed economies to compete with newly emerging and low-cost nations. On this basis, it is claimed that aerospace (including space activities) enables a nation to maintain its competitive and comparative advantage in international trade.

Economists critically assess such arguments. Their critique starts by relating the 'case for aerospace' argument to economic models of growth. Traditionally, economic models explained growth in terms of inputs of capital (machinery) and labour (numbers and skills of workers). However, empirical studies have shown that these inputs only explained a small fraction of economic growth and that the residual is explained by 'other factors'. These other factors include scale economies, the efficiency of resource allocation and technical progress which explains a large part of the residual. More recent models of endogenous growth theory identify internal factors as determinants of growth including human capital (skills), innovation and spill-overs. The policy implications of the model favour openness, competition, change and innovation. The important point is that economic models of growth identify a major role for technology in growth, but they do not identify a role for specific industries such as aerospace. Indeed, the endogenous growth models suggest that policies favouring or protecting existing industries will actually slow growth.

The case for aerospace is often based on its contribution to technological progress: it is a high technology industry which also provides valuable spill-overs to other industries. This chapter has provided evidence of both contributions reflected in product and process innovation and many examples of spill-overs within aerospace (military to civil aircraft) and to other sectors. Technical progress in aerospace has also contributed to national economic output through promoting beneficial market exchange. Civil aircraft which can fly faster and further with lower travel costs have improved market opportunities for both national and international trade and exchange. Military aircraft have also contributed to the development of markets by protecting national markets and international trade routes allowing the development of beneficial national and international trade and exchange. However, with military aircraft, problems arise in placing a market value on their contributions to security, protection and market development (e.g. compared with, say, a motor car, what is the valuation of a fighter aircraft?).

The case for aerospace as outlined above can be presented in a basic economic model of the following general form:

$$g = f(TP, S, Z) \qquad (5.1)$$

$$\text{and } TP = f(AS, X, Z) \qquad (5.2)$$

Where g is growth; TP is technical progress; S is spill-overs; Z is other relevant factors; AS is the aerospace industry; X is other industries. In both equations, the relationships are positive such that, for example, more technical progress results in more economic growth.

The above economic model needs to be developed and tested. To illustrate the approach, empirical tests were undertaken to identify possible correlations between the aerospace industry and measures of national economic performance. The European Union produces an annual Innovation Scoreboard. Data for 2011 showed that the EU's *innovation leaders* were Denmark, Finland, Germany and Sweden whilst the *innovation followers* were Austria, Belgium, Cyprus, Estonia, France, Ireland, Luxembourg, Netherlands, Slovenia and the UK. All remaining EU states were either *moderate* or *modest innovators*, including two with substantial aerospace industries (Italy and Spain: EU, 2011). On this basis, nations with a substantial aerospace industry accounted for only 5 out of 14 nations comprising the innovation leaders and followers group which does not provide convincing support for the importance of the aerospace industry in national economic performance. An alternative test correlated the size of a nation's aerospace industry measured by sales with its economic growth rate. Data for 2011 produced a Spearman's rank correlation coefficient of +0.98 which was highly significant showing larger aerospace industries associated with higher growth rates. These results are suggestive and provide some support for the view that the aerospace industry is associated with a successful economic performance. But correlations do not prove causation and the economic model and the associated tests are simplistic and need much greater development. The counter-factual also needs to be addressed: what has been the economic performance of those nations without an aerospace industry and are there other industries and sectors which might produce similar or even better economic performance than aerospace (e.g. motor cars; pharmaceuticals; general state support for R&D)?

CONCLUSION

Aerospace is regarded as a 'high technology' industry which also provides technology spill-overs. This chapter has outlined and assessed critically these technology arguments. More analysis and evidence on industry performance is presented in Chapter 7. In addition, technical progress resulting in new products and higher development and unit production costs is determining the industry's structure. Over time, the long-run trend has been towards a smaller number of larger firms which are developing new global relationships with their suppliers (e.g. European firms establishing new assembly plants in low-cost countries). Economists have a variety of models which analyse industry structure.

REFERENCES

Angelucci, E. (ed.). *World Encyclopedia of Military Aircraft*, Janes, Defence, London.
Davies, N., Eager, A., Maier, M. and Penfold, L. (2012). *Intergenerational Equipment Cost Escalation*, Defence Economic Research Paper, Ministry of Defence, London, December.
De Vijver, M.V. and Vos, B. (2006). The F-35 Joint Strike Fighter as a source of innovation and employment: some interim results, *Defence and Peace Economics*, 17, 2, 155–159.
DSTL (2010). *Historical Cost Data for RAF Aircraft 1935–65*, Ministry of Defence, using DSTL version, London.
EU (2011). *European Union Innovation Scoreboard 2011*, European Commission, Luxembourg.

Hartley, K. (2008). Collaboration and European defence industrial policy, *Defence and Peace Economics*, 19, 4, 303–315.

Lipczynski, J., Wilson, J.O.S. and Goddard, J. (2009). *Industrial Organization: Competition, Strategy, Policy*, Prentice Hall, London.

6.   Industry structure

INTRODUCTION

Why focus on the structure of aerospace industries? The world's aero-space industries have different industrial structures. How do economists explain the structure of an industry? Does economic analysis offer any guidelines for public policy towards industrial structures and which is the 'best' industrial structure? These are some of the issues addressed in this chapter.

Industry structure determines its performance. This chapter reviews the contribution of industrial economics to the analysis of aerospace indus-tries. Examples are taken from the US, European and UK aerospace industries. Significantly, aerospace industries depart from the economist's model of the perfectly competitive industry. Instead, aerospace industries are typically monopoly or oligopoly industries supplying military mar-kets which are dominated by national governments and civil markets dominated by large numbers of airlines. Ownership differs with some firms, industries and airlines being privately-owned and others being state-owned.

Various economic models can be applied to aerospace industries and these are reviewed in this chapter. It starts by explaining the industry structure–conduct–performance model and some of the newer develop-ments.

ECONOMIC PERSPECTIVES: THE SCP PARADIGM

A starting point for analysing an industry is the industry structure–conduct–performance model of industrial economics (SCP paradigm: Tisdell and Hartley, 2008). Using this approach, an industry is analysed in terms of its:

1.   *Structure* comprising the number of firms and their size together with entry and exit conditions for the industry. The number and size of firms will reflect the opportunities for achieving economies of

scale and learning which lead to lower unit production costs as the scale of output rises. These are known as decreasing cost industries and are typical of the aerospace sector which is characterised by learning economies (Chapter 4; Hartley, 2011). Where there are substantial scale economies in both R&D and production, firms have incentives to expand either internally or via mergers and acquisitions so creating large firms of the size seen in aerospace (e.g. Boeing; BAE Systems; EADS; Lockheed Martin).

2. *Market Conduct* reflected in price and non-price competition where non-price competition comprises advertising, marketing, political lobbying, R&D and product differentiation. In defence markets, competition is often based on non-price factors such as the technological features of equipment (e.g. speed, range and weapon load of a combat aircraft): hence, military aerospace firms are often R&D-intensive companies. Moreover, defence R&D might lead to beneficial 'spin-offs and spill-overs' to the rest of the economy (e.g. jet engines, composite materials and avionics for military aircraft applied to civil airliners).

3. *Market Performance* which is reflected in efficiency and profitability, growth and technical progress. Efficiency has two aspects comprising technical efficiency and allocative efficiency. Technical or productive efficiency requires that firms use the least-cost combination of factors of production to produce any level of output. Allocative efficiency requires technical efficiency plus outputs which are socially desirable (i.e. society's preferred or best output where price equals marginal costs so that additional benefits equal additional costs). The economists model of perfect competition leads to both technical and allocative efficiency (with price equal to marginal cost). This model provides a 'benchmark' for assessing the performance of markets (see Table 6.1). It is also a model which solves the defence equipment procurement problem by using competition to determine prices, profitability and the efficiency of contractors. In the absence of competition, all these variables have to be negotiated between the buyer and seller with myriad challenges to both parties. On this basis, competition is a high-powered efficiency mechanism and is a feature of a successful industry.

The SCP model predicts a simple causal relationship running from structure through conduct to performance with performance dependent on industry structure. Two extreme market types are identified, namely, perfect competition and monopoly. Typically, it is predicted that compared with perfect competition, monopoly results in higher prices, a lower output, monopoly profits and a misallocation of resources (reflected in monopoly prices exceeding marginal costs leading to a 'deadweight loss' of consumer welfare). In contrast, perfect competition leads to lower prices, greater output, long-run normal profits and an 'optimal' or best allocation of an economy's resources.

Such predicted benefits of competition are the basis for the Single European Defence Equipment Market (EDEM) and are reflected in competitive procurement policies as used by some national defence ministries (e.g. for equipment procurement and for military outsourcing). Competition has also been applied at various stages in a programme's life-cycle. For example, there is often competition at the initial design stage (i.e. between competing design proposals taking the form of a paper competition and usually based on technical features of the planned equipment). Next, there might be competition at the prototype stage usually with two firms invited to build competing prototypes (e.g. US combat aircraft prototype competitions leading to the Lockheed Martin F-16 and F-35 choices with associated competing engines: a 'fly before you buy' policy). Later in a project's life-cycle, there might be competition for production contracts. For example, the firm winning the development contract might be guaranteed an initial production order, but be required to compete for all subsequent production contracts. In all these cases, the aim of policy is to avoid the inefficiencies of monopoly and to retain some competitive pressures on the contractor. But there are no costless policies and options. Continuing competition to, say, the prototype stage involves the costs of two competing designs; but there are benefits in reducing programme risks and uncertainties and in retaining competitive pressures on contractor prices, efficiency and profitability.

The features of monopoly and competition industries are compared in Table 6.1 which also provides an analytical basis for identifying successful firms and industries. Each industry is defined with respect to the number and size of firms, entry and exit conditions, profitability and the form of competition (based on the SCP paradgm). Monopoly is a single seller of a product with no close substitutes so that the monopolist is the industry. Profits are defined in relation to the economic concept of 'normal profits' which are the minimum return required to keep a firm in the industry. Competition means that in the long-run, firms earn only normal profits. In contrast, monopoly leads to 'abnormal' or monopoly profits in the long-run (i.e. above normal or high). Immediately, questions arise about 'operationalising' the economic concepts of normal and abnormal profits and the associated long-run. Further problems arise since the standard measures of profitability based on company accounts data do not correspond to the theoretical concepts used by economists.

Accounting rates of profit usually show the ratio of profits to capital, equity or sales. Here, problems arise from the accounting interpretation of discretionary expenditure, depreciation, debt, risk, tax, inflation and mergers. Inevitably, data problems mean that accounting data are used to measure profitability but such data need to be adjusted for risk and need to be related to the cost of capital. A further qualification is required. The perfect competition model provides a benchmark for industrial analysis and is the basis for monopoly and competition regulatory policies used by nations.

Table 6.1   Market types: a taxonomy

Market type	Number of firms	Size of firms	Entry/exit	Profits	Form of competition
Perfect competition	Large numbers	Relatively small	Free entry and exit	Normal in long-run	Price
Monopoly	One	Firm is industry	Entry barriers	Monopoly profits in long-run	Price and non-price
Oligopoly	Few	Relatively large	Entry barriers	Monopoly profits in long-run	Non-price e.g. advertising; R&D/ technical progress
Monopolistic competition	Large numbers	Relatively small	Free entry	Normal in long-run	Non-price: product differentiation

Between the extremes of competition and monopoly, there are 'intermediate' types of industry structure, comprising oligopoly and monopolistic competition. Oligopoly is often present in national defence industries (e.g. US defence market) and is a market form which has some distinctive characteristics. Oligopoly comprises a small number of relatively large firms where there are close relationships between competitors (e.g. if one firm reduces price, its rivals will follow with price cuts so that rival behaviour cannot be ignored). Such interdependence between oligopoly firms has been analysed using game theory; but one critic has stated that when game theory is used to analyse competition 'almost anything can happen' (Schmalensee, 1990).

A further feature of oligopoly is relevant to aerospace industries. This concerns the likely impact of oligopoly on technical progress, where technical progress is a further indicator of industry performance (and hence its success or weakness). The presence of large firms with monopoly power but subject to rivalry provides the ability and incentive to undertake costly R&D together with opportunities for obtaining a return from investing in such costly R&D. However, defence R&D is usually financed by government rather than private industry (Tisdell and Hartley, 2008). Nonetheless, the technical complexity of modern defence equipment requires large firms with the R&D resources needed to undertake such complex programmes.

Monopoly is the typical market structure for prime contractors in most EU *national* defence markets. There is also an EU-wide monopoly for missiles (MBDA) and military airlifters (Airbus A400M) and a duopoly for helicopters (Airbus Helicopters, formerly Eurocopter; AgustaWestland). However, the presence of monopoly depends on the definition and extent of the market. If the defence market is defined as an EU-wide market, then the industry structure changes from monopoly to oligopoly (e.g. Airbus formerly EADS; BAE; Finmeccanica; Thales) and at the level of NATO and the world defence market, it becomes reasonably competitive. Also, monopoly power depends on the availability or absence of close substitutes. New technology often creates rival products, such as UAVs replacing manned combat aircraft for some missions. Industry structure also varies with the level of the supply chain. Suppliers to major prime contractors will involve more smaller firms operating in competitive markets (varying between perfect and monopolistic competition).

Two further aspects of the SCP model need to be addressed, namely, buyers and firm ownership. First, markets embrace both buyers and sellers. The SCP model focuses on the supply side in the form of industry structure. Buyers cannot be ignored and, as with the supply side, they can vary between large and small numbers. Typically, in most private markets, there are large numbers of buyers so that no one buyer has any power to determine prices (e.g. food; motor cars). But defence markets are different. Government is the dominant buyer of military equipment. For defence-specific equipment (i.e. lethal equipment), national government will be the major or for some equipment, it will be the only buyer: hence it is a monopsony buyer (e.g. nuclear-powered submarines in France and the UK; B-2 bombers in the USA). Other buyers for equipment will be foreign governments, reflected in defence exports. As a major or monopsony buyer, government can use its buying power to determine the size, structure, conduct, performance and ownership of its national defence industries. Where governments have buying power, they are a major determinant of the performance of firms and industries and hence whether they are 'strong or weak', successful or failures. Governments also purchase civil equipment (dual-use) such as food, fuel, motor cars, office equipment, clothing and a range of services (e.g. financial; consultancy) where they are one buyer amongst large numbers of buyers and where firm and industry performance depends on market structure.

Ownership also matters in determining firm and industry performance reflected in strengths and weaknesses, success and failures. State-ownership is believed to be associated with inefficiency, especially where state-owned firms are monopolies receiving state subsidies and are loss-making enterprises. Inefficiency arises from the absence of capital market pressures in the form of the threat of take-overs and bankruptcy and from the lack of competition in product markets (Tisdell and Hartley, 2008). Such an approach suggests that a 'weak' European Defence and Technology Industrial Base (EDTIB) will be characterised by loss-making monopoly state enterprises. Interestingly, a number of EU nations have 'privatised' their defence industries. For example, 25 years ago, the UK defence industrial base was mostly state-owned (BAe; Rolls-Royce; British Shipbuilders; Royal Ordnance; Shorts; research establishments), 'protected' by a 'buy British' procurement policy and receiving mostly cost-plus contracts. The UK defence industry is now privatised (except for the Defence Science Technology Laboratory (DSTL)) and foreign firms are often invited to bid for UK defence contracts, most of which are competitive (cost-plus contracts are no longer used (DASA, 2012)).

The SCP paradigm provides a 'tool kit' for analysing any aerospace industry. However, further developments have led to modifications of the basic SCP model. These newer developments include contestable markets; transaction costs; game theory; and the Austrian critique. *Contestable markets* are those where there is the possibility and threat of entry by domestic and foreign firms: hence, there is a *threat of rivalry*. With this approach, contestability rather than industry structure (number of firms) determines performance. *Transaction costs* recognise that all economic activity and exchange occurs in a world of imperfect information and knowledge and so involve costs of transactions. These embrace all the costs involved in planning, bargaining, modifying, monitoring and enforcing an implicit or explicit contract. Transaction cost economics offers some distinctive explanations and interpretations of economic organisations reflected in a variety of organisational forms in aerospace industries (e.g. the make or buy decisions of firms; vertical integration; internal organisations of firms; conglomerates).

Many real world markets, especially in defence, do not resemble the economists perfectly competitive model. They are dominated by small numbers of large firms (e.g. civil jet aircraft; computers; motor cars).

Game theory explains the behaviour of oligopoly firms where there are interdependencies between the behaviour of rival firms. Finally, the *Austrian economists* are critical of the standard SCP model with its focus on perfect competition and equilibrium. They assert that actual economies are never in equilibrium (i.e. never at a state of rest). Instead, economies are characterised by ignorance and uncertainty which leads to continuous change and continuous market disequilibrium (the future is unknown and unknowable). Entrepreneurs play a central part in Austrian economics. Ignorance and uncertainty create opportunities for profits and it is the entrepreneur's task to discover these profitable opportunities before their rivals with competition as continuous rivalry between entrepreneurs. The Austrian approach has two major implications for public policy. First, the role of profits: policies which reduce profits as the rewards of entrepreneurship will reduce future entrepreneurial effort so adversely affecting the competitive process. Second, Austrians believe that policy-makers should avoid making statements either about the most efficient form of industrial organisation or about the wastes of advertising and duplication. Austrians claim that no-one, especially politicians and bureaucrats, has sufficient knowledge and competence to judge which form of market structure is the most efficient for meeting future consumer demands (e.g. today's sunrise industries will be tomorrow's smokestack industries). Instead, it is entrepreneurs who have profit incentives to meet new and unexpected future consumer demands (Tisdell and Hartley, 2008).

ECONOMIC PERSPECTIVES: PORTER AND THE FIVE FORCES MODEL

The SCP model had a major influence on Porter's five forces model determining a firm and industry's competitive position (Porter, 1990, p35). The five competitive forces are:

1.   The threat of new entrants;
2.   The threat of substitute products and services;
3.   The bargaining power of buyers;
4.   The bargaining power of suppliers;
5.   The rivalry amongst existing competitors.

In the Porter model, the strength of the five competitive forces varies between industries and determines long-term industry profitability. For example, the threat of new entry and rivalry amongst existing competitors, the availability of substitutes as well as powerful buyers and powerful sellers will limit an industry's profitability. In turn, the strength of each of the five competitive forces depends on industry structure which is central to the SCP model. Porter's model which is part of the strategic management literature shows that a firm's strategies and conduct are determined by the presence and strength of the five forces. Indeed, management strategists focus on the distinctive internal characteristics of firms suggesting that each individual firm is different and its distinctive characteristics and capabilities determine its competitive advantage (e.g. innovation; reputation). It is the distinctive strategic choices taken by firms which are the main determinants of performance with firms maintaining their competitive advantage by protecting their strategies from imitation (Lipczynski et al., 2009).

Aerospace markets have all the features of Porter's five competitive forces model. Military aerospace markets are characterised by powerful buyers and powerful sellers, but industry competition and the availability of substitutes depends on a government's willingness to allow foreign firms to enter national defence markets (i.e. entry barriers).

CHARACTERISTICS OF THE AEROSPACE INDUSTRY

The aerospace industry has a number of characteristics which contribute to its distinctive industrial structure:

An Increasingly Long and Costly Development Process

Aerospace equipment is costly in both development and unit production costs and cost trends are strongly upwards. Also, on complex high technology aircraft projects, development can take many years. Some examples of cost levels and cost trends for military aircraft are shown in Tables 6.2a and 6.2b.

The Importance of Volume: Cost–Quantity Relationships and Learning Economies

Quantity is a major determinant of unit costs and competitiveness. Long production runs allow fixed R&D costs to be spread over greater volumes. There are also economies of learning leading to productivity improvements with greater cumulative output (Chapter 4; Hartley, 2011). As a result, aerospace industries are decreasing cost industries.

Table 6.2a   Examples of costs on military aerospace projects

Project	Unit production cost ($millions, 2012 prices)
Manned fighter/strike aircraft	134
Advanced trainer aircraft	33
Strategic transport/tanker aircraft	388
Attack helicopter	47
Anti-submarine helicopter	126
Stand-off missile	4
Reconnaissance UAV	10

Source: Pugh (2007).

Table 6.2b   Cost trends for UK combat aircraft

Aircraft	Year	Cost index
Spitfire	1934	100
Vampire	1946	170
Hunter	1954	200
Lightning	1959	670
Harrier	1969	1,670
Tornado	1979	2,900

Source: Hayward (1989, p6).

Costly Entry

Entry requires the high levels of technology and R&D spending to design, develop and produce modern military and civil aircraft and space systems. Costly military projects are usually funded by governments: hence, government can also be a barrier to entry (Laguerre, 2009).

Incentives to Collaborate

High R&D costs and the economies of scale and learning in production provide the economic incentives for two or more nations to collaborate. In the ideal case, international collaboration results in cost savings compared with a national programme as each nation shares R&D costs and benefits from scale and learning economies as the partners combine their production orders.

However, ideal case collaboration has never been achieved as each partner demands a 'fair share' of the high technology work, as well as its own flight testing centre and final assembly line, so increasing development costs by an estimated 50 per cent for each partner nation beyond the first (Pugh, 2007). Similar cost penalties apply to collaborative production whilst the international bureaucracy and international management arrangements inevitably add to development times (Hartley, 2008; see also Chapters 12 and 13).

Aerospace as an Economically Strategic Industry

Aerospace industries are high technology, R&D-intensive industries with technology spin-offs to the rest of the economy (e.g. radar; composite materials; jet engines). They are decreasing cost industries characterised by imperfect competition leading to monopoly profits. Government strategic trade policy providing state support for aerospace industries enables a nation to obtain a share of monopoly profits in world markets (e.g. Airbus: Lawrence, 2001; Flight, 2009).

MARKET FAILURES IN THE AEROSPACE INDUSTRY

Aerospace markets are characterised by significant market failure, especially in defence markets. Governments are central to determining military demands. They are 'monopsony' or major buyers of military aircraft, helicopters, missiles and space systems and they can use their buying power to determine the industry's size, structure, conduct and performance as well as its ownership.

For example, government determines entry and exit; it uses its contractual powers to determine industry structure (e.g. UK mergers of 1958–1960); it determines the form of competition for military contracts; it determines profits on non-competitive contracts and it controls military exports. As a result, government itself is a source of market failure in the sector and such failure is reinforced by the public goods characteristics of defence.

The role of government in aerospace markets suggests that these are political markets which might also be analysed using public choice models. These models identify various agents in political markets, comprising governments seeking re-election, relevant bureaucracies as budget-maximisers and producer groups as rent-seekers. Public choice analysis suggests that governments can also fail (see Chapter 9; Tisdell and Hartley, 2008, chapter 14).

Government is also highly influential in civil aerospace markets. It controls and regulates property rights determining landing and over-flying rights for national airspace. It has also provided targeted financial assistance and support through civil aircraft research and technology demonstrator programmes, as well as repayable launch investment (pre-viously known as launch aid in the UK: HCP 151-1, 2005).

Launch Investment

A distinctive feature of the civil aerospace sector is government financial support in the form of launch investment. Questions arise about the economic case for launch investment and whether such state support reflects genuine capital market failures. The economics of new large civil aircraft and engine projects involve high development costs, long devel-opment periods, substantial technical and commercial risks and long-term returns.

Compared with the motor car and pharmaceutical industries, large civil aircraft and engine projects are relatively few and each represents a large proportion of the enterprise value of the firms involved in such projects (e.g. Airbus; Boeing; Rolls-Royce). It appears that aerospace industries encounter difficulties in attracting finance in the early development stage of new projects; but difficulties in accessing private funds or in such funds only being available at 'too high' a price are not necessarily evidence of capital market failures (see Chapter 10). These features might reflect the efficient operation of capital markets and the market's judge-ment that there are more profitable alternative uses of such funds. Also, the fact that launch investment is, in principle, repayable inevitably raises the issue of why then cannot such funds be provided by private capital markets?

There are, however, a range of possible additional factors which might explain capital market failures to finance large civil aircraft projects. The more common *additional* arguments put forward in relation to launch investment for civil aircraft include uncertainty and the risk aversion of private investors; the presence of asymmetric information and the small number of programmes; short-termism; the dependence upon single companies (e.g. Airbus; Boeing); and the fact that rivals are subsidising their national aerospace industries. This is reflected in the availability of state support for civil aircraft in Europe, North America, Japan and elsewhere. Finally, the existence of significant beneficial externalities in the form of technology spin-offs from civil aircraft programmes. However, questions remain as to which, if any, of these additional arguments represent a genuine market failure which is specific to civil aerospace projects.

THE WORLD'S TOP AEROSPACE FIRMS

There is not a single market for aerospace equipment. Instead, there are national and world markets for military and civil aircraft, helicopters, missiles and space systems. There are further sub-markets within each of these groups. Military markets consist of markets for combat aircraft, bombers, trainers, helicopters, transports and specialist aircraft (e.g. air tankers; maritime patrol aircraft; reconnaissance and surveillance). Civil aircraft markets comprise markets for regional and large jet airliners, turboprops, helicopters, business and pleasure aircraft. Each market comprises different numbers of buyers and sellers. National military markets have a single buyer (national governments) with more buyers available in the world market. Civil markets are characterised by large numbers of buyers comprising publicly and privately-owned airlines, governments (VIP aircraft), companies (business aircraft) and individuals (pleasure aircraft).

Space markets are also dominated by governments who fund space exploration reflected in the development of rocket launchers and other space vehicles (e.g. moon landings). Governments also have military requirements for space systems (e.g. surveillance satellites). In addition, there are private commercial requirements for space systems (e.g. satellites for communications, TV, radio and broadband).

On the supply side, US aerospace companies dominate the world's top aerospace firms. In 2012, they accounted for 70 per cent of the top 10 and 52 per cent of the top 25. In contrast, European companies accounted for 30 per cent of the world's top 10 with firms from Brazil, Canada and Japan appearing in the world's top 25 list. France had four firms and the UK two firms in the top 25 (see Table 6.3).

The average US aerospace firm in the top 25 is some 40 per cent larger in terms of sales than its European rivals, so allowing American firms to achieve greater economies of scale, learning and scope. A comparison of average firm size for the US and European firms suggests excess capacity in Europe: if US average size applied to Europe, then Europe could produce its current output with some six firms rather than its current eight firms.

Table 6.3   World's top 25 aerospace firms, 2012

Company	Total sales ($Bn)	Defence share of total sales (%)
Boeing	81.7	46
Airbus (formerly EADS: N)	74.8	24
Lockheed Martin	47.2	78
General Dynamics	31.5	73
United Technologies	29.1	20
Northrop Grumman	28.1	81
Raytheon	24.4	90
Finmeccanica (It)	20.2	60
General Electric	20.0	3
SAFRAN (F)	15.9	32
Rolls-Royce (UK)	13.7	26
Honeywell	12.0	14
L-3 Communications	11.8	83
Textron	9.1	26
BAE Systems (UK)	8.7	95
Bombardier (Can)	8.6	n/a
Embraer (Br)	6.2	15
Thales (F)	5.8	52
Mitsubishi Heavy Industries (J)	5.5	10
Precision Castparts	5.5	12
Spirit Aerosystems	5.4	n/a
Dassault Aviation (F)	5.2	27
Rockwell Collins	4.7	59
Zodiac (F)	4.6	n/a
MTU Aero Engines (Ger)	4.5	15
US average firm	23.9	53
European average firm	17.0	30
Rest of World average firm	6.8	13

Notes:
1. n/a is not available. EADS was renamed as the Airbus Group in 2014.
2. Sales are for aerospace sales only estimated on the basis of those divisions which operate in aerospace only and reported in the Flight Top 100: hence, all non-aerospace business is excluded in the rankings. This explains what appears to be some strange rankings (e.g. BAE Systems which has much larger company sales than shown in the table and comprising sales of land and sea equipment) and the omission of some firms (e.g. missile specialist MBDA as a separate entity).
3. Defence shares of sales are all defence sales as shares of firm's total sales both aerospace and non-aerospace. The share figures are for 2011.
4. Brackets show country of origin. Br is Brazil; Can is Canada; F is France; Ger is Germany; It is Italy; J is Japan; N is Netherlands; UK is United Kingdom. All other companies where no brackets are shown are US firms. The table excludes Russian and Chinese aerospace firms.
5. Averages based on firms in World top 25: US average is for all US firms shown in table; similarly for European average; Rest of World average comprises Brazil, Canada and Japan. Defence shares of sales are medians.

Sources: Flight (2013a); SIPRI (2012).

Aerospace firms are large and economics explains their size in terms of the search for profitability and efforts to economise on transaction costs where transaction costs comprise all the costs of 'doing business'. Large firms exist where there are substantial economies of scale and learning in development and production, where size offers economies from the scope of the business and where making rather than buying offers lower costs.

Large size firms suggest an industry characterised by monopoly and oligopoly structures with large absolute size forming the basis for 'powerful producer groups' (see Chapter 9). Outside the USA, monopolies dominate a number of *national markets* (e.g. BAE Systems and Rolls-Royce in the UK; Finmeccanica in Italy). However, within the *world market*, oligopoly is typical. There are duopolies in the markets for regional and large civil jet airliners (Bombardier and Embraer for regional jets; Boeing and Airbus for large jet airliners). Oligopoly is typical for helicopters (AgustaWestland; Bell; Boeing; Airbus Helicopters; Sikorsky) and large aero-engines (General Electric; Rolls-Royce; SAFRAN; United Technologies). The small number of firms in oligopoly industries means that their behaviour is interdependent and is analysed using the new developments in game theory (see Chapter 7). Elsewhere, world markets are more competitive with substantial numbers of firms providing actual or potential competition for military combat and business aircraft.

The space industry often comprises national monopoly industries, especially for rocket launchers. Nations with a rocket launcher capability include China (Long March 3B), India, Japan, Russia (Soyuz) and the European Space Agency (Ariane 5). The US space industry is dominated by a monopoly in the form of the United Launch Alliance which is jointly owned by Boeing and Lockheed Martin and supplies three rockets, namely, Atlas V, Delta II and IV. However, there are potential new entrants to the US rocket launcher industry, including Orbital Sciences Corporation with its Antares launcher (originally known as Taurus II). In contrast, the space satellite industry is more competitive with substantial numbers of supplying firms, particularly in Europe and the USA.

Firms adopt different business models to organise their business and to seek lower transaction costs so not all firms are identical. Table 6.3 shows that there are different business models. For example, there is the *specialist aerospace firm* with a civil and military aircraft business reflected in the Airbus and Boeing models which are large firms based on a major civil jet airliner business with military markets forming less than 50 per cent of their business. In contrast, there is the *defence firm model* where defence sales account for over 70 per cent of the business and firms provide a range of air, land and sea equipment. Examples include Lockheed Martin, Northrop Grumman and BAE Systems. But within military markets, there are further specialisms: for example, Raytheon is defence-dependent and specialises in missiles whilst Boeing specialises in large military aircraft comprising transports, air tankers and maritime patrol/anti-submarine aircraft.

Elsewhere in the top 25, there are further specialisms reflected in aero-engines, avionics (electronics) and aero-structure firms. There are a small number of specialist aero-engine companies, none of which are vertically integrated with associated *aircraft* manufacture. United Technologies is different in that it is not an engine specialist with its Pratt and Whitney engine division and ownership of Sikorsky Helicopters (although Sikorsky Helicopters are often powered by rival engines). Similarly, SAFRAN comprises SNECMA which manufactures aircraft and rocket engines, Turbomeca which specialises in helicopter engines and SAGEM which is a security company. Also, SAFRAN owns Messier-Bugatti-Dowty landing gear specialists. Within the top 25, some firms have specialised in avionics (Honeywell; Rockwell Collins; Thales) whilst others are specialists in aero-structures (e.g. Spirit Aerosystems; Zodiac).

Typically, aerospace firms supply a range of aircraft so obtaining economies of scope. Examples include Bombardier and Embraer supplying both regional and light business jets; Airbus and Boeing supplying large jet airliners to both airlines and VIP customers; and Dassault supplying combat and business aircraft (e.g. Rafale and Falcon).

The supply side of aerospace markets is further complicated by international alliances. Europe's major combat aircraft firms have collaborated to produce the four nation Typhoon and there is a seven nation collaboration for the Airbus A400M airlifter. Other European collaborations include helicopters (Airbus Helicopters), missiles (MBDA) and space systems (ESA). Aero-engines have created international alliances involving European and US firms. CFM International is an alliance between General Electric and Snecma; and International Aero Engines is an international consortium originally comprising Pratt and Whitney, Rolls-Royce, the Japanese Aero Engine Corporation and MTU Aero Engines formed to produce the V2500 engine (Rolls-Royce withdrew from IAE in 2012).

Industry structure has also changed through take-overs, mergers and new entry. Take-overs and mergers led to major structural changes in the US and European industries (e.g. formation of BAE Systems and EADS; take-overs by Boeing and Lockheed Martin). Companies sold major divisions of their business where some sales led to the entry of new firms. Examples include the Boeing sale of its Wichita division to Spirit Aerosystems; and BAE Systems sale of its Airbus division to Airbus where the acquisition led to Airbus making rather than buying its wings. In the regional jet airliner industry, there are new entrants from China, Japan and Russia (China: Comac C919; Japan: Mitsubishi Heavy Industries; Russia: Sukhoi Superjet and Irkut MC-21).

Mergers and take-overs can be horizontal, vertical or conglomerate. Horizontal mergers involve firms at the same stage of production in the same industry; vertical mergers occur at different stages of production in the same industry; and conglomerate mergers involve firms whose production activities are unrelated. Aerospace industries have been involved in all three types of mergers reflecting their search for profitability (including lower costs). Horizontal mergers reduce competition; vertical mergers can also increase monopoly power; whilst conglomerate mergers enable a firm to diversify and reduce the risks from reliance on aerospace markets. Examples of horizontal mergers include Boeing's acquisition of McDonnell Douglas and Lockheed's acquisition of General Dynamics fighter business. Vertical mergers involve aircraft firms acquiring avionics firms (e.g. Finmeccanica ownership of Selex and DRS Technologies).

Interestingly, major airframe firms have not acquired major aero-engine companies (and vice versa): why is this? Usually, vertical integration occurs where it offers opportunities to reduce transaction costs or to achieve market power. The transaction cost explanation of vertical integration suggests that it arises where it is cheaper to perform productive activities itself rather than rely upon other firms. A major reason why it might be cheaper to produce internally rather than rely on markets results from the transaction costs incurred when using markets. Transaction costs comprise the costs of negotiating, policing and enforcing an agreement with another firm. No firm-to-firm agreement can deal with uncertainty and specify all possible future contingencies and the costs of renegotiating and modifying agreements represents an important transaction cost. Renegotiation of contracts also provides opportunities for either party to exploit its bargaining power (opportunistic behaviour).

Where transaction costs are believed to be high, a firm will prefer to undertake the activity itself rather than rely on the market (make rather than buy choices). High transaction costs occur where suppliers of a product require specialised assets for its production. Such specialised assets include specialised plant, equipment and labour which have no alternative use value: they are costly and cannot be used elsewhere in the economy. The owners of specialised assets need incentives to invest in them: without guaranteed markets, they are likely to invest in more attractive alternatives.

High transaction costs might also arise where market conditions are changing and where transactions involve the sale of information. No contract can specify all future contingencies and the more uncertain the future, the harder it is to specify a legally enforceable contract. Individuals have limited possibilities for identifying and understanding all future possibilities (known as bounded rationality). Transactions involving information create additional problems which might best be solved by undertaking the activity internally rather than using the market. Overall, the transaction cost explanation of the presence or absence of vertical integration predicts that firms will choose to perform activities internally rather than use market purchases when the costs of monitoring internal efficiency are less than the transaction costs of using markets. On this basis, the striking absence of vertical integration between aircraft and engine companies suggests that the transaction costs of such integration are too high and that reliance on markets is a lower cost solution.[1] But transaction costs and markets are always changing so that today's industrial structure might not be the most efficient for future production.

There are other explanations of vertical integration. These include opportunities to create or increase market or monopoly power. For example, by vertically integrating, a firm may create monopoly profits by price discrimination, by eliminating rivals or preventing entry. Elsewhere, vertical

---

[1]   Whilst the transaction cost approach is attractive it is difficult to operationalise and to test empirically.

integration might be restricted by government anti-monopoly and competition rules. Or, it might result from the need to assure the supply of important assets or it could be a means of creating countervailing bargaining power to offset existing monopoly power. Certainly there are numerous instances of vertical integration in the world's aerospace industries involving, for example, integration of aircraft and avionics activities, and engine and landing gear systems (Carlton and Perloff, 1994).

Overall, these economic explanations of the presence or absence of vertical integration provide a basis for understanding the different extent of such integration in the world's aerospace industries. There is, however, an alternative explanation, namely, the role of government either through its buying power or through its ownership of aerospace firms and industries (see Chapter 9).

US AEROSPACE INDUSTRY

US aerospace firms are privately-owned and dominate the domestic and world markets for military and civil aircraft. The large-scale of their operations results in economies of scale, learning and scope providing a competitive advantage in export markets. Data from the world's top 100 aerospace firms confirms the dominance of US aerospace firms. In 2012, US firms accounted for 70 per cent of the world's top 10 aerospace firms and 50 per cent of the top 50, falling to 38 per cent of the top 100. Aircraft, helicopter, missiles and aero-engine companies accounted for the US firms in the top 15; beyond the top 15, the remaining US aerospace firms were specialist suppliers in parts, components, electronics, sub-assemblies and aerosystems.

The US military aerospace market is protected by entry barriers in the form of the Buy American Act which typically requires the US government to prefer US-made defence equipment. Within the US national aerospace market, there are national monopolies for large civil jet airliners and large military transports (Boeing) and for missiles (Raytheon); a duopoly for aero-engines; and oligopolies for helicopters and combat aircraft (see Table 6.3). However, outside the US national market, the world aerospace market has more suppliers so creating potentially more competitive market conditions.

The size of the US aerospace industry is shown by its annual sales and employment. Table 6.4 shows that over the ten years 2002 to 2012, both real sales and employment have generally risen with a 'local maximum' in 2008 which reflected peak military demands for aircraft and missiles.

The sales-employment relationship is determined by labour productivity which rose by almost 30 per cent over the period.

Table 6.4   Size of US aerospace industry

Year	Sales ($ Billions, 2012 prices)	Employment (000s)
2002	190	618
2003	185	587
2004	189	592
2005	200	612
2006	212	632
2007	236	647
2008	242	660
2009	241	644
2010	240	624
2011	242	625
2012	250	631

Note: Figures are rounded.

Source: AIA (2013).

THE EUROPEAN AEROSPACE SECTOR

In 2011, total sales for the European Aeronautics and Space sectors were Euros 122.2 billion with direct employment of 513,630 personnel. Assuming a ratio of direct to indirect employment of 1.1:1.0 gives an estimated figure for total direct and indirect employment in Europe's aerospace industry of some 980,570 personnel (ASD, 2012; DASA, 2008). However, it is misleading to analyse the European aerospace industry as a single sector: it is distributed amongst its member states, especially in France, Germany, Italy, Spain, Sweden and the UK.

Both the European and US aerospace industries have shown considerable structural change leading to a smaller number of larger firms. The result is less competitive markets dominated by monopoly, duopoly and oligopoly. Structural change resulted from mergers and acquisitions and some exits from the aerospace industry. Table 6.5 shows the leading US and European aerospace firms in 1997. Comparisons with the leading firms in 2012 (see Table 6.3) shows that considerable structural changes have occurred.

Table 6.5 World's top 25 aerospace firms in 1997

Company	Aerospace Sales ($Bn, 1997 prices)
Boeing	45.0
Lockheed Martin	27.9
British Aerospace (UK)	14.0
Raytheon	10.6
United Technologies	10.3
Aerospatiale (F)	9.6
Northrop Grumman	9.2
DASA (Ger)	8.8
General Electric	7.8
Allied Signal	6.4
GEC (UK)	6.0
Thomson-CSF (F)	6.0
Alcatel Alsthom (F)	5.3
Rolls-Royce (UK)	5.0
SNECMA (F)	3.9
Finmeccanica (It)	3.9
Dassault Aviation (F)	3.6
Bombardier (Can)	3.3
Mitsubishi Heavy Industries (J)	3.2
Textron	3.1
TRW	3.1
Lagardere (F)	2.8
Litton Industries	2.6
Hughes Electronics	2.5
BF Goodrich	2.5

Notes:
1. Figures are rounded.
2. Countries are Can=Canada; F=France; Ger= Germany; It=Italy; J= Japan; UK = United Kingdom. All other companies are US companies.
Source: Flight (1997).

British Aerospace acquired GEC Marconi Electronics Systems to form BAE Systems (1999); Raytheon merged with Hughes Electronics (1997); United Technologies acquired BF Goodrich (2012); Aerospatiale merged with DASA and CASA (Spain) to form EADS (2000) now named Airbus; Northrop Grumman acquired Litton Industries (2001), Newport News Shipbuilding (2001) and TRW (2002); Allied Signal acquired Honeywell and re-named the new group as Honeywell (1999); Thomson-CSF became Thales; Alcatel Alsthom's satellite business was sold to Thales (2006); and SNECMA merged with SAFRAN (2005). Lagardere is more complex: its subsidiary was Matra which merged with Aerospatiale (1990) to form Aerospatiale Matra which is now part of Airbus (formerly EADS) whilst Matra BAe Dynamics became part of the missile company MBDA. General Dynamics showed both exit and re-entry into the aerospace industry. In 1993, it sold its F-16 combat aircraft business to Lockheed; but in 1999, General Dynamics re-entered the aerospace industry by purchasing Gulfstream Aerospace. More recently, a proposed merger between BAE Systems and EADS was abandoned (2012).

Industry concentration depends on the definition and extent of the market. Within Europe, the industrial re-structuring resulted in monopolies for large civil and military aircraft (EADS/Airbus) and missiles (MBDA); duopolies for helicopters (AgustaWestland; Airbus Helicopters, formerly Eurocopter) and aero-engines (Rolls-Royce; SAFRAN); and an oligopoly for combat aircraft (Dassault; Eurofighter; Saab). However, in national European Union markets, industry concentration is much greater than at the European market level. For example, concentration levels are much higher in the French, German and UK national markets, where monopolies are more typical in the aerospace sector.

Industry concentration is also determined by entry conditions. Protected markets are associated with monopolies. In European Union defence markets, national defence industries can be protected from competition through the use of Article 346 (formerly Article 296 of the Treaty on the Functioning of the European Union or TFEU) which allows national defence industries to be protected for reasons of 'essential security interests'. There is a further aspect of market entry, namely, the possibility that markets might be 'contestable'. In such markets, monopolies might be deterred from exercising their monopoly power by the *threat of entry* in the form of potential entrants.

A comparison of the top 25 firms in 1997 and 2012 shows major changes. A number of firms listed in 1997 were no longer listed in 2012 due to mergers, exits or no longer placed in the top 25. There were some new firms in the top group, namely, EADS (now Airbus) and General

Dynamics. However, Boeing remained the world's top aerospace firm (see Tables 6.3 and 6.5).

Between 1997 and 2012, the average size of US and European aerospace firms in the top 25 increased in real terms. US firms increased their average size from $15.6 billion to $23.9 billion and their average European rivals increased from $8.95 billion to $17 billion (2012 prices). Nonetheless, the US–European size differential remained but it declined over the period. In 1997, the average European aerospace firm in the top 25 was 57 per cent of the average size of the leading US aerospace firms; by 2012, the European aerospace firms were about 70 per cent of the average size of US firms. Indeed, by 2012, EADS/Airbus was similar in size to Boeing (see Tables 6.3 and 6.5).

The European aerospace sector has some distinctive features:

1. The sector has considerable experience of *international collaborative projects*. These involve the sharing of total R&D costs and the pooling of production orders between the partner nations. Aerospace has been involved in collaborative programmes for military and civil aircraft, helicopters, missiles and space systems. Some have led to the formation of European companies, namely, Airbus, MBDA, Eurocopter (now Airbus Helicopters) and ESA. Collaborations have ranged from the minimum two nation collaboration (e.g. Anglo-French Jaguar and the helicopter programmes) to 3–4 nation collaborations on advanced combat aircraft (e.g. Tornado; Typhoon) and the seven nation collaboration on the Airbus A400M airlifter. Collaboration is one of the distinctive features of European defence industrial policy; but it has been mostly confined to the aerospace sector. This reflects the high and rising costs of modern aerospace projects, especially for development (Hartley, 2008; Chapters 12 and 13).
2. Opportunities remain for improving the efficiency of European collaboration on military projects. Typically, work-sharing arrangements and the bureaucracy associated with these projects leads to increased costs and delays (Hartley, 2006). Also, there remain opportunities for creating European companies rather than relying on *ad hoc* loose federations of project-specific arrangements for managing such programmes. Airbus in the civil aircraft market shows that international collaboration can be successful.
3. Applying the US 'model' shows some of the opportunities for re-structuring the EU military aerospace sector. The USA has three major combat aircraft firms compared with six European firms in this market. Re-structuring also means reductions in excess capacity

in the sector. The possible end of future manned combat aircraft and their replacement with UAVs will mean capacity reductions in the military aircraft production sector. For example, in 2005, the UK predicted that the future number of its military aircraft plants would fall from four to two (DIS, 2005). However, so long as manned combat aircraft remain in service they will require support and up-grading over their life-cycle: hence, this capability will need to be retained.

4.   The trend towards internationalisation of the European primes. The major EU aerospace firms are seeking new market opportunities, especially in the US defence market (e.g. JSF; BAE; EADS/Airbus; Finmeccanica–AgustaWestland), but also in Asia (through acquisitions, partnerships and joint ventures). Over the longer-term such trends might have implications for employment and security of supply.

The following section presents a more detailed analysis of the UK industry as an example of one of Europe's largest aerospace industries. It describes the structure, ownership and regional location of the industry to illustrate how the approach can be applied to other European aerospace industries. It also describes how the UK industry has been affected by structural change.

THE STRUCTURE OF THE UK AEROSPACE INDUSTRY

The UK aerospace industry is dominated by privately-owned domestic monopolies for the supply of aircraft, helicopters, missiles and engines (BAE; AgustaWestland; MBDA; Rolls-Royce). Nonetheless, the domestic monopolies are, in principle, contestable markets, assuming that the UK government is willing to allow foreign firms to compete for UK defence contracts (Laguerre, 2009).

However, the Defence Industrial Strategy (DIS, 2005) identified key UK defence industrial capabilities which were to be protected, including BAE's design capability for combat aircraft, AgustaWestland's helicopter design capability and Rolls-Royce engine capability. Other capabilities were to be open to foreign competition (e.g. trainer aircraft; large transport aircraft; future helicopter requirements). But UK defence industrial policy changed in 2012 with the introduction of a policy based on open competition subject to the constraint of protecting the UK's operational advantage and freedom of action for 'essential national security interests'. Open competition means buying 'off-the-shelf' where appropriate based on open procurement providing 'best value for money' (Cmnd 8278, 2012).

Overall, the UK military aircraft sector is generally believed to be 'too large' and the 'current size of the air sector is not sustainable, and rationalisation and reduction in terms of both infrastructure and employment is inevitable' (DIS, 2005, p89).

In terms of ownership structure, significant parts of the UK aerospace industry are foreign-owned. For example:

- AgustaWestland is owned by Finmeccanica (Italy)
- MBDA is jointly owned by BAE Systems, Airbus Group formerly EADS (with plants in France) and Finmeccanica (Italy)
- Shorts (Belfast) is owned by the Canadian company Bombardier
- Smiths Aerospace was acquired by General Electric (USA) in 2007
- Shorts Missiles Systems was acquired by Thales (France)
- Airbus (UK) was acquired by EADS which is now Airbus Group
- Messier-Dowty is owned by Safran (France)
- TRW (Lucas Aerospace) is owned by Northrop Grumman (USA).

Similarly, the major UK aerospace firms, namely, BAE and Rolls-Royce, have substantial ownership of foreign aerospace and defence companies:

BAE Systems has a major presence in the US defence market, mostly in the ownership of US land systems and defence electronics subsidiaries; in Australia and Saudi Arabia; and for some years it had a 20.5 per cent shareholding in the Saab group of Sweden which has now been sold. BAE is also involved in European collaborative projects, including the Typhoon combat aircraft and MBDA missiles as well as being a partner company on the US Lockheed Martin F-35 combat aircraft (JSF: see Chapter 8).

Rolls-Royce owns Allison the US engine company and is involved in various European collaborative military aero-engine projects (e.g. Typhoon; A400M airlifter) as well as the US F-35 programme (including the alternative JSF engine with General Electric until both companies ended work on the engine in 2011).

The top 12 UK-owned aerospace firms in 2012 are shown in Table 6.6. They comprise a mix of prime contractors (BAE Systems), major suppliers (Rolls-Royce; Cobham; GKN; Martin Baker), avionics (Meggitt; Ultra), aerospace engineering (Senior) and maintenance services (Marshall Aerospace), all under private ownership. In 2011, the UK industry's total sales were divided almost equally between military and civil markets (51.3 per cent and 48.7 per cent, respectively) with exports accounting for 75 per cent of total sales (ADS, 2012).

Table 6.6   Top 12 UK-owned aerospace firms, 2012

Company	Aerospace Sales ($ Billions, 2012 prices)
Rolls-Royce	13.7
BAE Systems	8.7
Cobham	2.7
Meggitt	2.5
GKN	2.5
BBA Aviation	2.2
Ultra Electronics	1.2
Chemring	1.1
Senior	0.7
Marshall Aerospace	0.4
Doncasters	0.3
Martin Baker	0.3

Notes:
1. UK-owned only firms shown. Data not available on UK sales for UK divisions of foreign-owned UK-based firms (e.g. AgustaWestland; Smiths Aerospace).
2. Sales are for aerospace, excluding other group sales. This explains the position of BAE Systems which has major sales of land and sea systems.

Source: Flight (2013a).

Employment is an indicator of industry size. Table 6.7 shows the impact of war and peace on the size of the UK aerospace industry. Major employment reductions occurred after the end of World War I; employment rose during the rearmament of the 1930s and during World War II from 1939 to 1945 with a peak in 1944. Employment fell following the end of World War II and rose again during the Cold War. Since the end of the Cold War in 1990, the industry's employment has almost halved from 1990 to 2011.

Table 6.7   Employment in the UK aerospace industry, 1918–2011

Year	Employment (numbers)
1918	112,000
1924	11,735
1930	21,322
1934	23,775
1938	128,000
1940	750,000
1944	1,700,000
1948	171,800
1950	179,465
1957	311,936
1960	291,335
1965	259,025
1970	235,000
1980	241,997
1990	195,396
2000	150,651
2008	100,740
2011	100,658

Notes:
1. Data from different sources so they are not necessarily based on comparable definitions of the industry and of employment.
2. Data for 1980–2011 based on direct employment only (excluding indirects which are typically some 1.0 to 1.3 times direct numbers for 2000–2011).

Sources: Hayward (1989); Plowden (1965); SBAC (2000; 2009); ADS (2012).

REGIONAL DISTRIBUTION OF THE UK AEROSPACE INDUSTRY

The industry has regional concentrations associated with its major firms. There are major aerospace concentrations in the South-East (including London), the South-West (Bristol; Yeovil), the North-West (BAE located in the Preston area) and the Midlands (Rolls-Royce, Derby). Elsewhere, there are local concentrations in East Yorkshire (BAE, Brough), Scotland (Edinburgh) and Northern Ireland (Belfast).

The major regional concentrations attract clusters of high technology centres and small firms (SMEs) supplying first tier suppliers and prime contractors. Some of these SMEs have established 'niche markets' and are 'centres of excellence' in specialised areas of manufacturing.

A BRIEF HISTORY OF THE UK AEROSPACE INDUSTRY: AN EXAMPLE OF STRUCTURAL CHANGE

The Early Pioneers and World War I (1903–1918)

The early pioneers of manned flight were mostly privately-financed inventors using patents to capture any return on their investments. The Wright Brothers made the first manned and powered flight in December 1903 when they flew 120 feet in 12 seconds. The first British manned powered flight was made in 1908 (Brabazon).

Early British pioneers included Farman, Dunne, de Havilland, A.V. Roe, Handley Page, the Short Brothers and Thomas Sopwith. Even at this early stage, some inventors were sponsored by the British military. By 1912, the state-owned Royal Aircraft Factory had been created and became involved in the early British aircraft design and production for the Royal Flying Corps.

World War I led to a major increase in demand for both quantity and quality of aircraft for military roles. Fighter aircraft speeds increased from around 60mph in 1914 to over 120mph in 1918. The UK industry expanded rapidly with ever-increasing demands for speed and power which resulted in major technical advances (e.g. aircraft construction techniques; materials; aircraft design; engines: Angelucci, 1981).

The Inter-war Period: Civil Aircraft as an Infant Industry (1918–1934)

By 1918, the UK aircraft industry was the largest and one of the most technically capable in the world, with 122 firms employing 112,000 personnel (Hayward, 1989, p11). However peace resulted in cancellations of military orders and little prospect of any new significant military orders (there were large stocks of surplus aircraft). This led to exits from the industry (e.g. Airco; Sopwith who later joined with Hawker to create Hawker Engineering) and efforts to diversify (e.g. into motor vehicles, metal working and even using hangars for pig-rearing and mushroom-growing: Hayward, 1989, p12).

Eventually, the government introduced measures to support both military and civil aircraft developments. The Air Ministry provided sufficient work to support major design teams by allocating contracts to selected firms known as the 'family' or 'the ring' with the aim of promoting competition in design. To increase their prospects of survival, firms tended to specialise in specific product areas such as fighters (e.g. Bristol; Gloster; Hawker), flying boats (e.g. Blackburn; Shorts; Supermarine) and bombers (e.g. Fairey).

The 'family' system was criticised for its 'featherbedding' of the industry; for its continued support of existing firms rather than promoting rationalisation to create larger firms able to compete with the US rivals; for its failure to promote mass production; and for the Air Ministry's conservatism in design requirements (e.g. Empire policing in the 1920s did not require high speed aircraft). Instead, innovation was promoted by air races (Schneider Trophy) and the pursuit of world records as well as by imaginative designers willing to launch advanced types of aircraft mostly as private ventures (Hurricane; Spitfire; Wellington).

Civil aircraft was an infant industry in the 1920s and early 1930s but during this period civil aviation became the determining factor in the development of the aeroplane (Angelucci, 1981, p109). Government support in the UK for civil aircraft development involved subsidising the new Imperial Airways which was required to use British aircraft; but it was tasked with developing air routes to the Empire which represented a UK-specific requirement. In contrast, the growing demand for air travel in the USA with its large domestic market supported a number of rival firms and airlines with manufacturers achieving profitability levels which encouraged investment in large-scale production.

Rearmament and World War II (1934–1945)

Rearmament resulted in increased military demands for both quantity and quality leading to further innovation in military aviation (e.g. monoplanes; closed cockpits; retracting undercarriages) and increases in speed. Additional production capacity was financed by the state, with expansion achieved through a combination of:

- Capacity increases by existing firms in 'the family'
- Including second tier firms in 'the family'
- Contracting-out aircraft and engine production to other suitable manufacturing firms, mainly in the motor industry
- The shadow factory scheme (e.g. managed by Nuffield).

Nonetheless, the industry and the Air Ministry had much to learn about large-scale production. War demands for volume production exposed the limitations of the UK aircraft industry with its tradition of small-scale production based on a chief designer with no experience of 'designing for production'. In contrast, by the end of the War, US firms resembled the major car plants with moving production lines and larger research, design and development organisations (Barnett, 1986).

World War II led to the development of the jet engine as its single most important innovation affecting both military and civil aviation. The Gloster Meteor jet fighter flew in 1943, powered by the Whittle jet engine which was later developed by Rolls-Royce into the Derwent series (Hayward, 1989, p35). The War also destroyed Britain's European rivals in aircraft markets.

During the War, the UK concentrated on the production of fighters and bombers and relied on the USA for the supply of military transports: a decision which gave the US aircraft industry a competitive advantage in civil airliners at the end of the War. However, by 1942, the UK was considering the task of re-creating a UK civil aircraft industry. To this end the Brabazon Committee recommended various projects, including bomber conversions.

Post-war Adjustment and the Korean War (1945–1957)

The end of the War led to the inevitable reduction in demand for military aircraft. But, unlike 1918, the emergence of the jet engine created demands for new generations of jet-powered combat aircraft (Gloster Meteors; de Havilland Vampires), with plans to equip the RAF with supersonic jet fighters and jet bombers by the mid-1950s (Swift; Hunter; Canberra; V-bombers).[2]

The Brabazon Committee's recommendations provided the industry with funding for a civil aircraft programme to assist the adjustment from war to peace. The Committee's recommendations included a long-range piston-engined trans-Atlantic airliner (Bristol Brabazon); a short-range piston-engined airliner (Airspeed Ambassador); a short-range turboprop airliner (Vickers Viscount); a jet-powered mail carrier (which became the de Havilland Comet); and the Princess flying boat was added to the programme in 1946 (Hayward, 1983; 1986). However, the Brabazon Committee's programme was costly and had few commercial successes

---

[2] The 'ten year rule' required that for planning purposes the armed forces should not plan on fighting another major war for ten years.

(e.g. Vickers Viscount; de Havilland Dove: Barnett, 1995, chapter 12). Firms were also retained through the award of development contracts, some of which were duplicate projects to provide 'insurance' against project failures. In 1945, there were 27 airframe firms and eight engine firms with these divided into first and second divisions.

The technical failure of the Comet confronted de Havilland with possible bankruptcy. The company was rescued by the government through cash assistance and an RAF order for modified Comets as military transports. The nationalised airlines also continued to be required to 'buy British'. In 1951, the new Conservative government believed that aircraft firms should fund the development of new civil aircraft as private ventures (private venture policy).

The Korean War led to rearmament and increased demands for modern jet aircraft (some of which were ordered off the drawing board: e.g. Swift, which proved to be a failure). Again, problems emerged with delays in major projects, difficulties in achieving volume production, inefficiencies due to cost-plus contracting and firms being too small compared with their US rivals (Hayward, 1989, p63). The UK industry was now dominated by six firms, namely, Bristol, de Havilland, English Electric, Hawker Siddeley, Rolls-Royce and Vickers.

The Onset of the Cold War and Industry Mergers (1957–1960)

The 1957 Defence White Paper (Sandys White Paper) reflected the Cold War and signalled major changes in the industry. Aircraft were becoming technically more complex, taking longer to develop and becoming costlier leading to fewer being bought so making it more difficult to achieve volume production in small domestic markets.[3]

The Ministry of Supply recognised the need for industry rationalisation and the creation of larger firms and an end to the Buggins' turn of sharing development contracts between firms. Re-structuring was to be achieved by the selective allocation of contracts according to the following principles:

---

[3]   It was announced that nuclear weapons would replace conventional forces and that guided weapons would provide point defence of UK bases. The Ministry of Defence considered the abolition of RAF Fighter Command, but the proposal was rejected (Peden, 2007, p286). Instead some advanced aircraft projects were cancelled and there was to be one more manned combat aircraft (signalling the end of manned combat aircraft; but even in 2014, the UK plans to buy F-35 combat aircraft!).

- An ideal aircraft firm was one engaged in both military and civil aircraft and in industrial non-aircraft activities so that it could raise its capital on the basis of its entire diversified structure.
- Contracts would not be placed with the winner of a design competition but with a firm which had the technical ability to move quickly from development to production and with the financial strength to support the project when difficulties occurred (Hartley, 1965).

The next phase of re-structuring occurred between 1959 and 1960, when the government indicated that it wished to form a minimum number of competing groups in airframes and engines. There was an additional incentive from the financial problems being encountered by the private venture funding of civil aircraft. The outcome was the creation of five major groups, comprising:[4]

- The British Aircraft Corporation (Bristol Aircraft; Vickers; English Electric; Hunting).
- The Hawker Siddeley Group (including Blackburn, de Havilland and Folland).
- Bristol Siddeley Engines and Rolls-Royce as engine groups.
- Westland as a domestic monopoly for helicopters (including Bristol Helicopters; Fairey; and Saunders Roe).

The formation of the five groups was accompanied by a government announcement that except for specialised requirements of public policy, the government intended to concentrate its orders on the five major groups (Hartley, 1965, p848). It was also announced that the government would provide increased state support for promising civil aircraft and engine projects (launch aid: Hayward, 1989).

Unfortunately, maintaining competition in the airframe and engine sectors (duopolies) did not avoid the continued task of ensuring that government orders were shared between each of the rivals (Buggins' turn). The alternative (which was accepted for helicopters) would have been the formation of larger domestic monopolies in each sector.

---

[4]   Three firms remained outside the groups, namely, Handley Page, Scottish Aviation and Shorts (69% state-owned).

Plowden, Elstub and International Collaboration (1960–1970)

Despite the rationalisation of the industry in the 1950s and early 1960s, there were continued criticisms of the industry, in particular with regard to:

- It being too large and uncompetitive and it had been 'feather-bedded' for too long
- It absorbed an undue proportion of the nation's scarce R&D resources
- It was relatively unsuccessful in world markets (e.g. compared with the French industry: Hartley, 1996)
- The discovery of excessive profits earned by Ferranti on the Bloodhound missile (1964) and continued cost increases and delays on the TSR-2 project.

The newly elected Labour government of 1964 made two initiatives affecting the industry. First, it established a Committee of Inquiry into the future of the industry (Plowden, 1965). Second, it cancelled three major UK military aircraft projects, namely, TSR-2, P1154 and HS681. The cancelled projects were replaced by purchases of US aircraft (Phantom with UK engines and some UK equipment; Hercules transport) and Hawker Siddeley was partly compensated with a limited development programme for its P1127 (later to become the Harrier Jump Jet).

The Plowden Report (1965) considered the case for a national aircraft industry and concluded that none of the arguments provided conclusive evidence for maintaining an aircraft industry. The Report expressed doubts about the nominal competition in the UK market and recommended:

- Mergers between each of the groups which would offer economies and end the need to allocate work between each of the groups
- The level of support for the industry should be reduced to a level of similar to that given to comparable British industries
- Britain should collaborate with other European countries
- Costly projects should be purchased from the USA (with possible licensed production of US designs).

In 1966, Rolls-Royce acquired Bristol Siddeley Engines creating a domestic monopoly in engines and reducing the major groups from five to four. Also, in 1966, the government was involved in discussions about a merger between the airframe groups with a possible state share; but no agreement was reached.

During this period a number of international collaborative programmes were pursued, including:

- Development of a supersonic airliner (Concorde) with BAC and Sud Aviation as joint designers
- Jaguar strike aircraft (airframe development led by Breguet: 1965)
- A helicopter package (1967: involving Westland) and a missile package (Martel)
- Multi-role combat aircraft (AFVG, with BAC acting as project leader with Dassault)
- A civil aircraft initiative involving Britain, France and Germany for the development of an Airbus with Hawker Siddeley as the UK airframe firm in this joint programme.

However, these agreements were not always successful. In 1967 France withdrew from the AFVG aircraft and the UK later agreed a new three nation collaborative arrangement for the multi-role combat aircraft (Tornado with Germany and Italy in 1968). In 1969, France and Germany agreed to continue the Airbus without the UK government; but Hawker Siddeley decided to remain in the programme on a private venture basis.

In 1968, a new Profit Formula was introduced for non-competitive government contracts, and the productivity of the UK industry was reviewed in the 1969 Elstub Report. This Report found a productivity gap between the British and American aircraft industries, mainly due to the small scale of airframe production in Europe (Elstub, 1969, paras 186–192), noting that:

- After adjustment for output differences, the ratio of productivity in the USA and Britain was estimated to be between 1.2 and 1.5 to 1
- Quantity and learning economies were the major reason for this productivity gap
- The disadvantages of collaboration, reflected in the time needed to reach decisions at government level and in the role of national interests in agreeing inefficient work-sharing arrangements.

Nationalisation, Privatisation and Re-structuring (1970–1990)

Rolls-Royce was declared bankrupt in early 1971 and was immediately nationalised.[5] Next, in 1977 the Labour government nationalised the airframe firms and merged them to form British Aerospace (BAe); the case for nationalisation being based on the industry's dependence on the state, including civil aerospace projects (Hartley, 1996, p224). Shorts was already nationalised and its position remained unchanged outside the new group.

By contrast Westland remained in private ownership. However, between 1986 and 2004 its ownership varied from the USA (Sikorsky) to GKN (UK) and finally to Italy (Finmeccanica). Thus, foreign ownership of a UK helicopter company which was part of the UK's defence industrial base was accepted by the UK government.[6]

Two civil aircraft decisions dominated the nationalisation period. First, BAe was faced with a choice between being a subcontractor on the Boeing 757 airliner or joining the European Airbus consortium as a full partner: it chose to join Airbus. Second, the government approved the re-launch of the HS146 regional jet airliner.

The policy of nationalisation was reversed in 1979 by the new Conservative government which was committed to privatisation (Parker, 2009). As a result BAe was completely privatised by 1985, Rolls-Royce was privatised by 1987 and Shorts by 1989 (Shorts was purchased by Bombardier, the Canadian regional airliner firm).

In the 1980s, BAe and the UK aircraft industry were involved in a range of military aerospace programmes. These included national projects (Hawk; Harrier) and European collaborative programmes (three nation Tornado and four nation Typhoon). BAe was also involved in various civil aviation programmes including business jets (BAe 125), feeder airliners (Jetstream) and regional jets (146), an advanced turbo-prop airliner (ATP) and specialist wing work for Airbus aircraft. However BAe incurred losses on its civil aircraft programmes (see Chapter 8).

---

[5] Rising development costs and technical problems on the Rolls-Royce fixed price contract to supply the RB211 engine to Lockheed was the immediate cause of the bankruptcy (the new company was Rolls-Royce (1971) Ltd: Hayward, 1989, pp133–140).

[6] The US helicopter firm Sikorsky acquired a share in Westland in 1986; later in 1988, GKN acquired a stake in Westland; then in 2001, there was a merger between Agusta and Westland and in 2004, the Italian company Finmeccanica acquired Westland which became AgustaWestland.

End of the Cold War and UK Defence Industrial Policy (1990–2014)

Following the end of the Cold War, the search for a peace dividend resulted in cuts in defence spending leading to job losses and plant closures. The US defence industry underwent major re-structuring leading to the formation of four large aerospace and defence firms able to achieve economies of scale and scope so increasing their international competitiveness (Boeing; Lockheed Martin; Northrop Grumman; Raytheon: SIPRI, 1999).

In comparison, there were still too many relatively small European aerospace and defence firms. European governments preferred a European merger of their defence firms to form a single European Aerospace and Defence Company (EADC: in fact a merger was agreed between BAe and DASA in 1998). But, instead, BAe responded by acquiring Marconi Electronics Systems, the defence subsidiary of GEC (including its warship yards: 1999). This merger resulted in a vertically integrated company with warship building activities known as BAE Systems.

BAE focused on its core defence business by divesting all its non-defence activities; including its civil aircraft business. It made further acquisitions in the US and Australian defence markets. Also, BAE sold its Airbus (UK) business to EADS so ending any UK-owned involvement in civil aircraft development and production. These changes mean that the UK is no longer involved in the domestic development and production of civil aircraft marking the end of the post-1945 policy of re-entering this sector of the aircraft industry. Instead, the UK created a world class centre of excellence for wing design, development and production for the collaborative Airbus family of civil jet airliners (with plants at Broughton and Bristol).

In the civil aerospace sector, international collaboration has been successful with Airbus sharing the world's large civil jet airliner market with Boeing. However, UK specialisation on wing work has involved state assistance in the form of repayable launch investment (a policy which in 2009 was reviewed by WTO) and private venture funding of major civil aircraft and component wing work has not been achieved (see Chapter 10).

By 2005, BAE Systems was the dominant aerospace and defence firm in the UK market. However, by this point, BAE was encountering major problems with project management (Nimrod; Astute submarines) and with the adverse financial implications of fixed price contracts for some of its major UK defence programmes. Partly in response to this in 2005, the UK government published its new Defence Industrial Strategy (DIS, 2005). The DIS identified the key defence industrial capabilities which

MoD aimed to retain in the UK against expectations of major reductions in the future demand for military aircraft. The likely future for UK aerospace was outlined:

1. Fixed Wing Aircraft
    For fixed wing aircraft, the DIS did not envisage the UK designing and producing a new generation of fixed wing manned combat aircraft after the Typhoon and the F-35: hence, there will be a significant reduction in new military aircraft design and development work. But, BAE was expected to be involved in the life-cycle support of both these aircraft, together with Rolls-Royce.
2. Large Aircraft and Training Aircraft
    No sovereign requirement was envisaged for sustaining a domestic industrial capability in large aircraft and training aircraft. The expected decline in new programme work raises doubts over the future of all four of BAE's production sites (Brough in East Yorkshire; Samlesbury and Warton in Lancashire; Woodford in Cheshire). In 2009, BAE announced the closure of its Woodford plant by 2012 (with the end of Nimrod production).
3. Helicopters
    With helicopters, the DIS planned to retain in the UK the skills necessary for through-life support of UK designed helicopters, namely, AgustaWestland. However, the DIS stated that the UK 'will continue to look to the vibrant and competitive global market place for its future helicopter requirements with AgustaWestland's role neither predefined nor guaranteed' (DIS, 2005, p94).
4. Missiles
    For missiles, the DIS identified excess capacity in the UK and Europe and it expected major reductions in demand leading to substantial job losses with opportunities for industrial rationalisation and consolidation (DIS, 2005, p104; HCP 824, 2006, p18).

The 2005 DIS was replaced in 2012/13 by a new policy initiative for the UK's defence industry. This new initiative was based on a joint industry–government partnership focused on two industrial capabilities, namely, air capabilities and intelligent systems. The new Defence–Growth Partnership emphasised the importance of military aerospace exports which have dominated UK defence exports and were viewed as contributing to the government's wider agenda on export-led growth (BIS, 2013; MacKay, 2005; see Chapter 8).

Overall, structural change in the UK aerospace industry has been typical of many of the world's aerospace industries. The UK industry has changed from an industry consisting of a large number of small firms to one of a small number of large firms. In 1945, there were 27 airframe and eight engine firms; by 1960, re-structuring had reduced the industry to five major groups; and by 2014, only three groups survived (BAE; AgustaWestland; Rolls-Royce). Further structural change is inevitable and will involve international mergers and acquisitions.

OTHER AEROSPACE INDUSTRIES

Elsewhere in the world, other aerospace industries have various forms of industrial structure, ownership and industrial organisation. Typically, none resemble the economic model of a perfectly competitive industry. Instead, monopoly is the dominant industry structure for Russia, China, Brazil and South Africa.

The *Russian aerospace industry* was a dominant player in the world aerospace market during the Cold War. It had developed advanced military and civil aircraft and space systems. However, the end of the Cold War and the break-up of the Soviet Union led to falling defence budgets and the end of a protected market for its civil airliners leading some commentators to predict the end of the Russian aerospace industry. Instead, the industry has survived and adapted to its new market conditions and re-entered the sector.

In 2006/07, the fragmented Russian aerospace industry was consolidated into three state-controlled but independently managed groups comprising United Aircraft Corporation (OAK) for all military and civil fixed wing aircraft, Russian Helicopters and United Engines. The famous names of the design bureaux remain as subsidiaries of United Aircraft (e.g. Mikoyan MIG; Sukhoi; Yak; Antonov; Ilyushin; Beriev) but with closer links between the design bureaux and production plants. Future sales will be based on developments of new military combat aircraft, export sales of existing combat aircraft (upgrades of Su-27/30; MiG-29) and sales of two new civil jet airliners (Sukhoi Superjet; Irkut Yak MC-21: Flight, 2013c).

The new state-owned Russian Helicopters group consolidated the two helicopter design bureaux, namely, Mil and Kamov and five assembly plants. It aims to achieve military, civil and export sales of its existing and newly developed helicopters. Overall, the Russian aerospace industry is dominated by state-owned domestic monopolies for aircraft, helicopters and engines with the distinctive feature of a separation between design and production facilities.

The *Chinese aerospace industry* is state organised and state-owned and is a classic example of the inefficiencies of a state-owned monopoly. The industry consists of a single defence aerospace enterprise, namely, AVIC and a centre for civil aircraft development, namely, COMAC (which is developing two projects, namely, the ARJ21 regional jet airliner and the C-919 as a rival to the Boeing 737 and Airbus A320). The Chinese Academy of Aerospace Aerodynamics is the country's primary centre for aerodynamic research and testing. There is some limited privatisation to encourage private investment. Historically, China purchased much of its defence equipment from Russia followed by the licensed production of Soviet military aircraft and the reverse engineering of foreign technology to produce copies. The Chinese aerospace industry's major weaknesses include an 'over bureaucratic' management structure and inadequate jet engine technology (Hayward, 2013).

The *Indian aerospace industry* is dominated by Hindustan Aeronautics (HAL) which is a government-owned company. HAL has been extensively criticised for its poor performance reflected in production inefficiencies and delays in the development of its major programmes (e.g. Tejas combat aircraft). Further protection for India's aerospace industry is provided through its national offsets policy which requires offsets of 30 per cent on Indian aerospace imports (offsets of 50 per cent required for the sale of Dassault Rafales to India). However, some efforts are being made to subject HAL to competition. For example, a limited privatisation is planned (10 per cent of HAL shares) and HAL is being encouraged to outsource more work to Indian private sector aerospace companies (Flight, 2013b).

The *Brazilian aerospace industry* is dominated by its privately-owned prime contractor, Embraer. The company is a major supplier of regional jet aircraft and has a developing military aircraft, UAV and space programme. Embraer was privatised in 1994, but the Brazilian government retains a 'golden share' giving it veto powers. Embraer was the subject of a WTO ruling on regional jet airliner subsidies. WTO determined that in the late 1990s/early 2000s, Brazil operated an illegal subsidy programme (Proex) for its regional jet airliners in 1999/2000 and that Canada also illegally subsidised its regional jet airliner industry. Overall, Embraer forms a privately-owned domestic monopoly which was, for a period, protected by subsidies for its regional jet airliners.

The *South African aerospace industry* is dominated by the state-owned Denel aerospace and defence group. Denel has been involved in the development of an attack helicopter, work on the Gripen fighter aircraft, missiles, UAVs and aerostructures. Denel is a typical 'national champion' with a broader remit which includes the maintenance of South Africa's

defence capabilities and contributing to developing skills and manufacturing capabilities (Flight, 2012).

CONCLUSION: THE CONTRIBUTION OF ECONOMICS

This review of industry structure highlights a paradox. Economic models
identify the economic superiority of competitive industries and markets.
Competitive industries are characterised by large numbers of relatively
small firms with free entry and competition based solely on prices
leading to normal profits being earned in the long-run. However, aerospace industries and markets depart drastically from the competitive
model in two ways. First, aerospace is a decreasing cost industry
favouring large firms as monopolies or oligopolies in *national* markets.
But, national markets can always be subject to actual and potential rivalry
by allowing foreign firms to enter such markets. Second, governments
are central to understanding aerospace markets through their military
demands and their intervention in civil aircraft production. Governments
also intervene in aerospace industries by determining the size of aerospace firms and their ownership. State-owned monopolies in protected
markets result from government intervention. Austrian economists have
criticised such intervention arguing that governments and bureaucrats
lack the knowledge and incentives to determine the best structure for an
industry. They argue that profit-seeking entrepreneurs are the agents best
placed to deal with uncertainty about future consumer demands.

Industry structure determines performance. Typically, aerospace industries comprise small numbers of large firms forming monopolies, duopolies or oligopolies. Often major aerospace firms are regarded as 'national
champions' given protection by their governments. Industry structure
models provide insights into the behaviour of such industries, but more
analysis is needed on their conduct and performance (see Chapter 7).
Also, large firms form powerful producer interest groups which will seek
to influence government policies (see Chapter 9).

REFERENCES

ADS (2012). *UK Aerospace Survey 2012*, UK Aerospace, Defence and Security
    Industries, London.
AIA (2013). *Statistics*, Aerospace Industries Association, Washington DC.
Angelucci, E. (1981). *World Encyclopedia of Military Aircraft*, Jane's, London.
ASD (2012). *Key Facts and Figures 2011*, Aerospace and Defence Industries
    Association of Europe, Brussels.

Barnett, C. (1986). *The Audit of War*, Macmillan, London.

Barnett, C. (1995). *The Lost Victory*, Macmillan, London.

BIS (2013). *Securing Prosperity: A Strategic Vision for the UK Defence Sector*, Department for Business, Innovation and Skills, London, September.

Braddon, D. and Hartley, K. (2007). The competitiveness of the UK Aerospace Industry, *Applied Economics*, 30, 715–726, March/April.

Carlton, D.W. and Perloff, J.M. (1994). *Industrial Organization*, Harper Collins, New York, 2nd edition.

Cmnd 8278 (2012). *National Security Through Technology*, Ministry of Defence, TSO, London, February.

DASA (2008). *UK Defence Statistics 2008*, Ministry of Defence, London.

DASA (2012). *UK Defence Statistics 2012*, Ministry of Defence, London.

DIS (2005). *Defence Industrial Strategy*, Ministry of Defence, Cmnd 6697, TSO, London, December.

Elstub (1969). *Productivity of the National Aircraft Effort*, Ministry of Technology, HMSO, London.

Flight (1997). Aerospace Top 100, *Flight International*, Surrey, 2–8 September.

Flight (2009). A new trade war, *Flight International*, Surrey, 28 July to 3 August.

Flight (2012). South Africa: Special Report, *Flight International*, Surrey, pp30–36.

Flight (2013a). Top 100, *Flight International*, Surrey, 24–30 September, pp35–60.

Flight (2013b). India Special Report, *Flight International*, Surrey, 29 January to 4 February, pp31–33.

Flight (2013c). Russia: Special Report, *Flight International*, Surrey, 20 August to 2 September, pp22–43.

Hartley, K. (1965). The mergers in the UK Aircraft Industry, *Journal of the Royal Aeronautical Society*, 69, 660, 846–852.

Hartley, K. (1996). The defence economy, in Coopey, R. and Woodward, N. (eds), *Britain in the 1970s*, UCL Press, London.

Hartley, K. (2006). *The Industrial and Economic Benefits of Eurofighter Typhoon*, Eurofighter, Munich.

Hartley, K. (2008). Collaboration and European defence industrial policy, *Defence and Peace Economics*, 19, 4, 303–315.

Hartley, K. (2011). *The Economics of Defence Policy*, Routledge, London.

Hartley, K. and Braddon, D. (2002). *Aerospace Competitiveness Study*, Study for DTI, London, March.

Hayward, K. (1983). *Government and British Civil Aerospace*, Manchester University Press, Manchester.

Hayward, K. (1986). *International Collaboration in Civil Aerospace*, Frances Pinter, London.

Hayward, K. (1989). *The British Aircraft Industry*, Manchester University Press, Manchester.

Hayward, K. (2013). *The Chinese Aerospace Industry: A Background Paper*, Royal Aeronautical Society, London, July.

HCP 151-1 (2005). *The UK Aerospace Industry*, House of Commons Trade and Industry Committee, TSO, London, April.

HCP 824 (2006). *The Defence Industrial Strategy*, House of Commons Defence Committee, TSO, London, May.

Laguerre, C. (2009). Is the defence market contestable? The case of military aerospace, *Defence and Peace Economics*, 20, 4, 303–326.

Lawrence, P. with Braddon, D. (2001). *Aerospace Strategic Trade*, Ashgate, Aldershot.

Lipczynski, J., Wilson, J.O.S. and Goddard, J. (2009). *Industrial Organization: Competition, Strategy, Policy*, Prentice Hall, London.

MacKay, Sir Donald (2005). *UK Aerospace Industry*, Presentation to SBAC, London, September.

Parker, D. (2009). *The Official History of Privatisation: The formative years 1970–1987*, vol 1, Routledge, London.

Peden, G.C. (2007). *Arms, Economics and British Strategy*, Cambridge University Press, Cambridge.

Plowden (1965). *Report of the Committee of Inquiry into the Aircraft Industry*, Cmnd 2853, HMSO, London.

Porter, M. (1990). *The Competitive Advantage of Nations*, Macmillan, London.

Pugh, P. (2007). *Source Book of Defence Equipment Costs*, Dandy Books, London.

SBAC (2000). *UK Aerospace Facts and Figures, 2000*, Society of British Aerospace Companies, London.

SBAC (2009). *UK Aerospace Industry Survey 2009*, Society of British Aerospace Companies, London.

Schmalensee, R.C. (1990). Empirical studies of rivalrous behaviour, in Bonanno, G. and Brandolini, D. (eds), *Industrial Structure in the New Industrial Economics*, Clarendon Press, Oxford.

SIPRI (1999). *SIPRI Yearbook 1999: Armaments, Disarmament and International Security*, Oxford University Press, Oxford.

SIPRI (2012). SIPRI Top 100 arms-producing and military services companies in the world (excluding China) 2011, *Yearbook 2012*, Stockholm International Peace Research Institute, Oxford University Press, Oxford.

Tisdell, C. and Hartley, K. (2008). *Micro-economic Policy*, Edward Elgar Publishing, Cheltenham, UK and Northampton, MA, USA.

7. Industry conduct and performance

INTRODUCTION: THEIR IMPORTANCE

Industry conduct and performance are part of the structure–conduct–performance model which is often used by economists as a *starting point* in analysing an industry. In the basic model, industry performance is explained by industry structure with causation running from structure to performance. Reality, however, is more complex with industry performance and conduct often determining industry structure. Other economic models are also used to analyse an industry (e.g. game theory; contestable markets; transaction costs; Austrian economics: see Chapter 6). A non-technical description of the main features of game theory is presented showing its relevance to understanding the behaviour of major aerospace firms with examples from civil and military markets.

Conduct and performance are important in analysing aerospace industries. Conduct describes the form of competition between firms in the aerospace industry and the results of competition are reflected in industry performance. Analysis of performance also raises the more general question of how aerospace industry performance is measured and how it compares with the performance of aerospace industries in other countries and with industries in the rest of the economy. This chapter presents an analysis of the aerospace industry's conduct and performance, making a distinction between military and civil markets.

DEFINING CONDUCT

Industry structure determines the number and size distribution of firms in an industry and the conditions of entry into, and exit from, the industry (e.g. whether there is free entry and exit or barriers to entry and exit). The number and size of firms in the aerospace industry determines the form of competition and whether this takes the form of price and/or non-price competition. Price competition is typical of competitive markets where large numbers of relatively small firms in an industry produce identical products with free entry and exit and compete on the basis of price.

In contrast, in oligopoly industries, there are a few relatively large firms which compete on the basis of both price and non-price factors. In such markets, firms are price-makers rather than the price-takers of competitive markets. Price-makers might set prices to deter new entrants or eliminate existing rivals (predatory pricing) or they might adopt price discrimination charging different groups of consumers different prices for an identical product (e.g. domestic and export markets). Non-price factors include product design (product differentiation), advertising, marketing, sales efforts, research and development, collusion, location choices and political lobbying. These various price and non-price policies might be classified on the basis of the speed at which they can be changed. In the short-run or near-term, price can be changed quickly and so too can advertising and sales efforts. In the medium-term, product features and cost structures can be changed, whilst in the long-run, research and development might lead to new products and to new production processes. In aerospace industries, new military and civil products emerge after lengthy development periods.

Oligopoly industries have a distinctive feature, namely, they comprise a small number of relatively large firms with interdependence between rivals. New developments have seen the application of game theory to industrial economics which has offered new insights and challenged traditional theory.

GAME THEORY

Game theory uses formal models to analyse competition and co-operation between oligopoly firms. The small number of firms in such markets means that their decisions on price and non-price competition are mutually interdependent (my behaviour affects you and your behaviour affects me). Game theory views competitive behaviour by oligopoly firms as strategies which describe the actions of each firm. In the game, firms compete for profits using price and non-price strategies with game theory describing how firms develop their strategies and the impact of strategies on each firm's profits. In such markets, firms will try to anticipate the effect their actions will have on the behaviour and actions of their rivals; and with these expectations, each firm then develops their 'best' response to achieve profits (the pay-off from the game). Game theory offers solutions to a game in the form of a prediction of what each player in the game will do.

In game theory, there are two types of strategic behaviour, namely, co-operative and non-cooperative strategic behaviour. Co-operative strategic behaviour arises where the actions of firms make it easier for them to co-operate and co-ordinate their actions to raise profits by restricting competition. Cartels and price-fixing agreements are examples of co-operative strategic behaviour. In contrast, non-cooperative strategic behaviour arises where a firm aims to raise its profits by harming its rivals so reducing their profits. Examples include actions by firms to prevent rivals from entering the market (predatory pricing; entry deterrence), policies to drive rivals out of the market or to reduce the size of a rival. The success of a non-cooperative strategy requires first mover advantage and a commitment which forms a credible threat. First mover advantage requires that a firm can act before its rivals. Commitment requires that the firm demonstrates that it will follow its strategy regardless of the response and actions of its rivals: hence, its actions form a credible threat.

Game theory extends from simple concepts of firm interdependence to more complex situations comprising static and dynamic games. Static games include the 'prisoners' dilemma' game,[1] which can be applied to advertising competition (advertising trap) and to arms race situations. In contrast, dynamic games are played over a number of time-periods and might be one-off or repeated games, where repetition might lead to 'learning' behaviour (Romp, 1997).

Game theory also uses concepts of a Nash equilibrium, zero sum and non-zero sum games. A Nash equilibrium (named after John Nash who featured in the film: A Beautiful Mind) arises where each firm selects its best strategy in response to the best strategic choice being followed by the other firms (i.e. no firm has an incentive to change unilaterally its behaviour). A zero sum game arises where the gains and losses of all firms adds to zero; and a non-zero sum game means that the outcomes are greater or less than zero.

The behaviour and strategies of firms and players in game theory has various applications to the aerospace industry. In negotiating prices for defence contracts and for new civil aircraft, the buyers and sellers in the bargaining situation will resort to a variety of practices familiar to game theory. These include games of bluff, brinkmanship, chicken, threats and

---

[1]   An example occurred during trench warfare in World War I. As the front lines stabilised, non-aggression between the opposing troops emerged spontaneously along the front. For example, meal times were a period of mutual restraint from shelling and sniping; but each side reserved the right to retaliate if necessary.

promises. Each party has incentives to conceal or reveal valuable information; each can threaten 'tit-for-tat' policies; and bargaining is likely to be characterised by action-reaction behaviour.

Game theory can be applied to explain the behaviour of oligopolies and duopolies in the aerospace industry. Examples of duopoly include Airbus and Boeing in the large civil aircraft market and Bombardier and Embraer in the regional jet airliner market. Each duopolist will select its best mix of price and non-price strategies taking into account its beliefs about the reactions of its rival. For example, if one firm reduces prices, its rival is likely to follow with a price cut; but if a firm raises prices, its rival might not follow. A firm might also seek 'first mover' advantage aiming to launch a new type of aircraft before its rival follows. But once news of the new type is revealed, the rival can launch a similar but 'better' aircraft, leading to each firm producing similar aircraft (cf. competition between motor car firms where rival products might be similar). Here, it has to be remembered that development times for a new aircraft can be 5–10 years so that the 'first mover' might only gain a few years' sales advantage over its rival and buyers might delay ordering until they learn whether the rival will offer a similar but superior aircraft. There is some evidence from commercial airliners and business jets suggesting that 'first mover' is not always an advantage. For example, Boeing built the first all-metal twin-engined airliner, but the subsequent introduction of the Douglas DC-2 and DC-3 captured the market. Similarly, the UK de Havilland Comet was the first commercial jet airliner, but US firms, especially Boeing and Douglas later dominated the market (Phillips et al., 1994).

Game theory has been used to analyse and design auctions. Examples include Defence Departments using competitive auctions to award contracts. The aim of the Defence Department is to ensure low cost by selecting the most efficient firm. The Department's task is to design an auction to achieve its objective in a market which probably comprises a small number of bidding firms. Each bidder knows that it is competing against a few rivals, each with different valuations of the contract, each with different attitudes to risk and each with different cost levels. All bidders submit their best private estimates of minimum costs but the winner is likely to under-estimate costs and bid 'too low', later discovering that the contract is a potential loss-maker threatening the firm with bankruptcy (the winner's curse)! Nor can the Defence Department assume that its task is completed successfully with the award of the contract. Even where the winning firm is the most efficient, a losing firm might take-over the winning bidder: hence, the contract might be undertaken by a less efficient firm!

Whilst game theory is attractive in its efforts at analysing inter-dependence between oligopoly firms, critics claim that it is better at explaining past events rather than predicting behaviour. Some critics have even suggested that almost anything can happen in oligopoly and that oligopoly theory is indeterminate. 'There is no clear and unambiguous solution to the central issue of interdependence' and this is reflected in the large number and variety of models in the field (Lipczynski et al., 2009, p154).

CONDUCT IN DEFENCE MARKETS

Defence markets are different from normal commercial markets. They are dominated by a single or major buyer and often the product required does not exist. Defence Departments demand high technology equipment which has to be designed and developed for their specific national requirements. Aerospace examples include advanced combat aircraft, attack helicopters, maritime patrol aircraft, electronic surveillance aircraft and missiles. Elsewhere, armies demand main battle tanks, armoured fighting vehicles and artillery whilst navies require aircraft carriers, warships and submarines, all of which have to be built specially for the armed forces. In contrast, normal commercial markets provide a range of motor cars, TVs, computers and mobile phones which large numbers of consumers can buy off-the-shelf.

Defence Departments demand aerospace equipment specially designed and developed for their armed forces. Immediately, problems arise since the Defence Department has to specify an operational requirement for a product which does not exist and has to be developed to meet potential enemy threats over an uncertain future which might be some 30 or more years ahead. This marks the start of the game: potential suppliers will lobby the Defence Department about the requirement, its feasibility and the arrangements for contract award. At the next stage, the Defence Department will issue an operational requirement, inviting initial bids. For advanced aerospace equipment, there will only be a few potential suppliers (even fewer in national markets other than the USA). Suppliers will compete with a mix of price and non-price competition. They will offer various alternative paper design proposals to meet the requirement as well as an initial guideline price. At the initial design stage, there are considerable uncertainties and the price estimate will be no more than a 'guesstimate' offering a broad order of magnitude: even greater uncer-tainties arise in forecasting life-cycle costs. Also, the armed forces initially will place more emphasis on the technical features of each bid rather than on the price estimate. Price will be a factor in the competition since defence budgets are limited but more weight will be given to the technical features of the competing bids reflecting the desire of the armed forces to achieve technical superiority over their potential enemies.

Non-price competition based on technical proposals means that defence firms will recruit and retain teams of scientists, technologists and engineers, all aimed at giving a firm an advantage in the competitive process. The scientific team will be financed by government-funded defence R&D with the emphasis on development rather than research. Government funding reflects the risks and uncertainties of defence R&D which has to be undertaken for a project which initially has only one customer and where the technology is defence-specific with no alternative-use value (see Chapter 11). Once developed, the technology might be valuable in other uses, either within the aerospace industry or in completely different industries. Of course, where the technology is applied in other uses, it is the equivalent of a 'free gift' for the recipient firms.

In defence markets, prices are borne by taxpayers. Defence Departments will be allocated a budget to provide defence services and protection. The armed forces will administer their budgets and their emphasis will be on the operational performance of aerospace equipment. Costly equipment usually means smaller numbers which is where price factors become relevant in purchase decisions. However, the armed forces seek operational superiority over their potential enemies and their requirement for such superiority means that their demand is perfectly inelastic for a variety of prices (i.e. relatively unresponsive to higher prices). There is evidence showing a positive relationship but with diminishing returns between a nation's defence R&D and its military capability. In 2001, the USA had a time advantage of some 5–7 years over France, Germany and the UK (Cmnd 6697, 2005, p39).

Once a national Defence Department has funded the development and production of a new military aircraft, helicopter or missile for its armed forces, the supplier can seek additional income and profits by offering the equipment for export. Defence export markets are more competitive than national defence markets with more suppliers offering a range of competing equipment. For example, rival suppliers for combat aircraft include Boeing (F-18), Lockheed Martin (F-16; F-35), Saab Gripen, Dassault Rafale, Eurofighter Typhoon and the Russian Mikoyan and Sukhoi aircraft (Mig-35; Su-35). Similarly for attack helicopters, there are a substantial number of rivals creating a more competitive market. These include Boeing (Apache), Bell (Super Cobra), AgustaWestland

(AH129, Mongoose), Airbus Helicopters (Eurocopter Tiger), South African Denel (Rooivalk), together with Russian and Chinese attack helicopters (Russian Mi-24, 28 and 35M; Kamov Black Shark; Chinese Z-10).

Competition for military aerospace exports can be intense in both the price and non-price domains. In terms of prices, exporters can base prices on their additional unit production costs with a mark-up for profits and additional selling costs. Entering a new export market is not costless: there are costs of lobbying the national government and of providing aircraft for flight demonstrations. Export pricing might reflect a national government's desire to win the contract through waiving any requirement for an export levy to recover R&D costs. Other financial incentives might be offered, including generous financial assistance with the export sale. Non-price competition might embrace the exporting nation offering to provide interim equipment until the new equipment is delivered and generous offset packages.

Offsets take a variety of forms, including exporting firms offering work-sharing on the export order or on future military equipment or on civil projects or offering what appears to be a generous technology transfer package. In competing for business, defence exporting firms have incentives to offer attractive and generous offset deals (e.g. 100 per cent or 200 per cent offsets). Offsets are potentially economically inefficient and some might not represent genuinely new business.

Non-price competition in defence markets is reflected in technical progress and new technologies which can lead to changes in industry structure and conduct. Historically, the introduction of the jet engine revolutionised both military and civil aviation. The development of missile and rocket engine technology led to the entry of the industry into the space market. More recently, the development of unmanned air vehicles (UAVs) represents another major technical change leading to the entry of new firms into the aerospace industry. Examples include General Atomics (Predator and Reaper UAVs) and AeroVironment (Raven UAV). UAVs also create opportunities for substitution with manned aircraft in combat, surveillance and maritime patrol roles so affecting the structure of armed forces (e.g. armies operating UAVs replacing air force operated UAVs).

CONDUCT IN CIVIL MARKETS

Civil aerospace markets differ from defence markets. Price now becomes much more important in purchase decisions where the price dimension embraces the capital cost of a new airliner and its running costs. An aerospace firm considering the introduction of a new jet airliner faces choices similar to those faced by firms in private markets (e.g. motor car firms).

Aerospace firms have to make entrepreneurial decisions on whether to risk their funds on developing a new large jet airliner and a new jet engine. These are costly projects where development times are measured in years rather than months. Further lengthy periods arise between first deliveries and 'break-even' output, followed eventually by profitability. Civil aerospace markets differ from defence markets in that civil markets comprise large numbers of airlines of different sizes and different ownership patterns. Unlike defence markets, civil markets do not have a single buyer with sufficient funds to finance the requirements of its armed forces with national Defence Departments guaranteeing the market and underwriting development and production costs.

In civil markets, aerospace firms have to assess market opportunities before risking their funds in the development of a new and costly jet airliner. Typically, they will only proceed with developing a new jet airliner if they are assured of a minimum size of order and sales prospects greater than the 'break-even' output. For example, development costs for the CS100 and CS300 series of regional jet airliners were estimated at $4.4 billion (2014 prices). Similarly, development costs for the Airbus A380 were initially estimated at $8.5 billion (2000 prices) and the programme was launched with 50 firm orders from six launch customers. The break-even output for the Airbus A380 has been variously estimated at 270 to 420 units with a unit price of $414.4 million (2014 prices). However, programme development costs might increase if unexpected technical problems are encountered (e.g. wing and wiring problems on A380 which raised programme costs and led to delays in delivery) and sales prospects might change if airlines shift their demands to new and different types of airliners. Examples of such shifts in demand include the change from three jet to twin jet engine airliners and the rise and fall in demand for small jet airliners (37 to 50 seats). Such demand shifts might reflect new technology including new jet engine technology as well as rising fuel prices.

Competition between duopolists as occurs in the *large jet airliner and regional jet airliner markets* will lead to similar types of aircraft and similar unit prices. But aircraft and unit prices will not be identical: there will be some price competition but published prices are misleading and unreliable due to secret discounts (e.g. to attract a new or large order) and generous financing terms. Similarly, published data on aircraft operating costs and efficiency are generally unavailable. Furthermore, in assessing new aircraft, airlines will be conscious of their resale value (i.e. their value in used aircraft markets for sale to other airlines or as freighters or for scrap). Duopolists also compete through other forms of non-price competition including the use of new materials (e.g. composites); varying use of outsourcing and subcontractors (i.e. make versus buy choices) affecting both production costs and risk-taking by suppliers; offering different engine choices; and focusing on variants of existing aircraft types through upgrading rather than developing costly new types. Inevitably, intense competition between duopolists leads to accusations of rivals receiving 'unfair' state aid (Airbus versus Boeing; Bombardier versus Embraer: see Chapter 10).

As duopolists, Airbus and Boeing will compete by developing similar projects. For example, they have each chosen to develop their successful Airbus A320 and Boeing 737 series by adding new engines rather than opting for a completely new design of airliner (i.e. A320 new engine option or neo; B737 Max with new engines). Also, they have each developed a new but similar jet airliner, namely, the Boeing 787 Dreamliner and the Airbus A350. Typically, once one firm starts a new development, its rival responds by offering a similar product. With its Dreamliner, Boeing achieved 'first mover' advantage of some three years which was equivalent to extra deliveries of over 120 aircraft and some 200 additional orders before Airbus started delivery of its A350 aircraft. But, by starting later, Airbus was able to respond to the Boeing design and offer more recent technology and by 2014, it was not obvious which was the more successful strategy.

The example of the Airbus A350 and Boeing Dreamliner are summarised in Table 7.1 which shows their key price and non-price features. Whilst data are available on their features, they do not always show other important features and differences between the rival aircraft (e.g. use of composites; flight safety features, fuel efficiency, etc.). Superficial comparisons between the A350 and Boeing 787 series shows different unit prices with Airbus aircraft prices some 16 per cent to 20 per cent above those of Boeing; but the Airbus series generally offer greater numbers of passengers and longer range. However, comparisons of actual and potential rivalry are different. The A350-800 series is regarded as a rival for the Boeing 787-9 whilst the A350-900 and 1000 series are rivals for the Boeing 777-200ER and 300ER, respectively. The A350-900 is also regarded as a replacement for the A340-300 and the A350-1000 as a replacement for the A340-600. By end-2013, both the Airbus A350 and Boeing 787 series had each achieved orders in the region of 1,000 aircraft.

Table 7.1   Example of Airbus A350 and Boeing 787 Dreamliner

Type	Unit Price ($ million, 2014 prices)	Number of passengers	Range (nm)	Orders (end-2013)
Airbus				
A350-800	261	276	8,260	56
A350-900	295	315	7,750	567
A350-1000	341	369	7,990	189
Boeing				
B 787-8	215	242	7,650–8,200	495
B 787-9	253	280	8,000–8,500	404
B 787-10	293	323	7,000	132
B 777-200ER	265	314	7,725	422
B 777-300ER	325	386	7,930	452

Notes:
1. Seats are based on three class.
2. Range in nautical miles.
3. Orders include deliveries for B787-8 and B777 series. Orders can vary and should be regarded as broad orders of magnitude.
4. A350-900 is the first of the A350 series to be developed. Boeing 787-8 is the first of the Dreamliner series to be developed. The A350 series was also known as the A350 XWB (extra wide body).

Sources: Airbus and Boeing websites.

Duopoly is also a feature of the *regional jet market* which has been dominated by the Canadian firm Bombardier and the Brazilian firm Embraer. Competition embracing price and non-price forms between these firms has resembled that between Airbus and Boeing in the large jet airliner market. Bombardier's CRJ series (50 seats) first flew in 1991, entering service in 1992. Embraer entered the market and competed with Bombardier's CRJ series offering a range of small to medium size jet aircraft (e.g. 37 to 80 seats). Embraer's ERJ145 jet first flew in 1995, entering service in 1996 some four years later than the Bombardier CRJ service entry. As a new entrant and 'second mover', Embraer achieved considerable success with sales of its E jets exceeding 2,000 units compared with deliveries of over 1,600 units for Bombardier's CRJ series (sales include orders at end 2013). Bombardier responded to the rivalry from Embraer by developing its new larger C series (100–149 seats) which might be viewed as an attempt to achieve 'first mover' advantage.

Like the Airbus–Boeing rivalry, both Brazil and Canada were involved in an international trade dispute over government subsidies in the late 1990s and early 2000s (see Chapter 10).

The regional jet market has also been characterised by entry and exit. There are new entrants from China, Japan and Russia offering aircraft which are lower-priced for acquisition and with lower operating costs (Comac ARJ21; Mitsubishi Regional Jet; Sukhoi Super Jet). The new entrants have encountered technical problems leading to delays in development. There have also been exits from the market involving Fairchild Dornier, British Aerospace (BAe 146) and Fokker.

There is a *regional turboprop airliner market* which is also dominated by a duopoly comprising Bombardier and the European company ATR (jointly owned by Alenia Aermacchi and Airbus). There is some substitution between regional turboprops and regional jets, partly related to higher fuel prices. Regional turboprops represent a first entry point for nations seeking to create an aerospace industry. Possible future new entrants are likely to emerge in China, India and South Korea.

There is a further civil market for *business jets and light aircraft*. In the world market, business jets are produced by a relatively small number of major firms comprising Cessna (Textron), Gulfstream (General Dynamics), Bombardier (Learjets), Dassault (Falcon) and Embraer (Legacy). Interestingly, Hawker Beechcraft exited the business jet market where its aircraft were not profitable. It re-emerged as Beechcraft specialising in single engine turboprops and was acquired by Textron. In contrast, Honda is a new entrant to the business jet market with its Honda Jet (unit price of $3.7 million, 2013 prices). The major firms in the business jet market are part of larger groups with other aerospace or non-aerospace businesses. A good example is Textron which is a conglomerate owning Bell Helicopters, Beechcraft, Cessna and Lycoming Engines.

Competition in the *business jet market* is usually based on price and non-price elements consisting of speed, range, passenger capacity and passenger comfort. Some of these non-price elements are the result of technology transfers from a firm's military business (e.g. Dassault). The major buyers of business jets are large corporations which value speedy communications for long-distance travel for senior staff and where purchases are funded by the sales and profitability of the corporation.

Development costs for business jets are substantial and are usually privately-funded. For example, the Cessna Citation Columbus development costs were estimated at $800 million and a unit sales price of $27 million (2008 prices). The Citation Columbus is an example of a business jet which was planned but later cancelled (announced in 2006 and cancelled in 2009). Nor is there much evidence to support the 'first mover' advantage hypothesis in the business jet market. On the contrary, there is some evidence that followers learn from the first mover: they learn what the first mover did correctly and where the first mover made mistakes. This is not to suggest that the first mover never achieves an advantage: there are circumstances where the first mover wins (e.g. the early adoption of a significant cost-reducing technology leading to major learning economies and clear first mover advantages: Phillips et al., 1994, p212).

An economic study of the business jet market concluded that by the early 1990s, the profits of the major firms participating in the market had been negative resulting in a negative-sum game. This result reflected the positive profits of Cessna and Gulfstream and the sometimes profits of other firms, all of which were more than offset by the losses of the many who never succeeded in selling an aircraft, by those whose entry was quickly followed by their exit and by the once-successful firms who ceased to be profitable. Yet, entrepreneurs continue to believe that they are 'exceptional and different' and can achieve success when so many have failed. The long-run outcome of such entrepreneurial attitudes was expected to be market stabilisation with fewer firms and higher industry concentration (Phillips *et al.*, 1994, p213). There was some evidence that for business jets, this outcome *appeared* to be emerging by 2014 (e.g. exit of Hawker Beechcraft from business jets); but, as ever, new entrepreneurs were continuing to emerge (e.g. Honda Jet).

The market for *private and light aircraft* is also different from other aerospace markets. It is dominated by large numbers of individual private buyers as well as flying training schools and aviation clubs using light aircraft for pleasure and business flights. Individual consumers dominate this market where their demands are dependent on personal incomes and product prices embracing aircraft acquisition and running costs as well as the prices of close substitute aircraft. Typical unit prices for a four seat single piston-engine aircraft range from $190,000 to $290,000 (2014 prices). Non-price elements enter the competitive process, including simplicity of flying, reliability and safety. This market resembles the market for expensive motor cars and differs from military aircraft markets where the air force funds pilot training, provides combat aircraft and organises their repair, maintenance and disposal. Like motor cars, there is also a sizeable market for used aircraft.

Light aircraft are mostly single-engine types which are relatively cheap to develop and where firms can use private internal or external funds to develop such aircraft. US firms also have the advantage of a large home market offering opportunities for scale and learning economies from large-scale production. Indeed, the American Piper Company was based originally on the belief that everyone should fly.

At the world market level, the industry for light aircraft is competitive comprising at least seven major firms. These include three American firms, namely, Cessna, Beechcraft and Piper, the Canadian Bombardier group and three European firms, namely, Diamond (D-Jet: Austria), Piaggio (Italy) and Pilatus (Switzerland). Other firms in this sector include Daher-Socata (piston and turboprops: France) and Quest Aircraft (turboprops: USA). Entry costs are much less than for regional jets and large jet airliners so new entry is more likely. This is also a market where new entrants have offered novel ideas and concepts, not always with success. For example, the American Aviation Technology Group was created in 2000 to develop and produce the Javelin Very Light Jet. It failed to raise an additional $200 million for further development and the company went out of business and exited the market in 2008. Another example where potential new entrants offered to develop radical designs was the Aerion company with plans for a supersonic business jet with development costs of $2.5 billion to $3 billion (2007 prices).

Private firms are also entering the *space market* offering privately-funded space flights for space tourists. Virgin Galactic (part of the Virgin Group) is offering sub-orbital space flights at a price of $250,000 per person with reports of over 600 customers. The space flights are planned from a new space port facility in New Mexico, USA. Potential US rivals include Space X, Sierra Nevada Corporation and Orbital Sciences Corporation. Space X has also created a new market threat from its low-cost rocket launcher (Falcon 9). This new launcher represents a major challenge to the European Space Agency's (ESA) Ariane rocket launchers. Reports claim that Space X Falcon 9 is some 30 per cent cheaper than Ariane 5. The cost differences reflect the fact that Space X is based on an industrial structure built for efficiency whilst Ariane 5 has an industrial structure based on work-sharing between its member nations (Flight, 2014, p15). These are further examples of continued entrepreneurship embracing both product innovation and industrial organisation in the aerospace industry (cf. the early pioneers of manned flight: see Chapter 2).

The *civil helicopter market* has a variety of users, including the public sector (e.g. police forces), private industry and individual consumers with varying demands for helicopters of different sizes, ranges and passenger-carrying capacity. There is, for example, a substantial market for commercial helicopters to transport workers to remote oil platforms and for search and rescue operations. The result is a civil helicopter industry which comprises a variety of firms of different sizes. Some of the larger civil helicopter firms have military divisions. Examples include Bell, Sikorsky, AgustaWestland and Airbus Helicopters where there are opportunities for applying military technology to commercial helicopters (e.g. Bell/Boeing 609 civil tilt rotor now being developed by AgustaWestland as the AW 609). In contrast, other civil helicopter firms are relatively small focusing on the supply of small civil helicopters. Examples include the American firms of MD Helicopters and Robinson which is the world's leading supplier of civil helicopters. Typical unit prices for civil helicopters range from $4.2 million (AH/EC 135) to $17 million (Sikorsky S-92: 2013 prices).

The civil helicopter market places less emphasis on speed compared with the military helicopter market. In the commercial helicopter market, there is often an emphasis on non-price competition in the form of product improvements, including safety improvements, reduced maintenance requirements and fly-by-wire control systems. Operating costs are a major factor in commercial helicopter operations where such cost factors are less important for military helicopters. New technology is reflected in new, revolutionary designs in the form of the 'tilt rotor' and in new engine technology delivering savings in operating costs. Overall, the US military and civil helicopter markets comprise oligopolies whilst Europe is characterised by a duopoly (AgustaWestland and Airbus Helicopters, formerly Eurocopter) with the remaining markets consisting of national monopolies (e.g. Russian Helicopters; Hindustan of India; Denel of South Africa).

ASSESSING PERFORMANCE

Performance can be assessed at both the industry and firm levels. In each case, data problems arise, especially where aerospace firms are involved in non-aerospace activities and where firms have different combinations of defence and civil aerospace business. For the structure–conduct–performance model, various indicators of performance are recognised. These include profitability, productivity, productive and allocative efficiency, technical progress, growth and product quality. This section takes a more limited approach reflecting data availability. It presents an assessment of performance based on output, exports, development times, firm size, productivity and profitability. The examples are designed to illustrate the approach rather than provide a comprehensive evaluation of performance.

Output

Output is a major determinant of unit costs and hence of price competitiveness. Larger output allows a firm to spread its fixed costs, including R&D, over a larger output and also enables it to achieve learning economies leading to rising productivity. In assessing performance, a distinction needs to be made between military and civil aerospace equipment. Industry and firm performance on *civil aircraft and aerospace equipment* is a more accurate indicator of market competitiveness: defence markets are often subject to government protection from foreign competition with further restrictions from export licensing regulations.

Table 7.2 presents output levels for Airbus and Boeing large jet airliners. Airbus has achieved US scales of output. This is remarkable considering that in 1970 it was a new entrant into the fiercely competitive large jet airliner market dominated by US companies comprising Boeing, McDonnell Douglas and Lockheed. Its first aircraft was the A300B which by 1979 had orders for 256 units; by 2014, its successful A320 family had achieved sales of 6,132 units. Airbus, the new entrant in 1970, now forms a duopoly in the large jet airliner industry.

Table 7.2   Output levels of major jet airliners

AIRBUS		BOEING	
Aircraft type	Output	Aircraft type	Output
A300	561	707	1,010
A320 family	6,132	727	1,832
A330	1,046	737	10,499
A340	377	747	1,525
A350	812	757	1,050
A380	304	767	1,108
		777	1,431
		787	848
Average	*1,539*	*Average*	*2,413*

Note: Output based on deliveries and orders at end-2013. At this date, the following aircraft were no longer in production: A300; A340; B707; B727. Figures for 737 refer to all types, including NG and Max.

As a broad indicator, sales in the region of 1,000 units or more of a large jet airliner indicate a successful and profitable project. On this basis, the Airbus A320 family and the A330 together with all Boeing's jet airliners have been successful. Indeed, the Boeing 737 is the world's best-selling jet airliner. Airbus demonstrates a further aspect of successful performance: it is an example of a competitive European international collaboration (see Chapters 12 and 13).

Output levels for military aircraft and helicopters show major scale differences between Europe and the USA. Table 7.3 shows that typical output levels for US military aircraft have generally averaged almost 2,000 units compared with a European average of 621 units. Similar scale differences exist between US and European military helicopters. For example, output levels for the US Apache Longbow, Chinook, SuperCobra and Black Hawk helicopters ranged from 1,100 to some 4,000 units with an average output of 1,892 units. Comparable figures for the European Agusta A129 Mangusta, Puma, NH90 and Tiger helicopters ranged from 60 to some 700 units with an average output of 373 units (all output data at end-2013).

Table 7.3   Military aircraft output

| USA | | Europe | |
Aircraft type	Output	Aircraft type	Output
F-15 A-D	1,198	Mirage 2000	611
F-15E	814	Jaguar	543
F-16	4,570+	Hawk	1,000
F-18 A-D	1,480	Tornado	992
F-18E/F	665	Typhoon	571
F-22	195	Gripen	278
F-35	3,163	Rafale	351
Average	*1,726*	*Average*	*621*

Note: Output comprises orders and deliveries, including exports at July 2014. Defence budget cuts might lead to reductions in orders for F-35 and other current generation aircraft.

Exports

Exports are an indicator of international competitiveness. It might be expected that larger outputs are associated with export success due to the spreading of fixed R&D costs and the achievement of scale and learning economies all of which should lead to lower unit prices. However, this simple generalisation is subject to differences in the costs of factor inputs and difference in international comparative advantage. International comparisons encounter the usual data problems reflecting differences in definitions of the aerospace industry and of military and civil aerospace exports, and the actual availability of relevant data. There are also issues of causation and its direction. A correlation between output and success does not confirm causation: success depends on a variety of factors including output, R&D, choice of products, entrepreneurship and other relevant factors. Some broad assessments of performance can be made using both industry and firm level data.

At the *industry level*, there are data on the export performance of aerospace industries in the USA and the UK which are shown in Table 7.4. Comparing the US and UK industries, it can be seen that the greater output of the US industry is reflected in its greater exports, mainly reflecting its greater civil aerospace exports; but the UK exports a much higher proportion of its total sales.

Table 7.4   Export performance of aerospace industries, 2011–2012 (US$ million)

Nation	Aerospace Military	Exports Civil	Total	Total Sales	Export share of sales (%)
USA	11,290	84,171	95,461	217,870	43.8
UK	12,474	16,864	29,338	39,204	74.8

Note: UK data for 2011; US data for 2012.

Sources: Aerospace Industries Association of USA; UK Aerospace Survey, 2012.

At the *firm level*, company annual reports provide only limited information on a firm's defence exports. Typically, annual reports provide annual sales data by various product groups (e.g. commercial aeroplanes; defence, space and security; electronics; information systems) but often data on company export sales are not published (e.g. Boeing; BAE Systems). There are some exceptions including Lockheed Martin, Northrop Grumman and Dassault, as shown in Table 7.5. The company data confirm the industry data, namely, that larger sales are associated with higher export sales, but Dassault with the lowest sales and lowest exports in Table 7.5 has the highest share of exports in its total sales. The evidence for the UK industry and for Dassault Aviation suggests that despite the US scale advantage, the Europeans have a distinctive competitive advantage reflected in their relatively high export shares.

Table 7.5   Aerospace exports at company level, 2012 (US$ million)

Company	Sales	Exports	Export share of sales (%)
Lockheed Martin	47,182	8,021	17
Northrop Grumman	25,210	2,510	10
Dassault Aviation	3,579	2,970	83

Notes:
1. Lockheed Martin aeronautics exports were $3.3 billion or 22 per cent of its aeronautics sales of $15 billion; its missiles exports were $2.25 billion or 30 per cent of its missile sales of $7.5 billion; and its space exports were $0.33 billion or 4 per cent of its space sales of $8.3 billion.
2. Dassault export sales comprised military exports of $634 million and civil exports of $2.34 billion.

Sources: Annual Company Reports, 2012.

There are further firm level data on the exports of specific types of military and civil aircraft and helicopters. Some illustrative examples are shown in Table 7.6. Again, US scales of output are generally greater than for European combat aircraft with the US F-16 dominating the sample. However, on export shares, the UK Hawk and French Dassault Mirage 2000 compare favourably with the US F-16.

Development Times

The time taken to develop an aircraft from start to delivery is a further indicator of performance and competitiveness. Historically, the US aerospace industry developed both military and civil aircraft faster than its UK and European rivals. For example, between 1945 and 1969, the average UK development times for military aircraft were 100 months compared with 75 months for the USA; and for civil aircraft, the average

Table 7.6   Sales and exports for combat aircraft

Aircraft	Output (units)	Exports (units)	Export share of output (%)
Hawk	1,000+	797+	80
Mirage 2000	601	286	48
Tornado	992	120	12
Typhoon	571	99	17
F-111	563	24	4
F-16	4,570	2,339	51
F-18/A/B	1,480	431	29
F-18/E/F	665	36	5
F-35	3,163	720	23

Note: Output includes exports and orders where relevant. All numbers should be regarded as broad orders of magnitude at July 2014. The numbers for the F-35 are estimates at mid-2014.

UK development times were 52 months compared with 43 months in the USA (Elstub, 1969).

Since 1980, the position has changed, especially on large jet airliners where Airbus is now generally competitive with Boeing on development times. For a sample of Airbus and Boeing aircraft, the Boeing sample showed shorter average development times than the Airbus sample (67 months compared with 54 months, respectively). However, the averages conceal significant variations between different types: for example, the Airbus A320 and A330 series had shorter development times than the Boeing 767 series.

On military aircraft, there remains evidence that European aircraft continue to involve longer development times than similar US aircraft although the development time difference has been narrowing (Hartley and Braddon, 2014). This finding resulted from the statistical analysis of a sample of European and US combat aircraft and military airlifters with first flights over the period 1968 to 2009 (e.g. Jaguar; F-18E/F; F-15E; A400m: Hartley and Braddon, 2014). Such time differences reflect variations in the scale of US and European funding for defence R&D. However, a more limited analysis of a smaller sample gave completely different results. Development times on a sample of three current European projects averaged 203 months compared with an average of 263 months for two current US combat aircraft (i.e. Gripen, Rafale and

Typhoon versus F-22 and F-35). Since the end of the Cold War, development times have become relatively less important as the USA has placed less emphasis on speed into service in its procurement choices.

Industry and Firm Size

National aerospace industries differ considerably in their absolute size. Some examples are shown in Table 7.7 which confirms the dominant position of the US aerospace industry in both sales and employment. The European position is misleading in that it comprises a set of separate nation states rather than a single political entity (i.e. comprising 20 European countries consisting of 17 EU states plus Norway, Switzerland and Turkey). The Russian aerospace industry is relatively small but labour-intensive and similar in sales to Japan's industry. The Canadian industry is also distinctive in allocating a high share of its national output to aerospace: presumably, such allocative decisions reflect a government belief that aerospace represents a 'worthwhile investment'.

Table 7.7   National aerospace industries, 2012

Country	Aerospace Sales (US$ billion)	Aerospace Employment	Aerospace share in GDP (%)
USA	203.4	631,400	0.81
Europe	172.5	533,900	0.65
Canada	38.8	170,000	1.32
Russia	17.1	406,000	0.53
Japan	15.0	32,000	0.16
Brazil	7.0	23,368	0.19

Source: ASD (2013).

Data are also available on absolute firm size as measured by sales and employment. Examples are shown in Table 7.8. Again, these are illustrative of the approach and not meant to be comprehensive and definitive. In terms of sales and employment, Boeing and Airbus dominate the sample in Table 7.8. The 2012 averages for the US and European firms show that the US firms are some 60 per cent larger than the European firms in terms of sales and about 50 per cent larger in terms of employment. Two issues arise from the firm level data. First, the scale differences between US and European firms show the opportunities for further industry consolidation in Europe. Second, questions arise as to whether the scale differences are reflected in differences in labour productivity and profitability.

Table 7.8   Firm size, 2012

Company	Sales ($ billion)	Employment
Boeing	81.7	174,400
Lockheed Martin	47.2	120,000
Northrop Grumman	25.2	68,100
Average: US three	*51.4*	*120,833*
BAE Systems	29.1	88,200
Airbus (EADS)	70.0	140,405
Finmeccanica	21.6	70,474
Rolls-Royce	19.9	42,800
Safran	17.0	62,500
Average: EU five	*31.5*	*80,876*

Note: Finmeccanica data are for 2011.

Labour Productivity and Profitability

These are major performance indicators, especially profitability which is a key performance indicator for privately-owned firms. Such firms need to achieve profitability levels which are at least equal to the profitability of their assets if used in alternative activities: otherwise, firms will exit the industry.

Labour productivity can be measured at the industry and firm levels and in terms of sales per employee or value added per employee. Data are more easily obtained for sales per employee but value added per employee is a more accurate indicator of a firm's contribution to national output. Defined simply, value added consists of a firm's wages and profits. Value added data can be obtained from a company's annual accounts but assembling the data is time-consuming and requires knowledge of company accounts. Sales per employee reflect the value of a firm's sales which will be based partly on the value of a firm's purchases from other firms (e.g. bought-in parts and components).

Industry data on labour productivity are shown in Table 7.9. The Japanese aerospace industry has the highest labour productivity in the sample, followed by Europe and the USA. Whilst it might be surprising that the US industry does not top the list, it has to be remembered that sales per employee has its limitations as a performance indicator and that value added per employee is a better and more accurate indicator. Labour productivity in the Russian aerospace industry is the lowest in the sample and indicates the magnitude of inefficiency in the Russian industry (see also Table 7.7 which shows the labour-intensity of the Russian industry).

Table 7.9   Industry labour productivity, 2012

Industry	Labour Productivity (Sales per employee: US$)
USA	322,141
Europe	323,094
Canada	228,235
Russia	42,118
Japan	468,750
Brazil	299,555

Data on *firm* labour productivity are shown in Table 7.10. Airbus, Boeing and Rolls-Royce (aero-engines) dominate the sample. The results for Airbus and Boeing reflect their large-scale output of civil aircraft enabling them to achieve economies of scale and learning. In contrast, the productivity figures for Lockheed Martin, Northrop Grumman and BAE Systems reflects their focus on defence business with generally smaller outputs and fewer opportunities for scale and learning economies. Labour productivity at Rolls-Royce is substantially higher than at Safran which is a European rival aero-engine firm. Comparisons can also be made with the median productivity level for the sample (some $380,000) which shows some of the European firms with productivity below the median level for the sample in Table 7.10.

Profitability is the ultimate performance indicator for private enterprise firms. Profitability can be measured in different ways, usually as a return on sales or as a return on capital employed. Return on sales is often more readily available; return on capital requires a clear and consistent definition of capital employed which is more difficult to collect. Profitability data are shown in Table 7.10 where there are substantial variations

Table 7.10   Firm labour productivity and profitability, 2012

Company	Labour Productivity ($)	Profitability: Return on sales (%)
Boeing	468,463	7.7
Lockheed Martin	393,183	11.8
Northrop Grumman	370,191	12.4
BAE Systems	329,585	9.2
Airbus	498,557	5.3
Finmeccanica	306,851	(1.2)
Rolls-Royce	464,626	12.2
Safran	272,000	9.5

Note: ( ) shows a loss.

ranging from a loss of 1.2 per cent to profits of 12.4 per cent. Interestingly, the high productivity firms are not the high profitability firms (Airbus and Boeing). Instead, the high profitability firms are Northrop Grumman and Rolls-Royce, namely, a defence company and an aero-engine manufacturer. Rank correlations were estimated between productivity and profitability, between productivity and firm size, and between profitability and firm size (measured by sales). Only the relationship between firm size and productivity was statistically significant (with a Spearman's rank correlation of +0.7); none of the other relationships were significant. However, the profitability figures need to be treated with the usual caution: they are for one year only and do not reflect long-run trends, and they are for one measure of profitability, namely, returns on sales.

CONCLUSIONS

The structure–conduct–performance model provides a basis for analysing the world's aerospace industries. Other models can then be applied to provide further insights and add to understanding. Additional performance indicators can also be applied. Examples include data on cost escalation, delays in delivery, value added labour productivity and unit prices. Comparisons can also be made between aerospace performance and the performance of other industries (e.g. electronics; motor vehicles;

pharmaceuticals) and performance at the national economy level and between economies in the world market. Whilst statistical indicators confirm past and current performance and competitiveness, there are no guarantees of future successful competitiveness.

REFERENCES

ASD (2013). *Key Facts and Figures 2012*, Aerospace and Defence Industries Association of Europe, Brussels.
Cmnd 6697 (2005). *Defence Industrial Strategy*, Ministry of Defence, TSO, London.
Elstub (1969). *Productivity of the National Aircraft Effort*, Elstub, St. J., HMSO, London.
Flight (2014). ESA launches next stage of Ariane 6, *Flight International*, The Quadrant, Surrey, 18–24 February.
Hartley, K. and Braddon, D. (2014). Collaborative projects and the number of partner nations, *Defence and Peace Economics*, forthcoming.
Lipczynski, J., Wilson, J.O.S. and Goddard, J. (2009). *Competition, Strategy, Policy*, Prentice Hall, London.
Phillips, A., Phillips, A.P. and Phillips, T.R. (1994). *Biz Jets: Technology and Market Structure in the Corporate Jet Aircraft Industry*, Kluwer, Dordrecht.
Romp, G. (1997). *Game Theory*, Oxford University Press, Oxford.

8. A company case study. BAE Systems: achievements, rivals and prospects

INTRODUCTION: A COMPANY CASE STUDY

Previous chapters dealt with *industry* structure, conduct and performance. This chapter shows the opportunities for a *firm-level* analysis using BAE Systems as an example of a company case study approach. BAE Systems plc is the UK's largest defence contractor; in 2008 it was the world's top arms company and in 2011, it ranked third in the world (SIPRI, 2010; 2013). The company has undertaken a remarkable transformation involving changes of ownership, changes of business policy, extensive mergers and company disposals and a shift of focus from the UK to becoming a major participant in the US defence market. As a defence company, it has close relationships with the UK and foreign governments and has experienced problems in managing some of its major UK projects. From a public choice perspective, the company can be viewed as a powerful producer group with lobbying influence some of which has led to allegations of 'improper behaviour'(see Chapter 9).

This chapter presents a brief history of the company, its ownership and organisation followed by an assessment of its conduct and performance. There is an assessment of its achievements, its major rivals and its future challenges. Data for the survey were obtained from company annual reports which provided information on mergers and disposals, company organisation and statistics on sales, productivity and profitability. Since BAE Systems is a specialist defence company, its data on sales, productivity and profitability reflect its performance in defence markets. Other defence companies with a range of civil business often publish aggregate performance data which combines their military and civil businesses so that it is not possible to identify separately the company's defence business. As a result, BAE Systems provides a unique data base for the analysis of a specialist defence company.

A BRIEF HISTORY

BAE Systems was created on 30 November 1999 following the acquisition of Marconi Electronics Systems (MES) by British Aerospace (BAe). MES was the defence electronics and naval shipbuilding subsidiary of the General Electric Company plc (GEC). At the time, BAe was an aircraft, munitions and naval systems manufacturer and was the result of major mergers in the UK aircraft industry (Hartley, 2010). A description of the development of BAe is necessary for understanding the evolution of BAE Systems.

British Aerospace (BAe): Nationalisation

BAe was created in 1977 when the Labour government nationalised and merged the UK's two major airframe firms, namely, the British Aircraft Corporation (BAC) and the Hawker Siddeley Group (HSG comprising Hawker Siddeley Aviation (aircraft) and Hawker Siddeley Dynamics (missiles and space)) as well as Scottish Aviation. The two UK airframe firms were originally created in 1960 and were the result of earlier mergers involving famous UK aircraft companies. BAC was a merger of the aircraft interests of Bristol Aircraft, English Electric, Hunting and Vickers-Armstrongs. HSG was a merger of Hawker Siddeley Aviation (comprising Armstrong Whitworth, A.V. Roe, Gloster and Hawker) with Blackburn, de Havilland and Folland (Hayward, 1989). In 1960, the economic logic of forming two airframe groups was to create larger firms able to compete with US rivals whilst maintaining competition in the UK airframe sector. Industry re-structuring was achieved by the selective allocation of government contracts and offers of state support for promising civil aircraft and engine projects (Hartley, 2010). Similar re-structuring for aero-engines created two aero-engine firms, namely, Bristol Siddeley Engines and Rolls-Royce. An exception was helicopters where UK helicopter firms were merged to form a domestic monopoly, namely, the Westland Company. As a result, in 1960, the UK industry structure comprised five major groups, with duopolies in airframes and aero-engines and a domestic monopoly in helicopters (Hartley, 1965).

The case for the 1977 nationalisation was based on the industry's dependence on government, including state-funding of civil aerospace projects. Past issues of control and accountability were part of the case for nationalisation. Also, the industry's dependence on government funding for both military and civil projects meant that it was not regarded as a genuine example of private enterprise (Hayward, 1989, p150). Nationalisation was regarded as the only means of forcing the two airframe groups into a merger which was widely regarded as economically desirable.[1] However, ownership changed with the 1979 Conservative government committed to privatisation. As a result, BAe was completely privatised by 1985 (Parker, 2009).[2]

BAe: Privatisation and Diversification

On privatisation, BAe was a major aerospace company mainly involved in the design, development and production of a range of military and civil aircraft, missiles and space systems together with support services. Its UK military aircraft projects comprised (amongst others) the Harrier combat aircraft and Hawk trainer together with international collaborative projects, namely, the three nation Tornado and four nation Eurofighter Typhoon. Its civil aviation programmes included business jets (BAe 125), feeder airliners (Jetstream), regional jets (BAe 146) and specialist wing work for Airbus jet airliners.

Following privatisation, BAe adopted a new business model aimed at diversifying from aerospace into other defence and civil activities. It developed its electronics and communications capability (e.g. acquisition of Sperry Gyroscope: 1984) and it entered the land systems defence business when it acquired the ammunition and small arms division of the state-owned Royal Ordnance Factories (ROF: 1987). It also acquired civil activities in the form of a construction company (Ballast Nedam: 1987) to support its aspirations in developing prime contractor positions such as those in the Kingdom of Saudi Arabia; a property development firm (Arlington Securities: 1989) to manage the redevelopment of redundant industrial sites; and the Rover motor car company (1988). The acquisition of the Rover Group appeared to create a BAe version of Sweden's Saab company which also owned both aircraft and car divisions. BAe later acquired a 35 per cent share in Saab (1998).

BAe experienced major financial problems in 1991. The end of the Cold War meant reduced defence spending; the Rover Group recorded falling sales and losses; there were major losses in the civil aircraft business; and further market problems for the property company. Two major responses followed. First, in 1992, BAe announced a large

---

[1]   Short Bros was already nationalised and it remained outside the new BAe group. Similarly, the Westland helicopter company was privately-owned and also remained outside the BAe group.

[2]   The motivation for the privatisation of BAe was stated to be 'primarily political, not economic, reflecting a commitment made when the industry had been nationalised' (Parker, 2009, p124).

write-off of assets and large-scale redundancies, mostly in its civil aircraft business. Second, BAe abandoned its diversification policy and focused on becoming a specialist defence company which involved selling its non-core businesses. These non-core activities comprised civil aircraft, motor cars, property, construction and space systems. BAe Corporate Jets was sold to Raytheon; the Rover Group was sold to BMW; and BAe Space Systems was sold to Matra Marconi Space. In 1996, BAe and Matra Defense merged their missiles businesses to form a joint company, namely, Matra BAe Dynamics (Evans, 1999; Reppy, 1994; Taylor and Hayward, 1989).

The mergers in the US aerospace and defence industry by 1997 created larger and more competitive US defence firms (Skons and Weidacher, 1999). Pressure for similar industrial re-structuring arose in Europe with some interest in creating a single defence manufacturer in the form of a European Aerospace and Defence Company. In late 1998, a merger was agreed between BAe and Germany's DASA (DaimlerChrysler Aerospace). However, the situation changed when GEC announced the sale of its defence electronics business, Marconi Electronics Systems (MES) in December 1998. At the time, GEC was one of the world's top defence companies (ranked sixth in 1997: SIPRI, 1999).[3] BAe subsequently purchased MES leading to the formation of BAE Systems which became a vertically integrated company. A major reason for the change of merger direction for BAe was its fear that MES might be acquired by a US defence firm which would challenge both BAe and DASA.[4] Subsequently, DASA merged with the French company Aerospatiale-Matra and Spain's CASA to create the European Aeronautic Defence and Space Company which was a horizontal merger (EADS: July 2000).

For BAE Systems, the acquisition of MES was regarded as a transforming event. MES already held a substantial US holding (Tracor) which formed the basis for BAE Systems' initial North American operations and for its future US acquisition strategy. Its position in the US defence market was reinforced with the acquisition of Lockheed Martin Aerospace and Electronics Systems (Sanders: November 2000) which some commentators regarded as 'precedent setting' in establishing BAE Systems as a 'real' US defence company.

---

[3]   Between 1945 and 1999, GEC MES became one of the world's leading defence contractors with acquisitions of Associated Electrical Industries, English Electric Company, Yarrow Shipbuilders, Plessey and Ferranti, VSEL and Kvaerner Govan.
[4]   There were also reports that Thomson-CSF was a potential bidder for Marconi Electronics Systems.

At its formation, BAE Systems gave specific undertakings to the UK Department of Trade and Industry to avoid a reference to the Monopolies and Mergers Commission. For example, it gave undertakings ensuring fair competition between external companies and its subsidiaries and that there would be a 'firewall' between the former BAe and MES teams on defence projects (e.g. F-35 aircraft). In 2007, BAE Systems was released from the majority of these undertakings. Also, the Government Special Share was transferred from BAe which limited foreign share ownership in BAE Systems (to 15 per cent) and required the Chairman and CEO to be British nationals.

BAE Systems: Creating a Core Defence Business

BAE Systems continued to focus on developing its core defence business. This involved more acquisitions in the UK, USA and elsewhere. It exited the civil aircraft business by closing its regional jet airliner production line (2001) and selling its wing manufacturing business embodied in Airbus (UK) to EADS (2006). It acquired UK land and sea systems companies resulting in the UK's largest defence contractor with domestic monopolies in most air, land and sea systems. Its domestic monopoly in land systems was completed with the acquisition of Alvis Vickers which was the UK's main manufacturer of armoured fighting vehicles (2004). Similarly, it completed its domestic monopoly of UK warship building with the acquisition of the warship building business of the VT Group (forming BAE Systems Surface Ships Ltd: October 2009). At the European level, BAE Systems and Aerospatiale merged their Matra BAe Dynamics company with the missile division of Alenia Marconi Systems to create MBDA which is a European monopoly in missile manufacture (2001: BAE has a 37.5 per cent share). However, BAE Systems preferred to develop into the US rather than the European defence market. A 2004 review of the company's business decided on no further European acquisitions or joint ventures and a strategic bias for expansion in the USA.

BAE Systems: Developing its US Business

BAE Systems established a major presence in the US defence market which offered benefits from the large-scale of both total US defence spending and its defence R&D spending. Interestingly, in view of its traditional aerospace business, its American focus was on the US land systems sector. BAE Systems acquired United Defense Industries (2005) followed by Armor Holdings (2007), both companies being major US suppliers of land systems. Combined with its land systems businesses in the UK, Sweden and South Africa, BAE Systems is now one of the world's leading land systems firms (e.g. armoured fighting vehicles; tactical wheeled vehicles; artillery systems; munitions). This represents a major shift from its traditional military aerospace business (Hartley, 2003; Skons and Surrey, 2007).

Further acquisitions occurred in Australia with the purchase of Tenix Defence, a major Australian defence contractor (2008) making BAE Systems the largest Australian defence company. BAE Systems is also the majority shareholder in BAE Land Systems South Africa; it owns Hagglunds and Bofors of Sweden; it has a major defence interest in Saudi Arabia; and it entered the Indian defence market through a joint venture with Mahindra and Mahindra Ltd to create Defence Land Systems India (with a BAE Systems share of 26 per cent: 2010).

It developed its security and intelligence business with the acquisition of the Detica Group (2008) which specialises in counter-terrorism, serious and organised crime, border control and cyber threats for various UK government departments. Detica was renamed BAE Applied Intelligence in January 2014. Further acquisitions in this field involved ETI, the Danish cyber and intelligence company (2010) and parts of the US intelligence and security firm L-1 Identity Solutions (2011). In these cases, BAE Systems used acquisitions to enter a new market.

BAE Systems also developed new markets for military support involving maintenance, support and through-life management (military outsourcing markets). Its business was shifting from an equipment supply centred model to a service model. In this sphere, it acquired the US Atlantic Marine Holding Company (July 2010) which enhanced its ship repair and upgrading capabilities serving the US Navy (BAE, 2011).[5] By 2012, some 50 per cent of the group's sales were in services.

The BAE Systems focus on its core defence business led to further sales of non-core activities. Its space division was sold to Astrium (EADS: 2003); following internal rationalisation and consolidation, its share of SELEX Sensors and Airborne Systems was sold to Finmeccanica (2007); its German naval systems subsidiary (Atlas Elektronik) was sold to Thyssen Krupp and EADS; its aerostructures business was sold to Spirit Aerosystems (2006). In 2011, it sold its regional aircraft asset management business and its shareholding in Saab. The sale of its

---

[5] BAE's bid to acquire the US Marine Hydraulics International company was abandoned due to reported opposition from the US Departments of Defense, Justice and the US Navy on competition grounds.

Saab shares reflected its focus on Typhoon exports rather than Gripen sales and its focus on the US defence market. By 2008, BAE Systems was the world's leading defence firm (Table 8.2).

In September 2012, BAE Systems and EADS considered a merger of the two companies which would have created the world's largest defence and aerospace company. For BAE, such a merger would have provided access to civil aircraft markets as diversification from reliance on its uncertain and declining defence markets; it also represented a shift from the US market. EADS would have gained access to the US defence market. The proposed merger would have been shared 60 per cent for EADS and 40 per cent for BAE Systems. However, by October 2012, the proposed merger was abandoned on the grounds that 'no agreement acceptable to all parties could be reached' (BAE, 2012). Governments were centrally involved in assessing the proposed merger and Germany had major reservations about it. For the future, EADS now re-named Airbus faces challenges in improving its competitiveness, especially for its defence division (Cassidian). Similarly, with the collapse of the proposed merger, BAE Systems will need to reduce its costs via job losses and site closures.[6]

BAE Systems: Major Project Problems

BAE Systems' expansion was not trouble-free. There were reports of poor working relationships between some senior BAE Systems staff and the UK Ministry of Defence leading to management changes. Also, between 2000 and 2003, there were cost overruns and delays on two major UK projects, namely, the Nimrod MRA4 aircraft and the Astute submarine. BAE Systems made payments to the MoD for cost overruns of £800 million on the Nimrod MRA4 aircraft and £250 million on the Astute submarine (with the MoD also agreeing to contribute towards the cost overruns).[7] As a result of the adverse financial implications of fixed price contracts, the Nimrod contract was changed from a fixed price to a target cost incentive fee contract. Also, BAE Systems' continued concern that the UK operated an open and competitive defence market with fixed price contracts whilst the USA and most European nations protected their

---

[6]   For example, shipbuilding work at the BAE Portsmouth yard was ended in 2013.

[7]   The Nimrod MRA4 aircraft never entered RAF service and was cancelled in the UK's 2010 Strategic Defence Review. This Review also resulted in reduced military support contracts for BAES (due to scrapping of Harrier aircraft and reductions in the numbers of Tornado squadrons).

national defence industries was a major factor in the UK introducing a new defence industrial strategy in 2005 (DIS: Cmnd 6697, 2005). This new strategy committed the UK to retaining key defence industrial capabilities, many of which were dominated by BAE Systems (e.g. ammunition; armoured fighting vehicles; combat aircraft; core warship building; nuclear-powered submarines).

By 2014, BAE Systems was the prime contractor on the UK's major defence projects. These included its aircraft carriers, nuclear-powered submarines (Astute and Successor Deterrent Programme), the Type 45 destroyers, the new Type 26 warships, armoured fighting vehicles, the collaborative Typhoon combat aircraft and the F-35 combat aircraft. The Nimrod MRA4 maritime patrol aircraft was cancelled in 2010 as part of the UK's Strategic Defence Review. At cancellation, total spending on Nimrod was £3.4 billion (excluding cancellation costs); its costs had increased by £789 million since original approval; it was 114 months late; and the numbers to be purchased had fallen from an original planned 21 aircraft to nine aircraft. Cancellation was expected to save £1.9 billion in forecast operational and maintenance costs up to 2020 (and further savings beyond 2020: NAO, 2011).

Cost increases and delays in delivery are characteristic of major defence projects and such features affect two of BAE Systems' current projects, namely, the aircraft carriers and Astute submarines. On the two UK aircraft carriers, total costs have risen from an original cost of about £3.9 billion to a 2014 total cost of £6.1 billion and the in-service date is delayed by two years (NAO, 2014). The carrier contract has also been modified to a new target cost incentive contract where any variation above or below the target price will be shared 50:50 between the government and the contractor until all the contractor's profit is lost (compared with the original contract with a 90:10 sharing arrangement with 90 per cent borne by the government).

The Astute submarine programme has also been subject to cost overruns and delays. For the first four boats, total programme costs have risen by £1.9 billion and for the first three boats, the average delay has totalled 58 months. Over the planned order for seven boats, the delays range from 16 months to 37 months. Not all these delays are the responsibility of BAE Systems. The 2010 Strategic Defence Review delayed the introduction of the Successor Deterrent Programme and the Astute build programme was slowed to avoid a production gap in the submarine construction industry (NAO, 2011).

ORGANISATION OF BAE SYSTEMS

BAE Systems describes itself as a global defence, security and aerospace company with security added to the core business in 2008. It is organised into five major operating groups, namely, Electronic Systems; Cyber and Intelligence; and three Platforms and Services divisions for each of the USA, UK and International. Electronic Systems comprises the US and UK-based electronics activities (e.g. electronic warfare systems; electro-optical sensors). Cyber and Intelligence comprises the US-based intelligence and security business and the UK-based Applied Intelligence business (formerly Detica). Platforms and Services (US) comprises the US-headquartered Land and Armaments business with operations in the US, UK, Sweden and South Africa. Platforms and Services (UK) comprises the group's UK-based air, maritime and combat vehicle activities (e.g. aircraft carriers; Type 45 destroyers; Astute submarines; Typhoon; F-35). Platforms and Services (International) embraces the group's businesses in Saudi Arabia, Australia, India and Oman together with its share of MBDA activities. Table 8.1 shows details of these divisions.

Table 8.1   BAE Systems major divisions, 2013

Operating companies	Annual sales (£ millions)	Employment	Labour productivity (£000s)	Profits as return on sales (%)
Electronic Systems	2,466	12,500	197,280	14.0
Cyber and Intelligence	1,247	7,700	161,948	9.3
Platforms and Services (USA)	3,421	19,200	178,177	6.3
Platforms and Services (UK)	5,979	28,300	211,272	12.8
Platforms and Services (International)	4,063	14,600	278,288	10.6
Total	*18,180*	*84,600*	*214,894*	*10.6*

Notes:
1. Total includes HQ and Other Business (e.g. head office; research).
2. Labour productivity based on sales and employment for each operating company.

Source: BAE (2013).

The groups differ in size measured by sales and employment and in performance reflected in labour productivity and profitability. In 2013, the UK Platforms and Services sector was one of the largest divisions, approaching group average productivity and above average profitability (Table 8.1). The importance of the US defence market is reflected in BAE Systems being a top 10 US defence contractor in 2013 with 31,500 US employees. However, the budget deficit and the end of conflicts in Iraq and Afghanistan led to reduced US defence spending, especially for land systems. This explains the relatively poor performance of BAE's US Platforms and Services sector reflected in lower sales, job losses and reduced profitability. Elsewhere, in 2012, BAE Systems employed 5,500 personnel in Australia, 5,900 personnel in Saudi Arabia, 1,750 in Sweden, 600 personnel in South Africa and 350 in India (BAE, 2012).

The world's major defence companies have different businesses and organisations reflecting their varied efforts to economise on transaction costs. BAE Systems resembles the specialist US defence companies with 70 per cent or more of their business in defence (e.g. Lockheed Martin; Northrop Grumman: Table 8.2). In its range of defence activities, BAE Systems resembles Northrop Grumman being involved in air and sea systems as well as defence electronics (but not in land systems).[8] For BAE, both its size and range of activities offer opportunities for economies of scale and scope (a total of seven arms sectors). In comparison, Boeing and EADS are specialist aerospace companies with a large civil aircraft business and they are a duopoly in the world's large jet airliner market.[9] Table 8.2 also suggests other comparisons between the top 10 firms. BAE Systems is the most defence-dependent firm within the top 10 and it is involved in more defence sectors. However, there remain scale differences between the major European and US defence firms. European firms account for 30 per cent of the top 10 and the average European firm was some 88 per cent of the size of the average US defence firm (based on top 10). Similarly, the average European defence firm was less defence-dependent with more defence sectors

---

[8] In March 2011, Northrop Grumman announced the spin-off of its ship-building business to its wholly owned subsidiary Huntington Ingalls Industries (HII). The change will allow Northrop Grumman and HII to focus on their respective customers. The shipbuilding business of HII will be divided into two parts, namely, Newport News and the Gulf Coast segments.

[9] Whilst Boeing is less defence-dependent than BAE, Boeing has larger defence sales to the US DoD. In 2012, Boeing was ranked second in the list of top DoD contractors whilst BAE was ranked eighth (www.CBNC.com, December, 2013).

(European median of 60 per cent defence-share compared with US median of 78 per cent; and European average of six arms sectors compared with US average of four arms sectors: based on the top 10 firms in Table 8.2). Questions arise about the market structure, conduct and performance of BAE Systems.

Table 8.2   World's top 10 defence companies, 2011

Company	Arms sales ($millions)	Arms share of total sales (%)	Sectors
Lockheed Martin	36,269	78	Ac, El, Mi, Sp
Boeing	31,835	46	Ac, El, Mi, Sp
BAE Systems	29,161	95	A, Ac, El, MV, Mi, SA, Sh
General Dynamics	23,763	73	A, El, MV,SA, Sh
Raytheon	22,467	90	Ac, El, Mi, Sp
Northrop Grumman	21,394	81	Ac, El, Mi, Sh, Sp, Oth
EADS (Airbus)	16,399	24	Ac, El, Mi, Sp
Finmeccanica	14,572	60	A, Ac, El, MV, Mi, SA
L-3 Communications	12,521	83	Ac, El, Oth
United Technologies	11,638	20	Ac, El, Eng, Mi

Notes:
1. A = artillery; Ac = aircraft; El = electronics; Mi = missiles; MV = military vehicles; Sh = ships; Sp = space; Oth = Other.
2. Subsidiaries are not shown.
3. BAE (UK), EADS (Netherlands: later renamed Airbus) and Finmeccanica (Italy) are European defence companies. The remaining companies in Table 8.2 are US firms.
4. Ranking based on arms sales.

Source: SIPRI (2012).

STRUCTURE AND CONDUCT

Defence markets are far from 'perfect'. As the UK's major defence contractor with a domestic monopoly in a range of air, land and sea equipment, BAE Systems is a large firm in both absolute and relative size. Its sales to the UK Ministry of Defence (MoD) accounted for 41 per cent of all MoD procurement expenditure in 2011/12 with sales to the

UK MoD accounting for some 20 per cent of all BAE sales.[10] In contrast, Rolls-Royce sales accounted for some 3 per cent of MoD procurement spending in 2011/12 (DASA, 2012). As a large firm, public choice analysis identifies BAE Systems as a powerful producer group potentially able to influence UK government procurement and contracting policy. It can use its bargaining power to persuade governments to 'buy British', to provide guaranteed domestic markets and to offer 'fair and reasonable prices' with 'acceptable' profitability. It can threaten to close plants in vote-sensitive areas and in the final resort, it can threaten to exit the UK market (e.g. shifting its activities to the USA). It is believed that the UK's 2005 Defence Industrial Strategy was a response to BAE Systems' concerns about the UK's competitive defence procurement policy (Cmnd 6697, 2005).

BAE Systems is not the only UK domestic monopoly. There are other domestic monopolies in aero-engines (Rolls-Royce), helicopters (AgustaWestland owned by Finmeccanica) and repair and maintenance facilities for warships and submarines (Babcock International). Also, some of BAE Systems' potential domestic monopoly markets are in principle contestable from other UK defence firms, mainly in warship and submarine building[11] as well as from foreign defence firms. However, the UK's 2005 Defence Industrial Strategy provided BAE Systems and other UK defence firms with guaranteed and protected markets for key defence industrial capabilities so that these domestic markets are not contestable. Partnering agreements were the basis for achieving the Defence Industrial Strategy and more recent industrial policy initiatives. For example, BAE Systems has partnering agreements with the UK MoD for munitions supply (a 15 year agreement), warship building, nuclear-powered submarines, and for the maintenance and support of various UK aircraft fleets (e.g. Typhoon; Tornado).

BAE Systems' conduct has been reflected in its price and non-price behaviour embracing equipment quality and R&D. Defence equipment choices often focus on equipment quality reflected in its technical and performance characteristics in relation to potential enemy threats (e.g. speed; range of combat aircraft). Such non-price factors are promoted

---

[10]   There are no published data allowing estimates of BAE's relative size in each of the UK air, land, sea systems and electronics markets. Within the UK, BAE Systems has 7,500 suppliers.

[11]   Babcock International has facilities for the repair and maintenance of warships and submarines and is involved in the final assembly of the UK's two new aircraft carriers. Other UK domestic monopolies in helicopters and aero-engines are also contestable (e.g. Boeing and Airbus Helicopters for helicopters).

through major defence R&D activities most of which is funded by the government. Some of these R&D activities require defence-specific physical and human capital assets with no alternative uses. Examples include the development and production facilities for nuclear-powered submarines, combat aircraft, missiles, armoured fighting vehicles, artillery and ammunition. These markets are especially prone to information asymmetries between government and contractor leading to problems of moral hazard, adverse selection and hold-up (Laffont and Tirole, 1993; see Chapter 11).

Some limited evidence on the R&D and capital spending dimensions of BAE Systems' non-price behaviour are shown in Table 8.3 where comparisons are made with other major defence and aerospace firms. The data are limited since they are for privately-funded R&D embracing both military and civil markets for one year so they might reflect peaks and troughs in such spending. In 2012, BAE Systems had the lowest R&D share figure for the sample compared with other defence firms and a considerably lower R&D share compared with Boeing, Airbus (EADS) and Rolls-Royce each with a major civil airliner business. In contrast, Dassault and Finmeccanica had relatively high R&D shares. In recent years, BAE's total R&D expenditure was some five times its privately-funded R&D spending. For example, in 2012, its total R&D expenditure was £1,138 million of which £150 million was funded by the group compared with corresponding figures of £1,149 million and £222 million for 2011 (the balance comprised UK government and other sources of R&D funding: BAE, 2012).

On pricing, a significant proportion of BAE revenue is derived from fixed price contracts. However, BAE Systems has reduced its risks by reducing its exposure to fixed price contracts for design and development work which are usually much riskier than fixed price production contracts. Similarly, BAE Systems has reduced exposure to competitive contracting with such contracts accounting for 11 per cent of its MoD sales in 2011/12 compared with 20 per cent in 2009/10 (meaning that 89 per cent of its MoD sales were non-competitive in 2011/12). The corresponding figure of competitive contracts for Rolls-Royce Holdings was 7 per cent of its MoD sales compared with a national average of competitive contracts accounting for 56 per cent of the value of all MoD contracts placed in 2011/12 (DASA, 2012).

As a large defence company with lobbying powers, BAE Systems has been criticised for its business practices with allegations of bribery and corrupt practices, particularly in export markets such as Saudi Arabia, South Africa and Tanzania (Hudson, 2011; Tagarev, 2010). BAE Systems always denied these allegations and there have been two responses. First, BAE Systems created an independent committee (chaired by Lord Woolf)

Table 8.3   Company R&D spending, 2012

Company	R&D share of sales (%)	Capital expenditure share of sales (%)
BAE Systems	0.9	2.2
Boeing	3.6	2.1
EADS/Airbus	6.4	5.8
Lockheed Martin	1.3	2.0
Northrop Grumman	2.1	1.3
General Dynamics	2.1	1.4
United Technologies	3.7	5.1
SAFRAN	8.1	3.1
Rolls-Royce	5.2	3.6
Finmeccanica	10.5	4.9
Thales	4.9	3.1
Dassault Aviation	19.1	1.5

Source: EC (2013).

which examined the ethical principles and practices underlying its business with the aim of becoming a global leader in ethical business conduct. This committee reported in 2008 making 23 recommendations for further improvements, all of which were accepted by BAE Systems (including recommendations on anti-bribery policies and practices such as gifts, hospitality and donations: BAE, 2009a, p50). Second, in 2010, BAE Systems agreed to pay fines totalling £296 million to the UK Serious Fraud Office (SFO: £30 million) and the US Department of Justice (DoJ: £266 million). The US DoJ fines related to making false statements to the US government and violations relating to arms export controls in relation to contracts in the Czech Republic, Hungary and Saudi Arabia (DoJ, 2010). The UK SFO fine related to BAE Systems' accounting records for a radar contract in Tanzania (BAE, 2009b, 2011; Bean, 2010).[12]

---

[12]   Other UK and foreign defence companies have been subject to similar allegations. Examples in 2014 included Rolls-Royce being investigated by UK Serious Fraud Office over allegations of bribery and corruption involving contracts in China, Indonesia and other markets; and AgustaWestland (Finmeccanica) where India cancelled a helicopter contract over allegations of bribery.

PERFORMANCE

Published data are available to assess BAE Systems' performance in the form of productivity, profitability and international competitiveness. Table 8.4 shows data on sales, labour productivity and profitability for 2012. Compared with the firms shown in Table 8.4, BAE Systems' labour productivity compares unfavourably and is below the median figure for the group. The high labour productivity firms were each major manufacturers of civil jet airliners where there are economies of scale and learning from long production runs. For the firms in Table 8.4, rank correlations were estimated between labour productivity and sales and between labour productivity and profitability but the correlations were not significant.[13]

Table 8.4   Sales, productivity and profitability, 2012

Company	Sales (£ millions)	Labour productivity (£000s)	Profitability (% of sales)
BAE Systems	16,369	202,086	9.9
Boeing	50,775	291,141	7.4
EADS/Airbus	46,314	329,860	3.8
United Technologies	40,941	187,803	13.3
Lockheed Martin	29,323	244,358	9.5
General Dynamics	19,585	212,419	2.6
Northrop Grumman	15,673	230,147	12.4
Finmeccanica	14,119	209,450	−2.4
Rolls-Royce	11,927	278,668	11.3
Thales	11,610	175,930	5.6
SAFRAN	11,164	178,458	10.3
Dassault Aviation	3,232	279,778	37.3

Notes:
1. Companies ranked by sales.
2. Labour productivity based on sales and employment.

Source: EC (2013).

---

[13]   Rank correlations between labour productivity and sales were +0.38 and between labour productivity and profitability were −0.11 where the negative relationship was unexpected.

Labour productivity is a limited performance indicator since it reflects variations in a firm's make or buy choices. Some high productivity firms might have a large proportion of bought-in parts and components. Value added productivity is a more accurate indicator of a firm's productivity. Also, labour productivity figures for the firms in Table 8.4 reflect total sales and total employment where these totals relate to all military and civil sales comprising aerospace and non-aerospace products: the data do not show aerospace labour productivity only.

BAE Systems' profitability in 2012 was at the median level for the group of firms shown in Table 8.4. It was similar to the profitability of Lockheed Martin but higher than the major civil aerospace firms of Airbus and Boeing. Interestingly in considering size of firm and perform-ance, the leading firm in Table 8.4 was also the smallest in the group, namely, Dassault Aviation suggesting that size of firm does not guarantee successful performance.

BAE Systems' profitability depends on its internal efficiency, its competitiveness, contract types, its exposure to risks on large projects and the extent of profit regulation. Contract types affect risk and BAE Systems has reduced its exposure to fixed price design and development contracts which are riskier than fixed price production contracts (e.g. after its experience with the Nimrod MRA4 project: BAE, 2009a). However, losses on cost overruns affect profits so that such risk-related losses have to be recognised in estimating a true long-run average profit figure. Also, UK contracts which are non-competitive are subject to profit regulation and BAE Systems is a major recipient of such contracts: for example, in 2011/12, almost 90 per cent of BAE contracts from MoD were non-competitive (DASA, 2012). Traditionally, the 1968 UK Profit Formula for such contracts aimed to provide contractors with a return equal on average to the overall return earned by British industry with profits based on both costs of production and capital employed. In 2010, the baseline profit rate on UK non-competitive contracts was 9.05 per cent on costs of production (typically equivalent to a return of some 27 per cent on capital employed: Review Board, 2010). But target profit rates are not always achieved. Over the period 2007/08, the Profit Formula set a target profit rate of 7.01 per cent but the outcome was an actual profit rate of 10.82 per cent on costs of production (including some firms incurring losses on non-competitive contracts: Review Board, 2010). However, after a review of the 1968 Profit Formula, the govern-ment announced major changes for non-competitive contracts to be introduced from 2013 (e.g. Review Board to be replaced by a new Single Source Regulations Office: Cmnd 8626, 2013).

Exports are an indicator of international competitiveness although arms exports are influenced by both price and non-price variables, where the non-price variables include political factors, offsets and technology transfer packages. Published data are available on BAE Systems annual sales by geographical region. Private studies for BAE Systems estimated that in 2002, exports accounted for some 25 per cent of its total sales rising to 30 per cent in 2006 (OEF, 2004; OE, 2008). For 2006, BAE Systems accounted for over 85 per cent of UK defence exports (DASA, 2008).[14] In 2012, BAE Systems sales to the UK Ministry of Defence represented some 25 per cent of its total sales with the US Department of Defense accounting for a further 28 per cent of sales (BAE, 2012).

BAE has achieved some notable export sales, including Tornado, Hawk and Typhoon. Total sales of the three nation Tornado were 992 units with exports of 120 units (exports of 12 per cent of sales). Hawk sales have been most impressive with total sales of some 1,000 units comprising 203 units for the UK and some 800 units for export (with exports accounting for some 80 per cent of total sales). Typhoon is a four nation collaborative project with total sales of 571 units including 99 units for export (exports of 17 per cent of total output). However, by early 2014, its European rivals, namely, the Saab Gripen and the Dassault Rafale, had achieved greater export sales. Gripen has sold to the Swedish air force (original order for 204 units but 28 units leased overseas) with actual and planned export sales of 102 units (37 per cent of total sales). Similarly, the French air force and navy plan to buy 225 Rafales with a possible export order to India of 126 units giving a total output of 351 units (exports at 36 per cent of output). The sales and export performance of the Gripen and Rafale raise questions about the comparative performance of the multinational Typhoon collaboration. Gripen and Rafale demonstrate that European nations with relatively small firms, namely, Saab and Dassault, are capable of developing and producing successful and competitive advanced combat aircraft on a national basis without any collaboration.

---

[14] After 2008, the UK changed the official data published on its defence exports and excluded data on estimates of additional aerospace equipment and services (DASA, 2008; 2010). Also, in recent years, BAES export data were published in two private studies (OEF, 2004; OE, 2008); there are no published export data in BAES annual reports. However, data on UK defence aerospace exports are published annually by the industry trade association. In 2012, total UK defence aerospace exports were £7.5 billion and civil aerospace exports were £10.4 billion giving a total for UK aerospace exports of £18.1 billion (ADS, 2012).

Overall, BAE Systems is a major exporter accounting for a substantial proportion of the UK's defence and military aerospace industry exports. BAE Systems is now recognised not only as the UK's largest defence and security company but also as one of the UK's world class manufacturing firms.

CONCLUSION: ACHIEVEMENTS AND FUTURE CHALLENGES

Since its initial formation, BAE Systems has undergone a remarkable transformation. It originated as a state-owned aerospace company (British Aerospace) which was subsequently privatised and developed as a diversified company with a range of aerospace and other defence and civil activities, including motor vehicles, construction and property development. In the 1990s, BAe abandoned its diversified business model, it withdrew from civil aircraft activities and focused on its core defence business culminating in the acquisition of Marconi Electronics and the creation of BAE Systems. Its next phase led to the acquisition of US defence companies, especially in defence electronics and land systems. Its US business reflected a shift from investments in Europe. Over its life-cycle, BAE Systems has sold and closed a variety of plants, especially in the aircraft industry. In 1978, BAE owned 19 aircraft plants; by 2014, it operated from three aircraft plants (Brough; Samlesbury; Warton).[15] Further changes are likely as manned aircraft are replaced by unmanned systems.

BAE Systems faces major challenges concerned with future defence markets, new technology and new rivals. Changes in the levels and types of defence spending in world markets will determine BAE Systems' future as a defence firm (Hartley and Sandler, 2003; also Chapter 14). For example, future defence markets might focus on security and counter-terrorism systems and on space systems. There are also prospects of developing a European defence equipment market and a European defence industrial base which might make the European defence market more attractive to BAE Systems (Hartley, 2010). New technology will affect BAE Systems' future. For example, today's major defence firms did not exist in 1900 (e.g. BAE Systems; Boeing; Lockheed Martin) and it is highly probable that new names will enter defence markets over the

---

[15]   The Woodford plant was closed and acquired by a property developer in December 2011. Some design work is undertaken at Farnborough and further work has been transferred to UK front-line bases.

next 50 years (e.g. electronics firms). Some of these new rivals might be from nations such as Brazil, China, India, Israel, Japan and South Korea.

BAE Systems' monopoly position in parts of the UK defence market also has to be addressed. The standard monopoly problem might be resolved by treating BAE Systems as a regulated firm or by subjecting it to foreign competition. The challenge remains of ensuring that BAE Systems operates efficiently and that the profitability of UK defence contracts provides incentives to operate efficiently whilst avoiding generous profits for leading a 'quiet life' and relying on less demanding non-competitive contracts. These issues have been addressed by the UK government which in 2010/11 reviewed its defence industrial policy and its policy on pricing single supplier defence contracts, including profitability rules (Cmnd 7989, 2010). The new UK defence industrial policy will make greater use of competitive procurement in both European and world markets (buying-off-the-shelf) recognising affordability and budget constraints. There will also be greater emphasis on bilateral equipment collaboration and more military outsourcing. In response to unattractive UK market prospects, BAE Systems has the option of exiting the UK defence market and shifting its headquarters to the USA. Other possible business model options include an international merger with a major foreign defence and aerospace firm or diversification into civil, non-defence industries.

As a private company, BAE Systems' managers and shareholders have the task of developing a business model which will remain competitive, earning a rate of return at least equal to the returns earned in the next best alternative activity: they are the best judges of the company's future direction and prospects. But, the importance of BAE Systems in the UK defence market means that the UK government will not be indifferent to the future direction and ownership of the company. At this point, public choice models can be applied to the analysis of aerospace industries.

REFERENCES

ADS (2012). *UK Aerospace Industry Survey 2012*, ADS Group, London.

BAE (2009a). *Leveraging Global Capability*, Annual Report 2008, BAE Systems, London.

BAE (2009b). *Corporate Responsibility Report 2009: A Culture of Total Performance*, BAE Systems, London.

BAE (2010). *Delivering Total Performance*, Annual Report 2009, BAE Systems, London.

BAE (2011). *Annual Report 2011*, BAE Systems, London.

BAE (2012). *Annual Review 2012*, BAE Systems, London.

BAE (2013). *Annual Report 2013*, BAE Systems, London.

Bean, Mr Justice (2010). *Case No S2010565 Before Mr Justice Bean Between R and BAE Systems*, Crown Court at Southwark, London, December.

Cmnd 6697 (2005). *Defence Industrial Strategy*, TSO, London.

Cmnd 7989 (2010). *Equipment, Support and Technology for UK Defence and Security: A Consultation Paper*, Ministry of Defence, London.

Cmnd 8626 (2013). *Better Defence Acquisition*, Ministry of Defence, TSO, London.

DASA (2008). *UK Defence Statistics 2008*, Defence Analytical Services Agency, Ministry of Defence, TSO, London.

DASA (2010). *UK Defence Statistics 2010*, Ministry of Defence, London.

DASA (2012). *UK Defence Statistics 2012*, Defence Analytical Services Agency, Ministry of Defence, TSO, London.

DoJ (2010). BAE pleads guilty and ordered to pay $400 million in criminal fine, US Department of Justice, *Justice News*, Washington DC, March.

EC (2013). *EU R&D Scoreboard, 2013*, European Commission, Luxembourg.

Evans, R. (1999). *Vertical Take-off*, Nicholas Brealey, London.

Hartley, K. (1965). The mergers in the UK Aircraft Industry, 1957–60, *Journal of the Royal Aeronautical Society*, 69, 660, 846–852.

Hartley, K. (2003). The future of European defence policy, *Defence and Peace Economics*, 14, 2, 107–115.

Hartley, K. (2010). UK Aerospace Industry, BIS Economic Papers No 6, *Learning from some of Britain's successful sectors: An historical analysis of the role of government*, Department for Business, Innovation and Skills, London, March.

Hartley, K. and Sandler, T. (2003). The future of the defence firm, *Kyklos*, 56, 3, 361–380.

Hayward, K. (1989). *The British Aircraft Industry*, Manchester University Press, Manchester.

Hudson, J. (2011). Conflict and corruption, in Braddon, D. and Hartley, K. (eds), *Handbook on The Economics of Conflict*, Edward Elgar Publishing, pp172–194.

Laffont, J.J. and Tirole, J. (1993). *A Theory of Incentives in Procurement and Regulation*, The MIT Press, Cambridge, Massachusetts.

NAO (2011). *Ministry of Defence: Major Projects Report 2011*, HCP 1520, TSO, London.

NAO (2014). *Ministry of Defence: Major Projects Report 2013*, HCP 684-1, TSO, London.

OE (2008). *The Economic Contribution of BAE Systems to the UK in 2006*, Oxford Economics, Oxford.

OEF (2004). *The Economic Contribution of BAE Systems to the UK Economy and Implications for Defence Procurement Strategy*, Oxford Economic Forecasting, Oxford, January.

Parker, D. (2009). *The Official History of Privatisation*, vol 1: The Formative Years, Routledge, London.

Reppy, J. (1994). Defense companies strategies in a declining market: Implications for Government policy, *Peace Economics, Peace Science and Public Policy*, 1, 2, 3–10.

Review Board (2010). *Report on the 2010 General Review of the Profit Formula for Non-Competitive Government Contracts*, TSO, London.

SIPRI (1999). *SIPRI Yearbook 1999*, Stockholm International Peace Research Institute, Oxford University Press, Oxford.

SIPRI (2010). *SIPRI Yearbook 2010*, Stockholm International Peace Research Institute, Oxford University Press, Oxford.

SIPRI (2013). *SIPRI Yearbook 2013*, Stockholm International Peace Research Institute, Oxford University Press, Oxford.

Skons, E. and Weidacher, R. (1999). Arms production, *SIPRI Yearbook 1999*, Stockholm International Peace Research Institute, Oxford University Press, Oxford.

Skons, E. and Surrey, E. (2007). Arms production, *SIPRI Yearbook 2007*, Stockholm International Peace Research Institute, Oxford University Press, Oxford.

Tagarev, T. (2010). Enabling factors and effects of corruption in the defense sector, *Connections: The Quarterly Journal*, Summer, IX, 3, 75–86.

Taylor, T. and Hayward, K. (1989). *The UK Defence Industrial Base*, Brasseys, London.

9.   A public choice analysis

INTRODUCTION: SOME QUESTIONS

Economists are often attracted by their competitive market model which is based on large numbers of buyers and sellers. Aerospace markets depart from this competitive model. The military sector is dominated by governments as a major or the only buyer and by a monopoly or oligopoly suppliers, usually with entry restrictions with firms producing differentiated products and markets often in disequilibrium.

Observers of the aerospace industry see evidence of its dependence on government and the presence of a military–industrial complex with large firms forming powerful producer groups. Such groups will lobby governments for defence contracts, for national markets which are protected from foreign competition and for contracts which provide a guaranteed income and favourable profit rates. Producer groups will also lobby government for state-funding for civil aircraft and engine programmes. The result is aerospace industries operating in political markets which are more appropriately analysed using public choice analysis.

Government decisions are likely to be the result of actions by various agents and interest groups in the political market, each acting in their own self-interest and seeking to influence policy in their favour. This chapter outlines the possible role of these agents and interest groups in formulating policy towards the aerospace industry. Does public choice analysis provide a framework for analysing the military–aerospace industrial complex? Debates about the purchase of foreign weapons and policy towards the national aerospace industry (e.g. as part of the national defence industrial base) cannot ignore the behaviour and influence of agents in the political market on the formulation of aerospace policy, on the extent of competition for national aerospace contracts and the efficiency incentives for non-competitive defence contracts.

PUBLIC CHOICE ANALYSIS

Political markets are dominated by governments, political parties, bureau-cracies and other interest groups. Public choice analysis explains the behaviour of these groups in political markets by applying the ideas of self-interest and exchange to the political process. This approach shows that decisions about aerospace policy are made in political markets (Buchanan, 1986; Mueller, 1989; Tisdell and Hartley, 2008).

Political markets resemble other markets in that they contain buyers and sellers pursuing their self-interest by undertaking mutually beneficial exchange within the rules determined by the constitution. The agents within the political market comprise *voters, political parties, bureaucracies* and *interest groups* each of which will have preferences for various policies towards the aerospace industry.

In public choice models, voters act like consumers and are assumed to seek the maximum benefit from the policies offered by rival politicians and political parties. However, voters have only limited information and knowledge about such specialised topics as the opportunities for substitution between air, land and sea systems, the merits of buying British or foreign aerospace equipment, the economic impacts of international collaboration and the benefits of a privately-owned aerospace industry. Where the collection of such information is costly, there are opportunities for producers and other interest groups with specialist knowledge to influence voters and political parties. For example, UK aerospace firms can use their specialist knowledge to show that buying British is in the 'national interest', provides 'invaluable' independence and makes a socially desirable contribution to jobs, high technology and the balance of payments. The opportunities for such groups to influence policy are reinforced by the limitations of the voting system as a means of accurately reflecting society's preferences.

In theory, the individual tastes and preferences of large numbers of voters are recorded through the ballot box at elections. However, votes are usually cast for a general package of policies (e.g. a party's election promises) in which aerospace policy is only one amongst a diverse range comprising economic, social, environmental, international and other policies between which voters cannot register the intensity of their preferences. Nor are voters provided with the necessary information to evaluate the defence aspects of aerospace policy (e.g. due to secrecy and national security concerns). Furthermore, voters cannot bind politicians to a clearly specified set of policies, so that elected representatives have discretion in implementing their election promises. An elected government with, say, a commitment to privatise a state-owned aerospace industry can always delay the implementation of such a policy by claiming the principle of 'unripe time', the need for a thorough in-depth study and review of the issues and for 'full consultation' with the industry and trade unions. All of which suggests that the limitations of the voting system as a means of accurately identifying society's views on the aerospace industry allows opportunities for governments, bureaucracies and other interest groups to interpret the 'national interest' and to influence national aerospace policy. Ultimately, though, governments cannot ignore the need to be re-elected.

Exceptions occur where societies use referenda to make social choices on specific issues. For example, Swiss voters can request a referendum on a specific issue where a sufficient number of voters support a referendum. For example, in May 2014 Switzerland used a referendum to decide on its planned purchase of Swedish Gripen combat aircraft. The referendum resulted in Swiss voters opposing the purchase of Gripen aircraft.

Economic models of politics assume that political parties are vote-maximisers (Downs, 1957). Like firms, parties and politicians offer policies and legislation to win votes. Politicians are assumed to be self-interested, seeking the income, power and prestige which come from holding office, rather than seeking office to carry out preconceived policies. They will offer policies and legislation which appeal to specific groups of voters and offer income transfers between sectors of the population. Politicians have the choice of joining an established party or forming a new party. For example, opponents of nuclear weapons have to decide whether to influence party policy by attempting to change the policies of an established political party (cf. a take-over) or by creating a new party. Both solutions involve costs. Moreover, however attractive a specific policy might be to its supporters, it will never be implemented if the party fails to attract votes. The winning party at an election captures the entire market and forms the government. Its policies are then implemented by government bureaucracies.

Within public choice analysis, there are economic models of bureaucracies. These models start by assuming that bureaucrats are budget-maximisers (Niskanen, 1971). In the military aerospace market, the national Department or Ministry of Defence and the armed forces are analysed as bureaucracies, with the national Treasury and other departments concerned with aerospace budgets and the jobs, technology and balance of payments implications of aerospace policy. A government can be viewed as buying protection from its national Department of Defence which acts as a sole supplier of information and defence. Protection is supplied by the armed forces specialising in air, land and sea domains with each seeking to protect its traditional monopoly property rights. To maximise its budget, the Department of Defence can exaggerate the

threat, under-estimate costs and formulate programmes which are attractive to vote-maximising governments. Nevertheless, bureaucratic behaviour might be constrained by the activities of pressure groups and by the
investigations of various constitutional bodies (e.g. Congressional and
Senate bodies; Parliamentary Select Committees).

Public choice analysis recognises the influence of interest groups. In
formulating and implementing policies, governments and bureaucracies
are subject to the activities of pressure groups. Such groups of producers
and consumers will pursue their own self-interest by trying to influence
policy in their favour through lobbying, advertising campaigns, sponsorship of politicians, consultancy reports, mass demonstrations and civil
disobedience.

Producer groups will seek monopoly profits otherwise known as rents.
Governments can help to create, increase or protect a firm's monopoly
position. In this way, the government increases the monopoly profits or
rents of the favoured group at the expense of consumers of the firm's
products (leading to a re-distribution of income from consumers to the
monopoly which might not be regarded as socially desirable). The
monopoly rents which governments can create provide incentives for
firms to invest funds to acquire such monopoly positions. As a result,
firms will seek monopoly rents through contributions to political parties,
through advertising and lobbying or through illegal payments in the form
of bribes to officials who award monopoly rights. Or, monopoly rents
might be achieved by 'capturing' a regulatory agency and 'persuading' it
to award a higher regulated price which favours the monopoly (Mueller,
1989, p231). Other examples of behaviour by a rent-seeking monopoly
include lobbying for tariff and quota protection and for subsidies. In the
aerospace industry, further opportunities for earning rents arise from the
award of government contracts with the rent-seeking model predicting
that contracting will affect the flow of lobbying and political campaign
expenditures. It is predicted that spending on political campaigns will
come from firms seeking contracts and contracts will be awarded to the
firms making the political donations.

In public choice models, the various interest groups represent the
potential gainers and losers from different aerospace policies. Producer
groups of aerospace firms will support a buy-national policy, they will
demand protection from foreign competition and will seek favourable
rules for regulating profits on aerospace defence work. Trade unions and
professional associations with members in the national aerospace industry will also support domestic aerospace producers so as to protect the
jobs and favourable income prospects of their members. For example,
faced with the cancellation of a major UK defence aerospace project (e.g.

Typhoon; F-35 aircraft), it will be claimed that cancellation would involve writing-off large sums of taxpayers' money, potential losses of thousands of man years of work, lost exports, as well as adverse effects on the future competitiveness of the UK aerospace industry. It is not unknown for contractors to threaten the closure of plants, especially those in high unemployment areas and marginal constituencies.

SOME PREDICTIONS OF PUBLIC CHOICE ANALYSIS

Public choice models offer a variety of predictions which might explain public policy towards a national aerospace industry. To illustrate the approach, five predictions are presented. First, in a two party political system, both parties agree on any issues strongly favoured by a majority of voters (i.e. the median voter). The result is consensus politics, with party policies being vague, similar to those of other parties and less directly linked to an ideology than in a multi-party system.

Second, although political parties attempt to differentiate their policies, movements towards the political extremes of *laissez faire* or *collectivism* are likely to be constrained by the potential losses of moderate voters. In the case of aerospace equipment procurement policy, this suggests that parties are unlikely to favour complete free trade or total protectionism. Political parties also tend to maintain consistent ideological positions over time, unless they suffer drastic defeats, in which case they change their ideology to resemble that of the party which defeated them (Downs, 1957, p300).

Third, the policies of democratic governments tend to favour producers more than consumers. Examples include supporting a national aerospace industry as part of the defence industrial base and regulations which benefit producers rather than consumers (e.g. by guaranteeing the profitability of defence contracts). Producer groups dominate since they can afford the costly investments in specialised information needed to influence government and they have the most to gain from influencing policy in their favour. Also, the voters who are best informed on any policy issue are those whose incomes are directly affected by the policy change (i.e. producer groups), whereas such citizens are not as well-informed on policies that affect them as consumers. Professional associations and trade unions, for example, will oppose policies to import foreign military aerospace equipment pointing to the adverse effects on technology, spin-offs, exports and jobs, especially in communities dependent on defence contracts. They will be less informed on the possible costs to the taxpayer of buying from the national aerospace industry, particularly since they benefit by spreading such costs amongst large numbers of national taxpayers.

Fourth, there are political business cycles. Once elected, the governing party can use its policies to influence voter preferences, so increasing its chances of re-election. Popularity might be increased by an expansionary aggregate demand policy prior to an election (e.g. lower income taxes; higher public spending on roads, hospitals and schools). As part of such a policy, an aircraft plant which is 'vital' to a local community might be saved from closure; and orders for new aerospace equipment might be allocated to firms in marginal constituencies or in high unemployment areas. For example, in 2003, the UK's requirement for a new jet trainer aircraft was awarded to BAE Systems and its Hawk aircraft which was built at its plant near Hull (which was close to the then Deputy Prime Minister's constituency).

Fifth, bureaucracies aiming to maximise their budgets are likely to be too large and inefficient. To protect and raise their budgets, government departments which have a monopoly of specialist knowledge will use information to their advantage. Civil servants are experts: they have an infinite capacity for ingenuity and they can adjust and play any games. Civil servants are specialists with technical information on the possibilities for varying output and for factor substitution. These possibilities, which could result in undesirable outcomes for vote-sensitive governments, might be too costly for any individual minister to police and monitor. In the circumstances, bureaucrats have an incentive to hoard valuable information and to erect a set of myths around their preferred policies. They can support 'optimistic' cost estimates on new aerospace projects and neglect life-cycle costs (claiming that they are impossible to estimate). Once started, military aerospace projects are difficult to stop. They attract interest groups of scientists, contractors, unions and military personnel, each with relative income gains from the continuation of the work. Indeed, it has been claimed that one of the benefits of international collaborative defence projects (e.g. Tornado; Typhoon) is that they are much more difficult to cancel!

SOME APPLICATIONS

Public choice analysis contributes to understanding the political process and policy formulation. Questions arise as to whether there is any evidence supporting the predictions of public choice analysis. Consider the case of cuts in military spending. A public choice approach identifies some of the agents most likely to oppose policies designed to reduce defence spending and to change its composition. It shows the type of arguments used by bureaucracies to protect budgets and how the armed forces and domestic defence contractors are likely to respond to cuts and programme cancellations. Such an evaluation also exposes to critical scrutiny some of the myths of defence and procurement policy. Ideally, though, public choice models need to be compared with alternative explanations of defence spending and policy formulation, aiming to discover which theory best explains the facts.

Within the context of cuts in defence spending, a nation's armed forces are major interest groups which will seek to protect their traditional monopoly property rights and their prestige, and glamorous high technology weapons projects which often give satisfaction to their users rather than to society seeking protection and security. Faced with budget cuts, the armed forces are likely to respond by cutting reserve forces and civilian manpower and economising on training, exercises, support functions and stocks, rather than sacrificing their major new equipment programmes. Admirals like aircraft carriers, generals prefer tanks and air marshals yearn for air superiority fighters. As a result, preferences for inputs are likely to differ between the armed forces. The capital-intensive air force will be willing to sacrifice, say, personnel and its transport aircraft fleet, including helicopters, rather than its latest combat aircraft. The labour-intensive army will aim to protect personnel as its most valuable asset, especially its elite combat forces, and it will sacrifice trucks for tanks and attack helicopters. Similarly, each service will be keen to show that it can undertake more cost-effectively roles currently undertaken by its rivals. For instance, the army will claim that its attack helicopters and surface-to-air missiles can replace the ground-attack and air defence aircraft operated by the air force. Similarly, the air force will claim that its land-based aircraft can replace carrier-borne aircraft and that its maritime patrol aircraft can replace the navy's anti-submarine frigates.

Similarly, as a budget-conscious agency, the national Department of Defence will oppose efforts to cut military spending. It will emphasise the 'dire consequences' of budget cuts, pointing to the continuing threat from nations such as China, Iran and Russia, the continuing threats from international terrorism and failed states (e.g. Syria), and the employment and social consequences of cancelling weapons projects and closing military bases in remote rural areas lacking alternative job opportunities. References will also be made to the loss of national independence, prestige and high technology, resulting in a nation becoming a 'metal basher'. Other government departments concerned with employment, industry, technology and innovation are likely to support the arguments about jobs, technology and the international prestige of military spending. Furthermore, some of these arguments might influence a vote-maximising government concerned about the electoral harm of defence cuts, particularly their impact on marginal constituencies. In turn, to protect itself and the armed forces against substantial budget cuts, the Department of Defence will promise future efficiency savings from better acquisition policies including competitive procurement, military outsourcing and greater rationalisation within and between the armed forces.

Privatisation

Public choice analysis can also be applied to the debate about privatisation and state-ownership of aerospace firms. Popular belief claims that a change of ownership from public to private improves enterprise performance. It is argued that in the private sector, the prospect of profits, firm rivalry and the threat of take-over provides managers with incentives to remove organisational slack and to be efficient. In contrast, public sector managers lack efficiency incentives. Instead, in the public sector, policies are arranged to maximise votes, with managers subject to the detailed government controls affecting their pricing, investment and location decisions. Also, departmental budgets are expanded so that bureaucrats benefit from better jobs, tenure, on-the-job leisure and higher salaries, and public sector trade unions have opportunities to pursue high wage claims, restrictive practices and over-manning (forming 'soft' budget constraints under state-ownership). Public sector organisations will oppose privatisation where it is expected to make managers and workers 'worse-off'. Established interest groups will seek to minimise the costs imposed on them by favouring a change from a public sector monopoly to a private sector monopoly protected from competition. In fact, genuine efficiency improvements require *both* private ownership *and* competition.

The UK provides a case study of privatisation. By the 1970s, most of the UK defence industries were state-owned. The Conservative governments of the 1980s reversed the ownership position with the privatisation of British Aerospace (now BAE Systems: see Chapter 8), Rolls-Royce, Shorts, Royal Ordnance, the Dockyards and the warship builders. Some empirical work has examined the relationship between ownership and performance in the UK aerospace industry. A public choice approach suggests that the performance of an organisation improves with a change from state to private ownership (privatisation). Two aerospace firms were studied, namely, Rolls-Royce and British Aerospace focusing on the 1971 movement of Rolls-Royce from the private to the public sector; and on

the 1977 nationalisation of British Aerospace and its subsequent privatisation in 1981. Enterprise performance was measured by labour and total
factor productivity and the results are shown in Table 9.1. It is recognised
that empirical work in this area is fraught with difficulties. There are
problems of the counter-factual, changes in enterprise objectives, the
impact of other factors and the availability of a variety of performance
indicators (Dunsire et al., 1988; Parker, 2009).

Table 9.1   Ownership and productivity

Firm	Ownership change	Productivity (%)			
		Labour productivity		Total factor productivity	
		Before	After	Before	After
Rolls-Royce	1971 – from private to public ownership	–4.9	13.6	–0.4	4.7
BAe	1977 – from private to public ownership	6.3	2.4	1.8	1.3
	1981 – from public to private ownership	2.4	7.8	1.3	3.3

Notes:
1. BAe is British Aerospace.
2. Productivity figures are for average annual growth. Before and After refer to four years
   before and four years after the ownership change.

Source: Dunsire et al. (1988).

The results for Rolls-Royce were contrary to expectations. The 1971
take-over by the state was associated with a substantial improvement in
both labour and total factor productivity growth. This might be explained
by the 'shock effect' of financial collapse, inducing management to
remove organisational slack and over-manning, rather than to any beneficial effects of public ownership. In the case of British Aerospace,
nationalisation was associated with the predicted fall in productivity
growth and privatisation with an expected improvement (Table 9.1).

The Military–Industrial–Political Complex

By modelling the armed forces, the Defence Department and military
aerospace firms, public choice analysis provides a basis for understanding the behaviour of the military–industrial–political complex. Whilst

producer groups have a major role in public choice analysis, few efforts have been made to operationalise the concept. Critics of military spending claim that defence contractors are a powerful and influential pressure group. On this basis, an analysis of the major aerospace firms and their market environment indicates that powerful producer groups have some of the following features:

1. *Large firms in monopoly or oligopoly markets.* Examples of powerful producer groups in the aerospace industry include Boeing, Lockheed Martin, Northrop Grumman and Raytheon in the USA; Airbus and MBDA in Europe; Finmeccanica in Italy; and BAE Systems, AgustaWestland and Rolls-Royce in the UK.

2. *High dependence on military aerospace business.* Some aerospace firms and industries are dependent on national defence contracts, so that their fortunes are closely linked with government decisions affecting their size, structure, conduct and performance.

3. *Location.* Vote-sensitive governments seeking re-election are likely to be influenced by aerospace firms located in marginal constituencies or in high unemployment areas.

4. *Types of contracts.* Firms awarded non-competitive contracts (e.g. cost-plus or incentive contracts) will have close and continuous links with the national Department of Defence procurement agents. It is possible that procurement policy, the type of contract and the arrangements for regulating defence profits are the result of successful lobbying by producer groups, with both contracts and profit rules favouring producers.

5. *Lobbying activities.* This is another 'black box' which economists have neglected but it is an important mechanism in the operation of political markets. Aerospace firms lobby as a group through their specialist trade associations. Also, business appointments by staff leaving the national Department of Defence and the air force provide military aerospace contractors with valuable contacts and expertise in their search for government contracts. Lobbying is defined widely to embrace all efforts at rent-seeking by contractors. Examples include financial contributions to political parties; hospitality; and the employment of consultants to prepare 'independent' studies of the economic benefits of a national aerospace industry. It is not unknown for illegal or corrupt payments and bribes to be involved in the search for contracts. Some developing nations have a high risk of bribery (e.g. Africa; Asia; Middle East). In 2014, there were allegations of bribery and corrupt payments involving Finmeccanica and a helicopter contract with India as well as similar

allegations involving Rolls-Royce aero-engine sales to Indonesia and China. None of this is meant to suggest that only aerospace firms are involved in alleged bribery: firms in other industries are not immune.

CONCLUSION

Public choice analysis identifies the agents in the political market which will seek to influence national aerospace policy. The approach seems to offer a realistic description of the world. It provides explanations of producer groups and the military–industrial–political complex in the aerospace industry. But descriptive reality and intuitive appeal are not sufficient tests for the acceptance of a theory. It needs to be asked whether the approach offers any clear, testable predictions and does the evidence support these predictions? If there are alternative explanations of aerospace policy, it is necessary to determine whether the public choice approach is superior and out-performs existing models which ignore the political market.

Various interest groups in political markets will be involved in lobbying for government contracts and for state support for the aerospace industry. Subsidies are an obvious form of state support for the industry and the economic case for state subsidies is assessed in the next chapter.

REFERENCES

Buchanan, J. (1986). *Liberty, Market and the State*, Harvester, London.
Downs, A. (1957). *An Economic Theory of Democracy*, Harper and Row, New York.
Dunsire, A., Hartley, K., Parker, D. and Dimitriou, B. (1988). Organisational status and performance: a conceptual framework for testing public choice theories, *Public Administration*, 66, 4, 363–388.
Mueller, D.C. (1989). *Public Choice II*, Cambridge University Press, Cambridge.
Niskanen, W. (1971). *Bureaucracy and Representative Government*, Aldine-Atherton, Chicago.
Parker, D. (2009). *The Official History of Privatisation*, vol I, Routledge, London.
Tisdell, C. and Hartley, K. (2008). *Microeconomic Policy*, Edward Elgar Publishing, Cheltenham, UK and Northampton, MA, USA.

10. A case for subsidy?

INTRODUCTION: THE POLICY ISSUES

There are various ways in which governments can protect a domestic industry from foreign competition. These include tariff protection, subsidy, import quotas and public procurement. Such policies might be designed to protect domestic interest groups in the form of firms, scientists and workers in specific industries or they might be designed to increase society's welfare. Who gains and who loses from subsidies and other trade protection policies?

Military aircraft, helicopter and missile industries often receive preferential treatment in government procurement policy (e.g. a policy of buying American, British, Chinese, French or Russian equipment). Within the world civil aircraft market, there has been considerable controversy over subsidies. Airbus has been accused by Boeing of receiving large subsidies whilst Airbus has responded by alleging that the US aerospace industry benefits from US government subsidies through defence contracts. Similar controversy has arisen in the world regional jet airliner markets with claims that Bombardier and Embraer have each received government subsidies.

Arguments about state subsidies to national aerospace industries are dominated by myths, emotion and special pleading. Such myths and emotion need to be subject to critical appraisal based on economic analysis and empirical evidence. This chapter considers the economic case for subsidising the aerospace industry. The definition of a subsidy is explored; the distinction is made between military and civil aerospace markets; the aims of subsidy policy are assessed; some estimates of the size of subsidies for civil aircraft are presented; and consideration is given to who gains and who loses from subsidies. Subsidies are a further example of the relationship between government and the aerospace industry which provides an opportunity to apply public choice analysis.

DEFINITIONS

Subsidies have been subject to various definitions. They have been defined as financial contributions or the transfer of funds from government to firms or individuals with the aim of changing market prices and affecting the allocation of resources. Subsidies are paid to producers, consumers, workers, exporters, regions and to activities affecting the environment (e.g. wind farms; solar power). Applied to aerospace industries, subsidies defined widely can take a variety of forms embracing development, production and exports. Examples include:

1. Government funding of R&D, including demonstrator programmes.
2. Government subsidies for production, including plant and equipment.
3. Subsidies for employment and training and for the education of scientists and engineers.
4. Indirect support through regional assistance (e.g. tax allowances).
5. Export assistance, both financial and other forms (e.g. support for trade fairs; insurance to protect against currency fluctuations).
6. Preferential purchasing policy. Examples include buying from a national defence industry or a state-owned airline buying from its domestic industry or certification of domestically produced airliners.
7. Government support for other related industries and related R&D activities (e.g. electronics; materials).
8. Government measures to affect ownership and industry structure. Examples include support for state-owned aerospace firms; favourable terms and financial assistance for the privatisation of state-owned aerospace firms; and government assistance for industrial re-structuring (e.g. mergers; adjusting to disarmament).
9. Procurement policy reflected in competition or its absence, the types of contracts and profit rules. For example, cost-plus contracts for non-competitive contracts provide 'soft budget' constraints which might be reinforced by favourable profitability rules for such non-competitive contracts.

Overall, there are a variety of subsidies which are given to firms, industries, regions and to factors of production (labour; capital). Such variety means that it is difficult to make satisfactory international comparisons of state support for aerospace industries. Often, the focus is on the highly visible and easily identified items of state support to the neglect of the less visible and more difficult to identify items. For example, direct financial payments to aerospace firms are readily identified (but might be concealed by governments), but other indirect financial payments can be more difficult to identify and measure (e.g. regional assistance; transport subsidies). Further difficulties arise with non-financial support in such forms as protected markets (via entry barriers), favourable contract terms and regulatory requirements.

Whilst defining and measuring subsidies is difficult, there is a more general question to consider. Does economic analysis offer any guidelines for subsidy policy and are these guidelines applicable to the aerospace industry? In considering the case for aerospace, a distinction needs to be made between military and civil aerospace markets.

GENERAL ECONOMIC ARGUMENTS FOR SUBSIDY

Market Failure Analysis

There are two general economic arguments for subsidies concerned with market failure and strategic trade policy. Economic theory suggests that subsidies are required to 'correct' for specific types of market failures concerned with marginal cost pricing and beneficial externalities. Subsidies are required where firms determine price on the basis of marginal cost in decreasing cost activities. Aerospace is a classic decreasing cost industry but this argument is rarely used to justify subsidies for the industry. Instead, subsidies are more likely to be justified where there are substantial social benefits such that left to themselves private markets will provide 'too little' of a socially desirable output. R&D activities are likely to be under-provided by private markets due to the problems and costs of capturing returns to R&D investments: there are problems in establishing property rights in R&D results and spill-overs provide beneficial externalities. Here, aerospace is an R&D-intensive industry, so making it a potential candidate for subsidy.

But often, other arguments are included in the category of beneficial externalities, and are used as a case for subsidising aerospace industries. These include such claimed externalities in the form of jobs and balance of payments contributions of aerospace industries. In some cases, there is a focus on the Exchequer contribution of the industry in the form of tax receipts from home and export sales as well as savings on unemployment payments when projects might otherwise be cancelled. However, it needs to be asked whether some of these claimed beneficial externalities represent genuine market failures or are used as a pretext for subsidy.

Similarly, Exchequer contributions arise for all industries so these are not convincing arguments for subsidy.

Economic theory also identifies a major market failure which is a further form of externality, namely, defence as a public good: private markets will fail to provide such goods and services since once produced they are available for everyone to consume. Defence as a public good provides a case for subsidising the aerospace industry, especially the military sector (it might also provide a case for supporting the civil aerospace industry where it can be shown that civil aerospace retains industrial capacity for expansion of the defence sector).

It is not a simple matter to operationalise these broad guidelines for subsidy policy. Critics claim that it is all too easy to think up plausible arguments based on market failure and externalities for the subsidisation of almost any industry. Aerospace is not the only R&D-intensive industry and other sectors might be more attractive and offer society better returns from R&D investments (e.g. computers; IT; pharmaceuticals). Similarly, other industries support jobs, contribute to the balance of payments and make Exchequer contributions. Once introduced, subsidies attract interest groups opposed to their abolition and hostile to any attempts to evaluate the results of subsidy policy! In these circumstances, subsidies are likely to depart from the economist's market efficiency model and be based on *ad hoc* intervention reflecting the power and influence of various interest groups in the economy (Mueller, 1989).

A critical evaluation of the economic case for subsidising aerospace industries cannot ignore the opportunity cost question. Would the resources currently allocated to the aerospace industry make a greater contribution to national output if they were used elsewhere in the economy? Consideration also needs to be given to the counter-factual argument of what would happen to the aerospace industry in the absence of subsidy? The simple answer is that without subsidy, the industry would be smaller and society would have to take a view on the economic and other impacts of a smaller aerospace industry (e.g. fewer aerospace jobs). There is a further aspect of the market failure approach which cannot be ignored. The case for state intervention has to be related to significant failures in the relevant market. If it is claimed that there are beneficial externalities in the form of jobs, technology and exports, then there have to be clearly identified failures in the respective markets for labour, R&D and foreign currency (exports). Most of these markets work reasonably well without state intervention (i.e. labour and currency markets) leaving R&D markets as the ones most likely to fail.

Strategic Trade Policy

Standard economic theory explains international trade in terms of comparative advantage and large numbers of small firms operating in competitive markets. In reality, today's international trade is dominated by high technology monopoly and oligopoly industries with large fixed costs for developing their products. Examples include military and civil aircraft, computers, pharmaceuticals, telecommunications and silicon chips. These industries are decreasing cost industries reflecting economies of scale and learning; they are R&D-intensive with costly R&D programmes which result in technical spill-overs (externalities) to the rest of the economy; they operate in imperfect markets with domestic monopolies and oligopolies; and they are dependent on government where governments seek to maximise national economic benefits and rents. Strategic behaviour arises from the interdependence between national governments and oligopolies, between rival oligopolies and between different national governments.

This new strategic trade theory approach to international trade focuses on imperfect markets characterised by decreasing costs, innovation and spill-overs, with governments using trade and industrial policy, including subsidies, to influence national economic welfare (can subsidies make a nation better-off?). In this model, the aerospace industry is economically strategic in that it generates rents or 'excess returns' in the form of higher returns than could be earned elsewhere in the economy. Strategic trade theory shows that subsidies can create rents and shift rents between countries (Krugman, 1986; Lawrence, 2001; Tyson, 1992). The civil aircraft industry has the economic characteristics of a strategic industry where there appears to be room for only a few firms in the world market. Indeed, the strategic trade model seems to explain the story of the European Airbus and the rivalry between Airbus and the US manufacturers of large civil airliners. Interestingly, one economic study found that the entry of Airbus stimulated competition to the benefit of consumers throughout the world (including the US); it was also estimated that the US was a net loser from the Airbus subsidy because the decline in Boeing's profits offset the gains to consumers; and the European nations might have been net losers after paying the subsidy (Baldwin and Krugman, 1988).

Strategic trade policy appears attractive but it has its problems. The assumptions of the model are crucial with the optimal or best policy depending on the type of game played, whether firms or governments make the first move and the likely possibility that modelling and final outcomes will be further complicated by rivalry between governments and nations. A country selecting its best or optimal strategic trade policy needs perfect information about how all the oligopoly firms in the world market and national governments will react and behave in the unknown future. Inevitably, other nations will subsidise strategic industries leading to a subsidy race and a subsidy trap where all countries will be worse-off! Strategic trade policy also requires governments to 'pick the winners' where their track record has been far from impressive. Government mistakes and the selection of 'poor projects' involves the 'write-off' of the project's large development costs (e.g. Anglo-French Concorde). Strategic trade policy might be pursued for political and other objectives (e.g. national prestige) regardless of the costs of the policy.

Where strategic trade policy is pursued because of high entry costs for a decreasing cost industry, it resembles the *infant industry argument*. This maintains that a new domestic entrant with potential scale and learning economies needs to be protected from competition from low-cost established foreign firms so allowing it to achieve the scale enabling it to compete with rival foreign firms. Protection can take the form of tariffs and/or subsidies with an example being the entry of Airbus into the world civil aircraft market. However, the problem with the infant industry argument for protection is to know when the infant has grown-up and protection can be withdrawn. Alternatively, where strategic trade policy is based on externalities, it is using the traditional market failure approach to the case for subsidy policy.

A Public Choice Analysis of Subsidies

The central role of government in subsidy policy suggests that the policy can be explained by public choice models and the behaviour of various agents in the political market place. On this basis, vote-maximising governments and political parties can claim that a subsidy for a firm, industry or region is justified in the 'national interest'. Government departments and their bureaucracies will support subsidies where they help to raise a department's budget. The department will use various economic arguments about wider economic benefits to support the introduction of a subsidy. The behaviour of vote-maximising government and budget-maximising bureaucracies will be further supported by income-maximising producer groups. Firms and industries will lobby government for a subsidy which will protect them from foreign competition or from changing consumer demands or from the impacts of new technology (see Chapter 9).

Governments in developed nations such as the EU and North America often stress the need to subsidise high technology industries such as aerospace. It is claimed that aerospace is an R&D-intensive, high value-added, high skill and high wage industry which is crucial to a nation's future international competitiveness. Arguments about market failure and strategic trade policy are attractive to governments and other interest groups in justifying subsidies. Government departments might adopt a Buggins' turn principle to agreeing a subsidy: last year, Department X was allowed to introduce a subsidy, so this year it is the turn of Department Y!

Subsidies are often designed to protect specific interest groups such as domestic producers, scientists and technologists or workers. Firms and industries throughout the world lobby their governments for subsidies. Typically, producer interest groups are likely to be characteristic of large firms in highly concentrated industries because they are easier to organise into a lobby group. Governments might also choose to subsidise firms and industries because of their political power. An example would be a subsidy offered to firms in marginal political constituencies (e.g. an aerospace plant threatened with closure might receive a subsidy to keep it in business). However, subsidies enable inefficient firms to survive and they might induce firms to become subsidy maximisers, seeking revenue from governments rather than private consumers!

DEFENCE MARKETS: CAN THE PRIVATE SECTOR FUND DEFENCE PROJECTS?

Commentators on defence equipment projects often claim that such projects could, and should, be funded by the private sector. The reality is that on costly, advanced technology equipment, governments usually provide the necessary funding. Examples include the funding of advanced combat aircraft, specialised military transport and special mission aircraft, missiles, main battle tanks, surface warships and nuclear-powered submarines. Why are privately-owned firms unwilling to fund such projects? This section focuses on military aerospace projects.

Private firms and private capital markets often fund major projects such as exploration for oil and gas fields, new pharmaceutical products and new motor cars. But these products have some distinguishing features which differ from military aerospace projects. First, there is a genuine market comprising large numbers of private consumers each with different preferences and a set of market prices for products (e.g. prices for cars and computers). Second, firms have reasonable expectations that the market will be profitable so their investment decisions will be based on expectations of future profitability (but not the certainty of profitability). The firm's expectations of profitability will be reflected in the willingness of their shareholders to invest in the firm either through internal funds or external financing from the capital market. Third, the costs of the private sector project will be affordable for the firm and will not risk its future survival. Fourth, the technology involved will have alternative uses and will not be specific to one buyer.

Military aerospace projects are different. Defence is a public good where there are incentives to 'free ride' with tax-paying citizens reluctant to reveal their true valuation of defence: there are no market prices for air defence or maritime patrol activities. Military markets are also dominated by government as a major or only buyer (monopsony). Governments buy defence equipment for their Armed Forces and they are the only buyer for their nation's Armed Forces. Either as a large or sole buyer, government can use its buying power to determine the size, structure, conduct, ownership and performance of its national military aerospace industry. As a result, in defence markets, the government is the market. Moreover, in democracies, governments have a limited certain period of office. Defeat at the next election means a new government which might cancel the project (e.g. cancellation of the Nimrod MRA4 aircraft in 2010).

Military aerospace equipment is costly, and is reflected in both development costs and unit production costs. For example, unit production costs for an advanced combat aircraft are some £80 million; an electronic platform aircraft (e.g. for airborne early warning) might cost some £400 million per unit; a strategic airlifter some £230 million per unit; and a cruise missile with a unit cost of £5 million. Development costs are a multiple of unit production costs. For an advanced combat aircraft, total development costs are at least 100 times unit production costs and might be 200 times: for such an aircraft, development costs might be £8 billion to £16 billion (2012 prices: Pugh, 2007). These are large magnitudes to be funded by a private firm for one customer. High costs also mean that few units will be purchased (small production runs).

There are further features of military aerospace projects. They might involve technology which is project and defence-specific: for example, the technology required for stealth bombers is only of value on such aircraft and might have few alternative uses. Moreover, the technical requirements of advanced military aerospace equipment creates major uncertainties. Neither the buyer nor the contractor can anticipate correctly all future technological unknowns and their ability to resolve them at reasonable cost (internal uncertainties). There are also external uncertainties associated with changing threats, the emergence of new substitutes and a government's continued willingness to purchase the equipment.

The supply side of military aerospace equipment markets is also distinctive. Within each national military aerospace industry, there are few major firms and often only a single major supplier. As a result, military aerospace markets comprise a single buyer and often a single supplier. In such a market, the outcome is the result of a bargain between buyer and seller with each party using their bargaining skills to achieve their 'best outcome' (e.g. based on game playing using methods such as bluff, threats and 'tit-for-tat').

The distinctive economic features of military aerospace equipment markets are now clear: they explain why the private funding of costly and complex defence equipment projects does not occur. Government is the only buyer for the equipment and many of the technologies and labour skills needed to develop and produce the equipment are highly specific to defence industries (i.e. there are no alternative users). As a result, firms will be concerned that they will never recover their costly and specific investments in the human and physical capital needed for both development and production work: there are no attractive and profitable alternative uses for these assets and they will comprise a large proportion, if not all, of the firm's worth. Private firms will be unwilling to take such enormous risks with their own funds (the 'hold-up' problem). In these circumstances, government is required to bear the costs and risks of such projects (e.g. via guaranteed cancellation payments and cost-plus contracts: see Chapter 11).

This analysis does not mean that there will never be private funding of military aerospace projects. The defence market features which mean that private funding will not occur provide the basis for identifying where such funding might be available. Private funding might be available where military aerospace equipment is not too costly and risky, where it involves few new technical challenges and where there are substantial export market opportunities (i.e. other buyers). An example of private funding of a military aerospace project is the BAE Hawk. This was derived from a previous successful design where the technical problems had been solved (Hunter aircraft) and the original Hawk was sold to the UK RAF with an order for 175 aircraft (1972). BAE Systems subsequently used its own funds to develop an advanced jet trainer and light combat aircraft for export markets. By early 2014, sales and orders for the Hawk jet aircraft exceeded 1,000 units (including total sales to the UK of 203 units).

Governments often support their national military aerospace industry where such support embraces monetary and non-monetary transactions, all of which makes it difficult to estimate the magnitude of such support. Total government spending on the national military aerospace industry is *not* an accurate measure of subsidy and support for the industry. Governments buy military aerospace equipment but the purchase price might be higher than the minimum needed to obtain the equipment: the resulting extra payment can be regarded as a measure of state subsidy. For example, if a combat aircraft is available for purchase off-the-shelf from the USA for \$X billion and a European nation buys an identical or similar aircraft for \$X billion + \$Y billion, then \$Y billion represents a subsidy. But identifying and estimating subsidy is complicated where nations restrict entry for national defence contracts and where they prefer non-competitive markets with all the problems of determining costs, prices and profits in such markets. In the absence of competition, the government's procurement agency has to estimate efficient cost levels and add an acceptable profit margin to determine prices. Some types of contract might not promote efficient solutions (e.g. cost-plus).

Where governments are willing to subsidise their national military aerospace industry through a willingness to pay more for nationally produced equipment, they do so for wider economic, military–strategic and political reasons. Wider economic factors include the industry's contribution to supporting employment, technology, including spin-offs and the balance of payments (exports and import-savings). Military–strategic benefits include national independence, security of supply, aircraft designed to meet national military requirements and bargaining power when buying foreign equipment (for a critique, see Chapter 13).

CIVIL AIRCRAFT MARKETS: CAN THEY ATTRACT PRIVATE FUNDING?

Are civil aircraft markets different in their ability to attract private funding? A distinction can be made between three broad civil aircraft markets comprising large civil jet airliners, regional airliners together with business and private aircraft each with different abilities to attract private funding.

Large civil jet airliners and their engines raise the most challenging tasks for private funding. These aircraft have some distinctive economic characteristics which raise funding problems. The development of a new jet airliner and its engine involves high development costs, long development periods before production and long-term rather than immediate returns from sales. The result is that the development of large jet airliners involves substantial technical and commercial risks with only the prospect of long-term returns.

Other industries outside of aerospace use private capital to fund large-scale projects. Examples include motor cars, petroleum exploration (e.g. North Sea oil) and pharmaceutical products. So, why is civil aerospace different in its funding problems? Compared with other industries, large civil aircraft and engine projects are relatively few in number and each represents a large proportion of the value of the firms involved in such projects (e.g. Airbus; Boeing; General Electric; Pratt and Whitney; Rolls-Royce). Aerospace firms seem to encounter difficulties in attracting private funding in the early development stages of new projects. However, difficulties in accessing private funds or in such funds only being available at a price which is regarded as 'too high' are not necessarily evidence of a capital market failure. For example, if private capital markets are unwilling to provide funds at ruling prices for high-risk projects such as Concorde (supersonic airliner), this might be evidence that the market is working properly and believes that there are more profitable alternative uses for its limited and scarce funds!

Capital markets have provided some solutions to the aerospace financing problem. These include capital raised at the company level (compared with project funding) and finance provided by major suppliers where supply chain firms provide risk capital as risk-sharing partners on the project (e.g. Boeing 787). There are further factors which might explain possible capital market failures to provide funding for the development of large civil aircraft projects. These additional factors include:

1. Uncertainty and the risk aversion of private investors.
2. The small number of civil aircraft and engine programmes and asymmetric information. The small number of programmes and the small number of companies means that investors are unable to gather information and knowledge from a wide spread of sources to make informed decisions about the commercial viability of such programmes.
3. Possible short-termism in relation to the long-term nature of civil aircraft and engine projects: private investors will prefer projects offering immediate returns.
4. The availability of government funding for civil aircraft in other countries, including Europe, North America and Asia (which might be regarded as a government failure). Indeed, extensive government involvement in this market deters private investors.
5. Beneficial externalities in the form of technology spin-offs mean that civil aerospace firms are unable to capture all the returns from their investments.

The specific examples of capital market failures need to be reviewed critically. Questions arise as to whether these additional causes of market failure are genuine market failures and which are specific to aerospace and which are general, affecting all industries? One UK study of capital market financing concluded that 'the market has failed to provide finance to the UK civil aircraft industry but it was not possible to conclude that this reflected a capital market failure as viewed by economists' (AIGT, 2006, p16). But there is evidence of *government failure* demonstrated in an extensive system of state support for civil aircraft development in such countries as Europe, North America, Japan and China.

The arguments about capital markets failing to provide funding for the development of large civil aircraft and engines also apply to regional airliners, especially regional jet airliners. But, there are additional funding problems with regional airliners. Often, regional aircraft are the first stage of entry into the aerospace industry where new entry creates specific financing challenges. The new entrant might have no previous experience of civil aircraft development and production; it probably has little knowledge of the market; and it has to compete with established firms in a decreasing cost industry. Predictably, private investors will view the new entrant as a high-risk venture and will not be willing to provide funds at an acceptable price. In these circumstances, the new entrant has to provide private funds from other parts of its business (e.g. a large diversified firm) and/or from government funds. Governments are often willing to fund a new entrant to the aerospace industry as an infant industry which also offers prospects of competing in a high profile and high technology industry.

The remaining civil aircraft markets comprising business aircraft, light aircraft and civil helicopters are more likely to be privately-funded. Private venture finance has been available in these markets since development costs, development times and pay-back periods are relatively short; projects are small relative to company size with firms usually producing a number of projects; and there are large numbers of buyers, especially in the USA which has the economic advantage of a large domestic market. Even so, national and state governments might provide financial support to retain or attract a production plant for such civil aircraft (Phillips et al., 1994).

SUBSIDIES, TRADE DISPUTES AND LEGAL SOLUTIONS

The Airbus versus Boeing Trade Dispute

State support for civil aircraft has led to major trade disputes, especially between Airbus and Boeing. The starting point was the 1992 bilateral agreement between the European Union (EU) and the USA which limited the level of state support available for producers of large civil aircraft and engines. The agreement set an upper limit of 33 per cent of total development costs which could be supported by government *launch investment*. Such direct financial support was favoured by EU governments and was repaid with interest over 17 years (hence, it was termed repayable launch investment). The 1992 agreement included *indirect support* which is used mainly by the USA and takes such forms as military and NASA research contracts, other military contracts, tax incentives and support from state governments. Under the 1992 agreement, such indirect support was limited to 3 per cent of the large civil aircraft industry's turnover and there was no requirement to repay the support.

Boeing repeatedly complained that launch aid represented 'unfair competition' from Airbus with claims of the company receiving subsidies estimated at $15 billion to $20 billion. In retaliation, Airbus claimed that Boeing received illegal subsidies from military and research contracts and favourable tax treatment amounting to some $19 billion over the period 1989 to 2006. In 2004, the USA terminated the 1992 agreement and in 2005, the dispute was referred to the WTO. The original 2010 WTO report concluded that European governments unfairly financed Airbus and that Boeing had received unfair payments which broke WTO rules and should be withdrawn. Both parties appealed the original decision and after appeal, both parties claimed victory! After the appeal results in 2012, the WTO confirmed that Boeing had received $5.3 billion of illegal subsidies over the period 1989–2006. For Airbus, the appeal results found some limited evidence of subsidy but repayable launch investment was confirmed to be a legal instrument and that government support for Airbus did not constitute 'material injury' to Boeing. The WTO decisions represent legal solutions to subsidies as an economic policy issue with the opportunities for major policy changes on appeal and arbitration. Even if this issue is resolved between Europe and the USA, both parties cannot ignore possible new entrants into the large civil aircraft market where the new entrants will be recipients of major subsidy payments (e.g. Brazil; Canada; China; Japan).

Brazil versus Canada: Regional Jet Airliners

A similar trade dispute arose between Brazil and Canada over subsidy payments to their major aircraft firms, namely, Embraer and Bombardier in the late 1990s and early 2000s. The context was the entry of Embraer into the world regional jet airliner market in the mid-1990s. The incumbent firm, Bombardier, claimed that Embraer's success was due to unfair subsidies, leading to a challenge through the WTO. Embraer responded by claiming that Bombardier had received Canadian government subsidies in the form of interest-free loans for aircraft launch and low-interest loans on exports.

The WTO concluded that Brazil operated an illegal subsidy programme (an export financing programme known as Proex) which benefited its national aerospace firm, Embraer, from at least 1999 to 2000. Following this ruling, Brazil introduced a modified policy which satisfied the WTO (known as Proex III).

The WTO also ruled against Canada for illegally subsidising its national aerospace firm, Bombardier Aerospace. Brazil claimed that Canadian subsidies amounted to $2 million per aircraft. Whilst some of Brazil's claims against Canada were rejected by the WTO, it was found that some Canadian assistance programmes constituted illegal export subsidies. Both Canada and Brazil were allowed by the WTO to impose legal sanctions which would have caused some $3 billion in damages to each economy; but in the event, neither country imposed these sanctions.

CONCLUSION

There is no shortage of economic and other arguments for subsidising the aerospace industry. This can be presented as an 'attractive' industry for subsidy and state support. It provides defence and security benefits and it is R&D-intensive attracting scientists and technologists leading to innovations, new technology and spin-offs. It also provides the next generation of highly skilled and highly paid jobs needed to compete with low-wage countries which have a comparative advantage in labour-intensive goods and services. But today's national comparative advantage does not guarantee tomorrow's such advantage. New technology will create new high technology industries: the future is uncertain and no one can predict it accurately. Today's industrial successes might be tomorrow's failures!

Whatever the direction of new technology, the arguments for state subsidies will remain. The task for economists is to subject these arguments to critical analysis and evaluation. What are the costs of subsidy policy; what would happen without a subsidy; and who gains and who loses from subsidies?

Defence markets are an obvious focus of subsidy policy. National procurement policy provides opportunities for both direct and indirect financial support for national aerospace industries. The next chapter presents an economic analysis of national procurement policy.

REFERENCES

AIGT (2006). *Aerospace IGT: Finance Group, Final Report*, Commercial-in-Confidence, DTI, London.

Baldwin, R.E. and Krugman, P.R. (1988). Industrial policy and international competition in wide bodied jet aircraft, in Baldwin, R.E. (ed.), *Trade Policy Issues and Empirical Analysis*, University of Chicago Press, Chicago.

Krugman, P.R. (ed.) (1986). *Strategic Trade Policy and the New International Economics*, The MIT Press, Cambridge, MA.

Lawrence, P.K. with Braddon, D. (2001). *Aerospace Strategic Trade: How the US subsidizes the large commercial aircraft industry*, Ashgate, Aldershot.

Mueller, D.C. (1989). *Public Choice II*, Cambridge University Press, Cambridge.

Phillips, A., Phillips, A.P. and Phillips, T.R. (1994). *Biz Jets. Technology and Market Structure in the Corporate Jet Aircraft Industry*, Kluwer Academic Publishers, Dordrecht.

Pugh, P.G. (2007). *Source Book of Defence Equipment Costs*, Dandy Books, London.

Tyson, L. (1992). Industrial policy and trade management in the commercial aircraft industry, in Tyson, L. (ed.), *Who's Bashing Whom?* Institute for International Economics, Washington, DC.

11. Buying military aircraft

INTRODUCTION: THE POLICY ISSUES

National Departments of Defence are major buyers of military aircraft and other aerospace equipment and sometimes the only buyer. They buy a variety of equipment ranging from such simple items as paper clips, batteries, food and vehicles to complex aerospace products such as combat aircraft, helicopters, military airlifters, missiles and space systems. There is also spending on R&D for new aerospace equipment projects together with expenditure on equipment support. For combat aircraft and maritime patrol aircraft, equipment acquisition can account for some 60 per cent of life-cycle costs with support costs accounting for some 40 per cent of the total (e.g. Typhoon; Nimrod MRA4: NAO, 2011a; 2011b). National aerospace industries are usually major recipients of their national Department of Defence spending, involving contracts with small numbers of major prime contractors and large numbers of firms in supply chains.

When purchasing aerospace equipment, Defence Departments can choose to buy from their national aerospace industry, or they might import equipment, or they might be involved in international collaborative programmes. Inevitably, large-scale spending, especially on a single project (e.g. F-35 aircraft) by a single government department creates controversy. There are pressures to buy from the domestic aerospace industry rather than purchase foreign equipment and to support jobs by buying from firms in areas of high unemployment. Critics focus on project management by the Defence Department and on the performance of aerospace contractors. They criticise inadequate monitoring of projects, leading to cost escalation, delays, unsatisfactory equipment performance and cancellations. Similarly, defence contractors are often accused of waste, high costs and excessive profits achieved in a business which is believed to be not very competitive and where there is a 'cosy' relationship between defence contractors and national Defence Departments.

This chapter provides an overview of the general issues raised by aerospace equipment procurement policy dealing with the distinctive economic features of defence procurement, the choice set, the role of uncertainty and the incentive and profitability implications of different types of defence contracts.

MILITARY AEROSPACE PROCUREMENT

Government is central to understanding military aerospace markets. Often, government is a monopsony buyer or a major buyer and it can use its buying power to determine technical progress, ownership, the size of the national defence industry, its structure, conduct and performance (e.g. profits; exports: see Chapters 6 and 7). Typically, for costly, high technology aerospace projects, there is only one domestic supplier (e.g. BAE Systems in the UK; Finmeccanica in Italy) so that contract negotiations involve a single buyer and a single seller resulting in a bilateral monopoly bargaining situation. There are opportunities for each party to 'play games' using bargaining strategies of threats, bluff, chicken and brinksmanship. For example, contractors will seek to negotiate favourable cost and price targets and they will aim to shift the risks of cost overruns to the government. Similarly, governments will aim to shift risks to the contractor through their preference for fixed price contracts and government can always threaten to either cancel the project or buy from abroad.

There are information asymmetries between the contractor and the buyer. Contractors are experts on their costs which gives them a major advantage over the buyer in the bargaining process and they also know the minimum price at which they will accept the contract (adverse selection). Demands by the government for access to a contractor's cost data will be resisted and even where granted, accounting information is historical and does not indicate the extent of any contractor inefficiency. But the government is not powerless. It can use competition from foreign firms to check on a contractor's price bid; or it can use its competition agency or external consultants to provide an independent assessment of a contractor's efficiency and prices. Even where contracts are based on 'keen' competitive prices, there is likely to be some 'incompleteness' in the contract so allowing contractors to make cost-quality trade-offs. Firms have discretion in the amount and intensity of the effort which they allocate to a contract and the government's procurement agency cannot observe all aspects of such effort (moral hazard: Laffont and Tirole, 1993).

Contracting is not costless and there are transaction costs involved in specifying, negotiating, agreeing and monitoring contracts. Firms have to invest considerable resources in preparing a tender, especially for complex high technology equipment (e.g. a new combat aircraft or missile). Where contracts involve rivals, each potential bidder has to assess the probability of success against the costs of preparing the tender. Transactions are characterised by limited information (bounded rationality), opportunism (incentives to hoard valuable information) and inevitably, many contracts are incompletely specified. For example, a contract for a complex new combat aircraft or missile has to identify all contingencies for a project which does not exist and will take years to complete: typically, such contracts are incomplete (Arrowsmith and Hartley, 2002).

A TAXONOMY: THE CHOICE SET

The award of contracts for new aerospace equipment involves the national Defence Department and ultimately the government in a set of choices about what to buy, when to buy, who to buy from and how. Decisions are needed on the following issues:

1. *What to buy?* Equipment purchases require the selection of a project reflected in decisions about the performance requirements of new aerospace equipment. Decisions are needed about a project which might not exist and which will involve considerable uncertainties. For example, for a new combat aircraft, decisions are needed about its speed, range, weapons capability and landing and take-off requirements, all of which will be related to the need to meet the future threat over a time-horizon of some 50 years. Also, the operational requirement for new equipment will determine technical progress in the aerospace industry.
2. *When to buy?* All projects have a life-cycle starting with research and development, through to production, followed by operational use in the armed forces which might require mid-life updates and finally, disposal. Choices have to be made as to whether to allow competition at each stage and when competition should end and selection both of a project and a contractor should occur. For example, in the early 1950s, the UK purchased a number of advanced combat aircraft off-the-drawing-board after only a design competition, with the successful bidder receiving a contract for both development and production work. Alternatively, competition can continue through various stages in a project's life-cycle up to, say, the award of a production contract. As a result, design contractors could not assume that they would be guaranteed the first production

order: they might be subject to competition for both the initial production work and for any subsequent production orders (including orders for spares during in-service operations and mid-life updates). In this way, Defence Departments introduced and extended contestability into markets which were previously non-competitive. However, if development and production work are undertaken by different contractors, there are transaction costs in establishing and protecting property rights in new ideas and in transferring technology.

3. *Who to buy from?* A contractor has to be selected, using either competition based on price or non-price criteria (e.g. technical quality), or direct negotiation with a preferred supplier. In addition, in any competition, the Defence Department has to determine the extent of the market. Should the competition be restricted to domestic firms or should foreign firms be invited to bid? A further dimension of contractor selection involves a choice between the extremes of buying from national suppliers or purchasing directly from abroad, or selecting an intermediate solution in the form of a joint project with another nation or producing foreign equipment under licence in the country (see Table 11.1).

4. *How to buy?* A contract type has to be selected ranging between the extremes of firm or fixed price and cost-plus contracts or an intermediate type of incentive contract. Often, cost-plus contracts are used for advanced technology work characterised by considerable uncertainty. In contrast, firm or fixed price contracts are used for production work where there are fewer uncertainties. With firm price contracts, the contractor receives the contract price, no more and no less. For equipment programmes extending over several years, where there are uncertainties about inflation and exchange rate movements, fixed-price contracts are used where the price paid to the contractor reflects variations in an agreed price index. Some Defence Departments might also use fixed price contracts for development work, so placing contractors at risk and giving them an incentive to control costs. Alternatively, where the development work cannot be defined clearly, a target price incentive contract might be used where the Defence Department and the contractor share any cost savings or cost overruns up to a maximum price beyond which the contractor assumes total liability.

UNCERTAINTY AND COSTS

Uncertainty complicates aerospace equipment procurement decisions. Questions arise as to what are the most appropriate market, institutional, organisational and contractual arrangements for coping with uncertainty? The options range from open competition to selective competition to direct negotiation with a preferred contractor.

At one extreme of the procurement choice, uncertainty is absent and the competitive model is relevant. As a buyer, the Defence Department knows what it wants; the products exist and are being bought and sold in a competitive market (e.g. computers; motor vehicles; existing combat aircraft). Here, the Defence Department acts as a competitive buyer, specifies its requirements and invites competitive tenders. The lowest bid is selected and a firm or fixed price contract is awarded. These arrangements for open competition *reduce* the opportunities for favouritism and corrupt payments in contract awards.

Selective competition is an alternative to open competition where rivalry is limited to a group of invited firms selected from an approved list of known reliability (e.g. members of a trade association). It is claimed that selective competition reduces the transaction costs for buyers and reduces tendering costs for industry. Public choice analysis suggests an alternative explanation, namely, that selective competition benefits producers on an approved list (with incentives to gain access to the list) and also benefits bureaucrats seeking a 'quiet life' avoiding the transaction costs of organising a genuine open competition (Tisdell and Hartley, 2008, chapter 15).

Non-competitive and negotiated contracts are also used. Air forces are not always certain about the type of product they wish to buy, particularly with high technology equipment such as combat aircraft, attack helicopters, special missions aircraft and missiles. It might also be the case that the national aerospace industry is dominated by domestic monopolies and there are no other buyers. In this case, uncertainty occurs in a bilateral monopoly bargaining situation where both buyer and seller have opportunities for exercising bargaining power. In such a non-competitive market, the Defence Department will enter into direct negotiations with a preferred contractor. The Defence Department will have to choose a contractor and select a contract for a project which does not exist and which is likely to involve a substantial advance in technology. For example, a modern combat aircraft might take 15 years to develop and will remain in service for a further 30 years, so that the Defence Department has to anticipate a variety of technical developments as well as economic and political changes among both allies and potential enemies over a 45-year time period. Such advanced technology equipment is often associated with cost escalation and overruns, time slippages and major modifications, leading to allegations of contractor inefficiency, especially where the work is undertaken on a cost-based contract with no incentive provisions. Sometimes projects are cancelled, giving rise to further allegations of 'waste and incompetence' by both the Defence Department and the contractor.

Critics of a Defence Department's project management can always be wise with the benefit of hindsight! But there are challenges in formulating policy rules for improving *ex ante* decision-making under uncertainty. Often, there are alternative methods of coping with uncertainty and economists are interested in identifying the costs and benefits of the various options. Basically, the problem is one of acquiring information and knowledge where such acquisition is not costless. Information and knowledge can be purchased at different points in a project's life-cycle, ranging from the initial design and development stage to the construction of a prototype and, ultimately, a production decision.

Advanced technology aerospace equipment projects are the classic example of defence choice under uncertainty. They can be bought 'off the drawing board', with only paper or design competition and the successful bidder receiving a contract for development and production work. It is claimed that this policy reduces the costs of competition but, there are higher risks of technical failure as well as the removal of competitive pressure on the successful contractor. Alternatively, competition could be continued beyond the design stage through, say, the Defence Department's purchase of relatively cheap competing prototypes. In this way, the Department might postpone its final choice until it has more information on the actual performance of competing designs. An example was the US 'fly before you buy' policy which has been used to choose between competing prototype combat aircraft and aero-engines. For example, in the competition for the US Joint Strike Fighter (JSF), Boeing and Lockheed Martin were selected as competing contractors, with Lockheed Martin awarded the contract for its F-35 Lightning aircraft. However, competitive prototyping is frequently rejected because it is believed to lead to delays and to involve higher development costs through competitive 'duplication'. But the critics often compare an *actual* competitive procurement policy with an *ideal* (but never achieved) project, ordered off-the-drawing-board, which never encounters any technical problems, cost escalation or delays! The general point remains. In buying advanced technology equipment, the Defence Department has to choose the point in the life-cycle at which competition should cease and selection occur. Economists can make a contribution by showing that alternative policies involve different costs and benefits and, where possible, offering evidence on orders of magnitude (e.g. on the costs of competing prototypes and the magnitude of any delays: Hartley, 1983). Of course, the Defence Department's procurement choices can always be justified as offering good value for money!

There is one apparently low-cost and low-risk solution to acquiring information and knowledge about advanced aerospace equipment. This involves a national Defence Department agreeing to buy an established product 'off-the-shelf' from a foreign supplier where the equipment is already in operational service. Importing military aerospace equipment means that a foreign nation bears all the R&D costs, all the risks and uncertainties and the importing nation acquires equipment which has been proven in operational service. Whilst importing appears to be a cheap solution, there are costs, some of which might not be apparent. For example, the exporting nation might require a contribution to its R&D costs; it might not be prepared to export its latest advanced aerospace equipment (e.g. US F-22 aircraft) or it might not be willing to sell the latest version (e.g. Apache without Longbow). The price for the imported equipment is also vulnerable to exchange rate fluctuations; imported equipment might not meet the operational requirements of the importing nation's air force; and key software might have to be returned to the exporting nation for repair. Furthermore, the exporting nation might refuse to supply during emergencies and conflict; and even if the equipment is cheap, you will pay for the spares!

The buying power of the Defence Department raises questions about the aims of its procurement policy. The possibility arises that procurement contracts can be used to pursue other policy objectives which need to be recognised in assessing the purchased 'product'. This has occurred where aerospace equipment contracts have been awarded to achieve wider economic and defence policy objectives concerned with jobs, technology, exports and maintaining the defence industrial base. Once these wider policy aims become part of the procurement choice and the purchased 'product', they make it difficult to evaluate efficiency in procurement. Choices and decisions are always subjective and will reflect the values of policy-makers (e.g. policy-makers can always claim and assert that their choices represent efficiency and value for money!).

COMPETITION: NATIONALISM, IMPORTING AND OTHER OPTIONS

The Case for a National Aerospace Industry

All policies involve benefits and costs which need to be identified and valued in monetary terms. For a nation with an established aerospace industry, the choice set can be illustrated by considering two extreme policy options. At one extreme is the nationalist or complete independence solution where a nation buys all its military aerospace equipment domestically. Independence offers military and economic benefits. These include equipment designed to meet its specific military requirements as well as jobs, technology and balance of payments benefits. Costs involve acquisition and life-cycle costs on a unit and total fleet basis. But independence is costly, involving the sacrifice of potential gains from international trade based on specialisation by comparative advantage (cf. a nation growing its own bananas: see Table 11.1).

The Case for Importing

At the other extreme, the nation could 'shop around', acting as a competitive buyer purchasing its military aerospace equipment from the lowest-cost suppliers within the world market (buying-off-the-shelf at lower prices than comparable equipment bought from a domestic industry). For most nations, this would mean buying more abroad, especially from the US, with the attendant worries of 'undue' dependence on one nation, fears of an American monopoly and concerns about supply during a conflict. Opposition to such a policy would arise from domestic interest groups of defence contractors and trade unions, supported by bureaucrats with a preference for domestic suppliers. Vote-sensitive governments might also believe that there are more votes in allocating contracts to national rather than foreign firms. As a result, an importing nation might prefer to link its overseas purchase with an *offset* providing some work to its national aerospace industry.

Offsets

Offsets are designed to achieve a relocation of economic activity from the country of the equipment supplier to the purchasing nation. In most cases, offsets are economically unattractive since they involve trade diversion (inefficiency) rather than trade creation (which is efficient).

They involve the transfer of work from lower-cost suppliers in the exporting nation to higher-cost firms in the importing nation. As a result, the exporting nation loses aerospace industrial capability and wider economic benefits and these losses become gains to the importing nation (i.e. a transfer of economic activity). Nor do all offsets represent genuinely new business to the importing nation (i.e. work which would not have occurred without the offset). Evidence suggests that genuinely new business might be 25 per cent to 50 per cent of the total offset (Sandler and Hartley, 1995).

Licensed Production

Between these policy extremes, there are some intermediate policies. A nation could undertake the licensed manufacture or co-production of foreign equipment. This is likely to be costlier than purchasing 'off-the-shelf' from the established supplier since the existing supplier will benefit from scale and learning economies. In contrast, a new entrant will be commencing production at the top of the learning curve. For example, the European governments could have purchased the F-16 aircraft directly from General Dynamics. Instead, their preference for European co-production resulted in a cost penalty of 34 per cent (Rich et al., 1984). But there are believed to be benefits from licensed and co-production through domestic jobs, the saving of foreign exchange and research and development resources, tax contributions and savings in unemployment benefits, together with access to new technology. Such claimed benefits need to be assessed critically. What are the alternative uses of resources allocated to licensed production; how much extra is paid for licensed produced aircraft; what are the resulting benefits; how highly are they valued; and do the benefits exceed the costs making it a worthwhile investment?

International Collaboration

Alternatively, a nation could participate in a collaborative aerospace project with other countries. Examples have occurred with European aircraft, helicopters, missiles and space systems. Collaborative or joint projects involve two or more nations sharing the R&D costs of a project and combining their production orders so leading to cost savings in both development and production. Collaboration enables a nation to retain a domestic industry while being involved in high-technology work which would be 'too costly' to undertake alone. An example is the European four nation Typhoon combat aircraft (Germany, Italy, Spain and the UK:

see Chapters 12 and 13). But collaborative aerospace programmes have been characterised by inefficiencies reflecting bureaucratic procurement arrangements and duplicate industrial organisations. There have also been inefficient work-sharing arrangements requiring each partner to have a share in each sector of advanced technology on the project (e.g. airframe; engine; avionics) together with duplicate flight-testing centres and final assembly lines.

A Rand study published some evidence which can be applied to international collaboration. The study assessed whether joint aircraft programmes where two or more services from the same nation participate in the acquisition and operation of a single aircraft design results in savings in life-cycle costs. Such joint aircraft programmes are believed to lead to cost savings through eliminating duplicate development programmes and achieving scale and learning economies in both production and in operations and support: these arguments about cost savings are often used to justify international collaborative projects. Rand asked the question: do joint fighter aircraft programmes cost less overall over their life-cycle than an equivalent set of specialised, single service aircraft? The US Joint Strike Fighter (JSF) aircraft is the classic example of a joint acquisition programme between different US armed forces (Air Force; Navy; and Marines). Rand concluded that historical joint aircraft programmes had not saved overall life-cycle costs compared with single service aircraft programmes and this conclusion also applied to the JSF (Lorell et al., 2013). The failure to deliver life-cycle cost savings resulted from higher rates of acquisition cost growth compared with single-service aircraft programmes with the problems of reconciling diverse service requirements into a common design being a major factor in cost growth. Rand concluded that 'unless the participating services have identical, stable requirements, the DoD avoid future joint fighter and other complex joint aircraft programs' (Lorell et al., 2013, pxix). These conclusions apply to joint programmes within one nation which illustrates the problems of international collaboration.

Table 11.1 provides a general conceptual framework for assessing the costs and benefits of alternative military aerospace procurement options. In reality, each policy option will be reflected in a choice between different types of aerospace equipment (e.g. Rafale versus Typhoon versus imports of F-18 or its licensed production).

Table 11.1   Policy options: a choice framework

Policy Option	Costs	Benefits
National Project (Independence)	———————	———————
Collaboration	———————	———————
Licensed Production	———————	———————
Import Foreign Equipment	———————	———————

Note: Costs and Benefits need to be identified and valued. Costs include acquisition and life-cycle costs on a unit and fleet basis. Benefits comprise military–strategic benefits and wider economic benefits such as jobs, technology and exports.

THE ROLE OF COMPETITION

Contractor selection involves wider choice issues about entry and the extent of the market. In addition to encouraging new entrants from domestic suppliers, competition can be extended by opening the national military aerospace market to foreign firms. For example, while there might be domestic monopolies in aerospace equipment (aircraft, helicopters, missiles and aero-engines), there are also rival suppliers elsewhere in the world market, particularly in Europe and the USA. In other words, a domestic monopoly can be subjected to competition by allowing foreign firms to bid for national defence contracts. Alternatively, foreign firms form the threat of entry so making the national aerospace market contestable.

Some of the limitations of a competitive procurement policy have become apparent. Competitions take time and are costly to organise for both the Defence Department and industry. It is claimed that competitions have unintended behaviour and consequences for both the Defence Department and industry. These consequences include unrealistic timescales, an over-optimistic assessment of both risk and costs and the potential loss of flexibility for timely insertions of technology in the future. It is also felt that increasing technological complexity, globalisation and industry consolidation mean that price-based competition might not result in the best opportunity for successful acquisition or for maintaining key sovereign capabilities. Industry became increasingly concerned about cost overruns and reduced profitability (losses) on competitive fixed price contracts. There was also the recognition that defence does not correspond to the economists' model of a perfectly competitive market. As a result, some national Defence Departments modified their procurement policy away from competition to partnering approaches: the aim was to deliver value for money in situations where competitions are not held. For example, some Defence Departments identified key defence industrial capabilities which they aimed to retain through guaranteed work and partnering agreements with key firms. These agreements involved target cost incentive fee contracts with gainsharing and risk adjusted profit rates providing adequate rewards to induce firms to remain in the defence market.

The argument often arises that competition is costly and a 'waste of scarce resources' and that efficiency requires the selection of a single aircraft to replace a variety of different types. However, there is a different dimension which needs to be considered. Joint aircraft programmes lead to a reduced combat aircraft industrial base and increase the operational risks to warfighters. For example, the US fighter aircraft industrial base has reduced from eight prime contractors in 1985 to three in 2014, with only Lockheed Martin involved in a major fighter aircraft programme. Industrial re-structuring has reduced the potential for future competition with potential impacts on innovation and the incentives to control costs. Also, the availability of a variety of fighter aircraft provides a hedge against design faults and increases the options available to meet unexpected enemy capabilities (Lorrell et al., 2013). Again these options are not costless and sensible policy choices on such issues require a comprehensive evaluation of the costs and benefits of the policy and its alternatives. All policies involve costs and there are no costless options.

CONTRACT TYPES

Firm and Fixed Prices

Once a contractor, either national or foreign, has been chosen, an appropriate contract has to be selected. There are two limiting cases, namely firm or fixed prices and cost-plus contracts, with various intermediate types offering different incentives related to, say, cost, or equipment performance or delivery dates. Firm or fixed price contracts can be determined by open or selective competition, or by direct negotiation with a preferred contractor. Nations will have different contractual arrangements and this section provides an outline of the general economic principles of contracting.

Firm prices are generally used for contracts of relatively short duration (e.g. up to two years). Where the work is long term, fixed price contracts contain escalation clauses allowing for variations in the prices of labour and materials (i.e. variation of prices). However, there are no obvious market failures preventing firms from bearing risks and estimating future inflation rates over the period of the contract, whatever the length. Someone in the economy either in the private or the public sector has to bear risks and the process is not costless.

Typically, fixed price contracts are used where the work required can be clearly specified and the uncertainties are removed, as in production work. The aim is to place the contractor at risk and provide the maximum efficiency incentives, both of which require the price to be agreed before the work begins. If the contractor beats a competitively determined fixed price, it retains the whole of any extra profits or, in the opposite case, bears all the losses. Fixed price contracts form 'hard' budget constraints.[1]

Problems arise with *non-competitive* fixed price contracts. Since competition is absent, the market cannot be used to determine prices, to provide competitive pressures for efficiency, and to 'regulate' profits through entry and exit. Instead, in non-competitive situations, prices and profits have to be estimated and negotiated. A Department of Defence procurement agency will aim to minimise the taxpayers' liability by negotiating 'fair and reasonable' prices. Non-competitive fixed price contracts are prices based on *estimated* costs plus a government-determined profit margin. Such contracts assume that firms are profit-maximisers and that governments can estimate X-efficient costs. In principle, fixed price contracts specify the price to be paid for an agreed quantity and quality of product, together with delivery dates. A typical non-competitive fixed price contract will be based on estimated costs plus profits determined by the Department of Defence profit formula:

$$P_f = E_o + \pi_g \tag{11.1}$$

---

[1] Terminology differs between nations. For example, US defence contracts include cost reimbursable contracts; fixed price incentive fees; fixed price where prices are fixed regardless of actual costs; and time and material contracts where payments are made for labour at agreed rates and for certain expenses. The US Department of Defense (DoD) allows bid protests on contract awards. Also, the US DoD provides government-owned facilities. For example, in 2013, Lockheed Martin Aeronautics owned 5.8 million square feet of space but also used 14.2 million square feet of government-owned space (LM, 2013).

Where:

E_o = total *estimated* expenditures for the required output. This total comprises direct labour, materials and bought-out parts (variable costs) and overheads (fixed costs). Direct labour costs might be estimated using a labour learning curve for calculating man hours worked and an agreed wage rate applied to estimated man hours. Fixed outlays might be recovered by applying an overhead recovery rate to estimated direct labour costs;

π_g = the government-determined profit margin, which might be calculated as a rate of return on costs of production.

With fixed price contracts, profits will exceed the government-determined margins whenever a firm's actual costs are *below* the original estimates. For example, if costs are estimated to be £1 billion and the Ministry allows a profit margin of 10 per cent on costs, the firm will receive a lump sum payment of £1.1 billion on completion of the work. The firm's profits or losses will depend on how well it controls its costs in relation to the lump sum payment.

Firms can reduce actual costs below the estimated level through two sources. First, they can increase efficiency. Second, there might be errors in the Department of Defence cost estimates, so that the negotiated price is not based on X-efficient behaviour. As a result, the actual profits earned on fixed price contracts will be 'excessive' in the sense of exceeding the rate allowed by the Department of Defence profit formula. The determinants of a firm's actual profits on fixed price work can be shown as follows:

$$\pi = \pi_g + s\,(E_o - A_o) \tag{11.2}$$

Where:

π = actual profits received by the contractor;

π_g = profit sum negotiated and agreed by the Department of Defence and the firm;

s = the rate at which any difference between E_o and A_o will be shared between the firm and the government;

E_o = estimated outlays;

A_0 = actual expenditures.

With fixed price contracts, $s = 1$, so that the firm retains the whole of any difference between estimated and actual outlays: hence, $\pi > \pi_g$ when $E_0 > A_o$. This provides a basis for determining excessive profits, especially if $E_o > A_0$, not as a result of increased efficiency but due to inaccuracies in the Department of Defence cost estimates. Such inaccuracies can result from the estimating techniques used by the procurement agency, differences in the information available to both parties, and their behaviour in the bargaining process. With non-competitive fixed price contracts, a firm wishing to increase its profits above the government-determined level has every incentive to maximise its estimated, and minimise its actual, outlays. Some nations allow for post-costing and re-negotiation of non-competitive prices.

Profit regulation can affect the behaviour of defence contractors. Firms in imperfect and regulated markets have opportunities to pursue non-profit objectives, so that procurement and regulatory policy formulated on the assumption of profit-maximising behaviour under competition might not produce the expected outcomes. For example, a defence contractor subject to profit regulation has an incentive to substitute staff or other discretionary expenditures for profits (e.g. luxury offices; company cars; leading a 'quiet life': see Tisdell and Hartley, 2008, p180).

Cost-plus Contracts

Advanced technology projects confront government procurement agencies with the classic problem of choice under uncertainty. They have to determine the optimal distribution of risks between the buyer and the contractor. In these circumstances, the traditional solution was some form of cost-reimbursement contract with the state bearing most, if not all, of the risks. Under a cost-plus percentage profit contract, the firm recovers all its actual outlays regardless of their level, plus a government-determined percentage profit. Such contracts are believed to offer little or no efficiency incentives: they have been called 'blank cheque' contracts and form 'soft' budget constraints. Since the profit sum is directly related to costs, the contractor is almost encouraged to incur higher costs and to search for perfection!

Cost-plus contracts in non-competitive markets provide contractors with the financial framework for escalation in costs, time and quality. It is not unknown for defence equipment projects, especially those involving advanced technology, to cost substantially more than their original estimates, to be considerably delayed and to be 'gold plated'. Cost escalation factors of 2.0 or more have been recorded on defence development projects, with actual costs being twice the initial estimate, expressed in constant prices (see Chapter 7).

The possibility arises that contractor behaviour is a possible cause of escalation (optimism bias). Cost escalation might be due to the deliberate under-estimation of costs. Such behaviour might reflect the efforts of an income-maximising contractor to 'buy into' an attractive new programme by offering optimistic cost, time and quality estimates, thereby establishing a temporary monopoly. In competitive markets with firm or fixed price contracts, this optimism, especially in costs, would result in losses and possibly bankruptcy. But in non-competitive markets with cost-based contracts, a firm's optimism would be financed by the Defence Department, so that the penalties for under-estimation might be absent. Similar behaviour can also arise with fixed price contracts. Once a fixed price contract has been awarded, the contractor might persuade the armed forces and the Defence Department that design changes are 'essential' which will require a new price! Or, increased costs with a fixed price contract might mean that the contractor faces bankruptcy and has to be rescued by the national defence ministry (paying the loss-making firm sufficient to induce it to remain in the industry). The situation could be reinforced by any budget-maximising aim of bureaucracies sponsoring the project, supported by interest groups of scientists and engineers with a preference for new technology and new designs: they would have an incentive to under-estimate costs. Once a contractor has been selected, then cost-based contracts are unlikely to deter modifications, ambitious technical proposals or X-inefficiency (Hartley, 2011, p111).

There is substantial evidence of both contractors and Defence Departments seriously under-estimating the technical risks, difficulties and costs of achieving an operational requirement. These outcomes reflect the set of incentives in the procurement system which is characterised by 'optimism bias'. Participants in the procurement system have a vested interest in optimistically mis-estimating outcomes. The Armed Forces competing for scarce funding seek to obtain the largest share of resources for their own needs and so have incentives to under-estimate equipment costs (Gray, 2009). Under a regime of cost-plus contracts, firms have incentives to offer 'optimistic' cost estimates so that projects appeared 'cheap' and Defence Departments rarely cancel an equipment order. During the Cold War, the continual search for technical superiority in defence equipment meant that both the armed forces and contractors were encouraged to aim for the most advanced weapons and cost-plus contracts meant that this process occurred regardless of costs! Moreover, the armed forces have little incentive to economise since they were not subject to clearly specified budget constraints and output targets. The more-performance requirements approach the frontiers of knowledge, the greater the additional costs of an increment of performance and the more uncertain are the cost estimates (McNaugher, 1989). An extra few miles of range for a combat aircraft might double its cost, with drastic implications for the numbers purchased.

Cost-plus contracts in non-competitive markets are further criticised because they are believed to provide the financial basis enabling defence contractors to hoard labour, especially valuable scientists and technologists. This belief arises from the frequent observation that the cancellation of defence projects leads to threats of 'massive' job losses and plant closures; but in the event, employment reductions are usually much less than the numbers involved on the project (e.g. cancellation of TSR-2). This suggests the hypothesis that cost-plus defence contracts are associated with labour hoarding and 'excess' employment which is reflected in a sluggish employment response to cancellations and a relatively labour-intensive reaction to an increase in sales.

There could be alternative explanations of labour hoarding and sluggish employment behaviour by defence contractors. For example, the announced redundancy figures associated with the cancellations of a major aerospace project might be deliberate exaggerations, reflecting an attempt by producer interests, supported by budget-conscious bureaucracies, to influence the decisions of vote-maximising governments (Hartley and Corcoran, 1975; see Chapter 9).

Continued concern about cost escalation on aerospace equipment projects resulted in some Defence Departments shifting away from non-competitive cost-plus contracting for development work. The alternatives included either fixed prices agreed at an early stage or a maximum price with some form of target cost incentive. Where the unknowns and uncertainties in a development project make it difficult to agree a fixed price, Defence Departments often preferred a target cost incentive contract with a maximum price, so limiting the taxpayers' liability. A target cost contract is based on estimates and consists of an agreed target cost, a profit rate based on the target, and a sharing ratio whereby cost savings or losses are shared in a specified proportion between the Defence Department and the contractor. For example, the target cost could be £10 billion, the target fee £100 million, and the sharing ratio 80:20. If the actual cost equals the target, the firm receives the target fee of £100 million. If actual costs exceed the target, the firm bears 20 per cent of the extra cost, with adverse effects on its fee; and vice versa where actual costs are below the target. Similarly, with such a sharing ratio, the Defence Department bears 80 per cent of any cost overruns and receives the same percentage share of any cost savings. The Defence Department's preference for a maximum price introduces an additional constraint and incentive into a target cost contract. Of course, with a target cost contract and a bilateral monopoly bargaining situation, a contractor has an incentive to bargain for the maximum possible target cost and for a favourable sharing ratio. As a result, a firm's observed performance on an incentive contract might reflect its relative success in the bargaining process!

CONCLUSION

The procurement of military aerospace equipment raises a range of analytical, empirical and policy issues to which economists can contribute. It embraces the study of government and firm behaviour in various market and bargaining situations and the choice of the most appropriate contractual arrangements for coping with uncertainty. But the evaluation of aerospace procurement policy raises a fundamental question: what criteria are to be used to evaluate a Defence Department's project management and procurement performance? Is the model of a perfect or ideal project which encounters no technical problems and no slippages in costs and time-scales to be used? Or, is a Defence Department's project management performance to be assessed against some average or typical national defence project, or is it to be compared with foreign experience such as France and the USA (see Chapter 7)?

REFERENCES

Arrowsmith, S. and Hartley, K. (2002). *Public Procurement*, The International Library of Critical Writings in Economics 144, Edward Elgar Publishing, Cheltenham, UK and Northampton, MA, USA.

Gray, B. (2009). *Review of Acquisition for the Secretary of State for Defence*, Ministry of Defence, TSO, London.

Hartley, K. (1983). *NATO Arms Co-operation*, Allen and Unwin, London.

Hartley, K. (2011). *The Economics of Defence Policy: A New Perspective*, Routledge, London.

Hartley, K. and Corcoran, W. (1975). Short-run employment functions and defence contracts in the UK aircraft industry, *Applied Economics*, 7, 223–233.

Laffont, J.J. and Tirole, J. (1993). *A Theory of Incentives in Public Procurement and Regulation*, The MIT Press, London.

LM (2013). *2013 Annual Report*, Lockheed Martin Corporation, Bethseda, Maryland, USA.

Lorell, M.A. et al. (2013). *Do Joint Fighter Aircraft Programs Save Money?* Rand Corporation, Santa Monica, California.

McNaugher, T. (1989). *New Weapons, Old Politics*, Brookings, Washington, DC.

NAO (2011a). *Ministry of Defence. Management of the Typhoon Project*, National Audit Office, HCP 755, TSO, London, March.

NAO (2011b). *Ministry of Defence. Major Projects Report 2011*, National Audit Office, HCP 1520, TSO, London, November.

Rich, M. et al. (1984). *Cost and Schedule Implications of Multi-National Co-Production*, Rand Corporation, Santa Monica, California.

Sandler, T. and Hartley, K. (1995). *The Economics of Defense*, Cambridge University Press, Cambridge.

Tisdell, C. and Hartley, K. (2008). *Microeconomic Policy: A New Perspective*, Edward Elgar Publishing, Cheltenham, UK and Northampton, MA, USA.

12. The political economy of international collaboration: an overview of benefits and costs

INTRODUCTION: THE POLICY PROBLEM

Both military and civil aerospace equipment is costly, their costs are rising and these trends affect all nations. For example, the unit cost of combat aircraft has grown at an exponential rate with time; typically by a factor of four every ten years. Similar trends but at different rates apply to commercial airliners, bomber aircraft, helicopters, ships and tanks (for ships and tanks the cost growth has been at a rate of two every ten years; Augustine, 1987, p140). For military aerospace equipment, the historical cost trend arises from technical progress for each new generation of equipment with nations seeking to acquire the latest high technology defence equipment to maintain their superiority in the technical arms race. Technical progress in commercial airliners reflects similar competitive pressures between airlines searching for aircraft which are faster, with greater range and seating capacity and lower operating costs (see Chapters 4, 6 and 7).

Costly equipment and continued rising unit costs provide the economic context for international collaboration in aerospace programmes. The cost incentives to collaborate with other nations result from large 'fixed' development costs and high unit production costs where small national orders for costly equipment are unaffordable. On this basis, international collaboration for the development and manufacture of costly military and civil aerospace equipment appears economically attractive; but appearances can be deceptive. This chapter reviews experience with such programmes and the economic case for collaboration. But international collaboration is characterised by inefficiencies: why do inefficiencies arise; how large are they; and with continued inefficiencies, why do international collaborative programmes continue to be supported by governments? These issues and proposals for improving the efficiency of collaboration are presented in Chapter 13.

BRIEF HISTORICAL OVERVIEW

Europe has considerable experience of collaborative projects, especially in aerospace programmes. Indeed, collaboration has been a distinctive feature of European defence industrial policy. Table 12.1 shows the major European collaborative aerospace projects since 1959. These have comprised military and civil aerospace projects, including combat, trainer, transport and maritime patrol aircraft, helicopters, missiles, civil airliners and space systems (Hartley, 2012; Hayward, 1986).

Table 12.1   Major European collaborative aerospace programmes

Collaboration: Partner Nations and Dates	Major Partner Firms	Project
France–West Germany 1959	Breguet; Aerospatiale; Alenia; Dornier; MBB; Sabca-Sonaco (SECBAT)	Atlantic Maritime Patrol Aircraft
France–UK Treaty 1962	Aerospatiale; BAe	Concorde supersonic airliner (civil airliner)
France–UK 1966	Breguet; BAC (SEPECAT)	Jaguar strike aircraft
France–UK 1967	Aerospatiale; Westland	Helicopter agreement
France–West Germany 1969	Dassault; Dornier	Alpha Jet trainer aircraft
Germany–Italy–UK 1969	Alenia; BAe; DASA (Panavia)	Tornado combat aircraft
France–Germany–UK 1970	Aerospatiale; BAe; DASA	Airbus Industrie (civil airliners)
EU Member States: 10 founding members 1975	Arianespace (launchers); Airbus Defence and Space (including Astrium)	ESA: civil space agency
Italy–UK 1980	Agusta; Westland	EH Industries: anti-submarine helicopter
France–Italy 1981	Aerospatiale; Alenia	ATR: regional civil transport aircraft
France–Germany–Italy–Netherlands 1985	Agusta; Eurocopter France and Germany; Fokker (NHI)	NH90 multi-role military helicopter
Germany–Italy–Spain–UK 1986	Alenia; BAe; CASA; DASA (Eurofighter)	Eurofighter Typhoon combat aircraft

Collaboration: Partner Nations and Dates	Major Partner Firms	Project
France–Germany 1992	Aerospatiale; MBB	Eurocopter: military and civil helicopters
France–UK 1996	Matra; BAe Dynamics	In 2001, became MBDA
France–Germany–Spain 1999	Aerospatiale-Matra; CASA; DASA	EADS including Airbus and Eurocopter. Renamed Airbus in 2014
Seven nations with France, Germany, Spain and UK as major nations 2003	Aerospatiale; BAE; CASA; MBB (Airbus Military)	Airbus A400M Atlas airlifter

Notes:

1. Collaborations are for those involving European nations only, and exclude collaboration between European nations and other non-European nations (e.g. US and the JSF). Collaboration countries and dates refer to initial agreements. In some cases, there were additions and/or exits.
2. The company names were at the date of the original agreement. Since then, many companies have merged and have new names (e.g. BAe is now BAE Systems; EADS is now Airbus; Westland is AgustaWestland).
3. Company names in brackets show the name of the relevant international organisation (e.g. SECBAT for international consortium for production of Atlantic; SEPECAT for Jaguar).
4. ESA was created by 10 founding member states and by 2011 there were 19 member states, mostly EU states.
5. Italy withdrew from the A400M airlifter project leaving Belgium, France, Germany, Luxembourg, Spain, Turkey and the UK as the partner nations.

Table 12.1 shows that European aerospace collaboration has involved a small group of nations. In the 1960s, these comprised France, West Germany and the UK, with France and the UK collaborating on two high technology projects, namely, a supersonic airliner (Concorde) and an advanced combat aircraft (Jaguar). From the late 1960s, two new partner nations entered European collaborative programmes, namely, Italy and Spain. Aerospace projects have dominated European collaboration which raises the question of why the general absence of such collaboration for land and sea systems?

There is a further feature of Table 12.1 concerning the industrial arrangements for European collaborations. Most of the collaborative defence programmes involved the creation of defence and product-specific industrial consortia with the sole task of producing the collaborative project. For example, the Anglo–French Jaguar aircraft was designed and produced by SEPECAT; the Tornado was produced by Panavia; the NH90 helicopter is managed by NH Industries; and Typhoon is produced by Eurofighter. There are some significant exceptions where collaboration has been associated with the creation of permanent and multi-product European-wide companies. Examples include Airbus (civil jet airliners: formerly EADS), Eurocopter (helicopters: now Airbus Helicopters) and MBDA (missiles). The varying industrial arrangements and the different numbers of partner nations associated with different European collaborative projects raises further questions. Which is the most appropriate industrial organisation for collaboration; which form of organisation has been most successful; and is there an ideal or optimum number of partner nations in any collaboration?

THE ECONOMICS OF COLLABORATION

Economics in the form of costs are a major determinant of collaboration. Initially, any economic evaluation of collaboration requires a definition followed by consideration of methodology issues and then the 'perfect' case scenario.

Multinational collaboration involving European nations has a distinguishing feature. It involves two or more nations sharing all aspects of the development and production of aerospace equipment.[1] Aerospace examples have dominated European collaborations (see Table 12.1) where two or more nations have agreed to share the development costs of aerospace projects and combined their production orders to achieve economies of scale and learning from longer production runs. European collaboration is distinctive in its sharing of all aspects of the *acquisition* of the project. In contrast, US-dominated collaborations have involved American defence companies acting as prime contractors and design leaders with groups of nations participating in the *production* of a US-designed and developed aircraft (co-production). The US Joint Strike Fighter (F-35) is an exception where there is some international participation and cost sharing in the development of the aircraft (e.g. the UK is the only Level 1 partner in the project contributing some 10 per cent of planned development cost).

---

[1] In this chapter, collaboration is variously described as multinational collaboration or joint ventures or joint projects. These terms are used interchangeably.

METHODOLOGY: HOW CAN COLLABORATIVE PROJECTS BE EVALUATED?

Typically, the economic evaluation of collaboration involves an assessment of both benefits and costs of each project compared with its alternatives. Immediately, this approach encounters major methodological problems. An obvious starting point is to compare a national project with an identical collaborative programme. But collaboration means that no such national identical comparators will exist. This approach also raises the counter-factual problem of what would have happened without the joint venture: which type of aerospace equipment would have been purchased by each partner nation?

One solution to these problems is to compare actual collaborative projects and actual similar national programmes between nations. European collaborative projects can be compared with similar European or US projects. For example, the multinational Eurofighter Typhoon can be compared with the French Rafale, the Swedish Gripen and rival US combat aircraft (e.g. F-15; F-16; F-18; F-22; F-35). In principle, these projects can be compared on the basis of total development costs, unit production costs, cost escalation, delivery dates and schedule overruns as well as data on total output and export sales. Problems arise because such data are not always available in the public domain. Also, projects differ in their performance capabilities. For example, for military aircraft, there are differences in the speed, range, altitude, weapons carrying capacity and type of weapons carried. Similarly, civil airliners will differ in their speed, range, number of passengers carried and operating costs. However, comparisons of actual collaborative and actual national aerospace projects is often distorted where the comparator national project is some ideal, problem-free national project which has never existed (the grass is greener fallacy).

Further problems arise in such comparisons since there is a very limited and heterogeneous population of collaborative aerospace projects (e.g. combat, transport and trainer aircraft; helicopters; missiles; civil aircraft) involving different partner nations and different organisational arrangements. More data points can be obtained by combining military and civil collaborative aircraft projects (e.g. Airbus and Boeing civil jet aircraft). However, before assessing the available evidence, it is necessary to outline the predictions derived from economic models of collaboration. A starting point requires a comparison of collaboration with alternative procurement choices.

PROCUREMENT CHOICES

For military aerospace equipment, international collaboration is one of a range of procurement choices for a nation. The options range from the extremes of buying from a national defence industry, or importing foreign equipment, or selecting an 'intermediate' option of building a foreign design under licence or multinational collaboration. Table 12.2 outlines a conceptual cost–benefit framework for assessing these broad procurement choices.

Table 12.2   A framework for procurement choices

Policy Option	Costs (acquisition; life-cycle)	Military Benefits (e.g. performance; delivery)	National Economic Benefits (jobs; technology; exports)
National Project			
International Collaboration			
Licensed Production			
Import of Foreign Equipment			

The procurement options range from the extremes of complete independence, namely, buying nationally (e.g. buy British or French) to complete dependence in the form of importing foreign defence equipment (e.g. from the USA). The importing option can have a variant in the form of offsets where the buying nation requires some work to be awarded to its domestic industry (the offset work can be in either its defence industry or elsewhere in the importing economy). Between the extremes, there are intermediate options embracing licensed production and collaboration. Licensed production of foreign defence equipment also has a variant, namely, co-production where a group of buying nations might share in the total production order. Finally, international collaboration involves two or more nations sharing in the acquisition costs of a defence project with the sharing of both development and production work forming the distinctive feature of multinational European collaborations. Of course, more partner nations increase the complexity and the transaction costs of the collaboration.

Each procurement option in Table 12.2 involves a variety of costs and benefits. For costs, data are required on acquisition and life-cycle costs both on a per unit and fleet basis. On the benefits side, a distinction can be made between military and national or wider economic benefits. Military and strategic benefits comprise equipment performance, delivery dates (and their reliability), the possibility of re-supply in a conflict and the contribution to NATO standardisation.

There might also be wider economic and industrial benefits in the form of jobs, skills, technology and technology transfer (spin-offs) as well as exports and import-savings contributions to the balance of payments. Such wider economic benefits need to be identified and assessed critically. For example, alternative public expenditure programmes might be more cost-effective in job creation compared with a multinational defence project (cf. construction work). Here, the opportunity cost question has to be considered, namely, whether alternative uses of resources will make a greater contribution to jobs, technology, the balance of payments and, ultimately, to national output (GDP)? There is a further concern, namely, whether wider economic benefits are the proper concern of national defence ministries: is the aim of defence to protect jobs or a nation's citizens? Moreover, these wider economic benefits have to be valued and converted into financial terms to be included in any cost–benefit analysis. Inevitably, published data are not available to enable a complete and independent economic evaluation of a nation's procurement options.

THE ECONOMICS OF COLLABORATION: THE IDEAL CASE

Cost savings are believed to be the major economic benefit of collaboration. Such savings apply to both R&D costs and production costs. Partner nations can share costly R&D outlays which are regarded by economists as a fixed total cost which have to be incurred regardless of the output to be produced. Then, by combining their national orders, the partner nations can achieve economies of scale and learning from a longer production run.

Consider a simple example of two nations independently producing a similar combat aircraft with development costs of $10 billion, each with a national requirement for 200 units. Without collaboration, this is the classic case of duplication of costly R&D and the failure to exploit economies of larger scale production: it demonstrates the costs of independence which is typical of both European and NATO nations. Collaboration between these two nations offers substantial cost savings

compared with a national venture. *Ceteris paribus* a two nation collaboration with equal sharing will save $10 billion on development costs
($5 billion for each nation) plus savings in unit production costs from a
larger output. Typically, a doubling of output from 200 to 400 units might
lead to savings in unit production costs of some 5 per cent. On unit
production costs of $100 million per aircraft, such savings are worth
$5 million per aircraft. The total cost savings for this example are shown
in Table 12.3. Compared with two duplicate national programmes, a two
nation collaboration offers cost savings totalling $6 billion for each
nation. But these estimated cost savings assume the ideal or perfect case
scenario where collaboration involves no extra costs and inefficiencies.
Actual collaboration usually involves a collaboration premium and
departs from the perfect or ideal case scenario.

A similar analysis applies to international collaboration for civil
aircraft programmes: two nations share development costs and combine
their national orders to achieve savings in unit production costs. However, with civil aircraft programmes, national governments will either
provide subsidy or repayable loan support for financing development
costs and the airlines of each nation will combine their orders. For civil
aircraft, the partner nations will also share the risks of the programme.

Table 12.3   Cost savings from collaboration (all costs in $s)

	Independence		Collaboration	
	Nation A	Nation B	Nation A	Nation B
Total R&D costs	10 billion	10 billion	5 billion	5 billion
Unit production costs	100 million	100 million	95 million	95 million
Total production costs	20 billion	20 billion	19 billion	19 billion
Total costs	30 billion	30 billion	24 billion	24 billion

The ideal case of collaboration is represented in Figure 12.1. Total R&D
costs for the projects are shown in Figure 12.1(a). With a two nation
collaboration, total R&D costs are shared equally (shown by the reduction from 1.0R to 0.5R where R is R&D costs). Figure 12.1(b) shows
unit production costs and the unit cost savings of increasing output from
200 to 400 units (shown by the reduction in unit production costs (upc)
from C_1 to C_0).

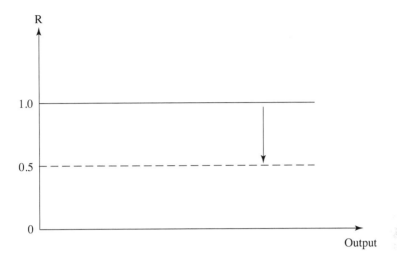

Figure 12.1a   Research and development

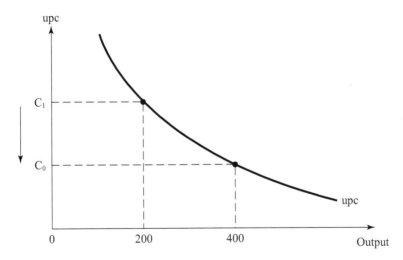

Figure 12.1b   Production

OTHER BENEFITS OF COLLABORATION

In addition to cost savings, there are other benefits of collaboration comprising economic, industrial and military–political benefits. Wider economic benefits arise in the form of jobs, skills, technology, spin-offs and export contributions. Collaboration also enables partner nations to retain a domestic defence industrial capability in high technology equipment (e.g. aerospace). Furthermore, it allows European nations to create larger industrial groups to undertake costly R&D and to achieve a larger scale of output enabling them to compete with their US rivals. Military and political benefits arise in the form of greater equipment standardisation and the ability of Europe to be independent of the USA (Heuninckx, 2008).

These benefits are not free gifts: they come at a price reflected in the price of collaborative equipment compared with the price of imported equipment from the lowest-cost supplier (e.g. USA). The wider economic benefits need to be assessed in relation to market failure analysis. Economists usually justify state intervention in markets where there are clear indications of market failure. For example, benefits relating to jobs and exports suggest failures in labour and foreign exchange markets, respectively. Here, the causes of market failure have to be identified and appropriate solutions determined which are related to the causes of failure. For example, labour markets generally work reasonably well as clearing mechanisms and where there are failures (e.g. due to lack of skills or mobility and a lack of labour market information about job opportunities), it has to be shown that defence aerospace equipment procurement policy is the most cost-effective solution to such market failure. Similarly, claims about technology spin-off benefits from collaboration raise two problems. First, they might reflect genuine failures in R&D markets which might justify state intervention to 'correct' such failures; but it does not follow that collaborative aerospace programmes are the most cost-effective method of correcting such failures in R&D markets. Second, the technology spin-offs need to be identified and valued. There are examples of spin-offs from defence and aerospace programmes including the jet engine, radar, the Internet, composite materials, racing cars and the turbine blades for wind turbines. However, a list of interesting examples is not very helpful without some valuations: what are the market values of these spin-offs? The difficulties of measuring and valuing such spin-offs might mean that they do not exist and reflect the lobbying behaviour of producer and scientific interest groups with an interest in promoting the collaborative programme!

DEPARTING FROM THE IDEAL CASE:
COLLABORATION INEFFICIENCIES

Actual collaborations depart from the ideal or perfect case scenario: they are not costless. Collaboration involves additional transaction costs reflecting the costs of 'doing business with strangers' in the form of different partner nations and different industrial companies. Transaction costs are the costs of trading above and beyond the product price such as the costs of writing and enforcing contracts. Differences in transaction costs can explain why structure, conduct and performance vary between industries.

Transaction cost economics regards all complex contracts as inevitably incomplete and collaboration involves complex contracts: their incompleteness allows agents opportunities for pursuing their own self-interest. Transaction costs are the costs of creating and running the multinational organisation.[2] They comprise the costs of search, acquiring information, negotiating, bargaining, reaching contractual agreements together with monitoring and enforcing contracts. Collaboration provides extensive opportunities for international transactions in reaching complex multinational contractual agreements.

Collaboration can also be analysed as an international club between nation states based on an international agreement. Creating and maintaining a club involves transaction costs. Most clubs are voluntary organisations which are formed so long as they are expected to be beneficial and worthwhile. Members join a club so long as they expect to receive benefits which are at least equal to the costs of membership[3] (e.g. clubs for angling, gliding, golf, swimming and tennis). A similar approach applies to collaborative aerospace equipment programmes where governments create an international club. They determine the type of club, its size, the rules about entry and exit, the entry and exit fees and the distribution of benefits. For such clubs, nations will join and remain members so long as membership is worthwhile.

Club rules will reflect the objectives and behaviour of the different agents in the political market of each nation: hence, public choice analysis provides an alternative analytical framework for explaining

---

[2] Transaction cost economics has been criticised for being a tautology. Some critics have suggested that transaction cost economics has not been operationalised and is often introduced into the analysis in a casual way with no empirical support (Williamson, 1999, pxv).

[3] The economic theory of clubs regards a club good as a variant of a public good which is excludable but non-rivalrous.

international collaboration (see Chapter 9). International collaboration will reflect the interests of different groups, namely, governments, bureaucracies and producer groups. Within a collaborative programme, governments will be focused on vote-winning implications, bureaucracies in the form of Defence Ministries and the Armed Forces will be seeking opportunities to increase their budgets and firms will be seeking large-scale contracts and the associated income and profits.

Each partner nation will seek business for its national champions, including favourable work shares especially of high technology work. Government ministers and bureaucracies will welcome the opportunities for regular international travel and meetings in each partner nation. There is the prestige involved in negotiating and monitoring an international agreement with opportunities for 'protecting the national interest', award-ing contracts, making it costly for any partner nation to withdraw unilaterally and maximising their involvement in programme decision-making and monitoring (under the guise of public accountability and protecting national taxpayers). Decision-making by committee will domi-nate with major decisions often requiring unanimity. Committee deci-sions take time and will not be characterised by entrepreneurship! Adding more partner nations to a collaborative programme will mean more delays. Changes in national budgetary positions further add to pro-gramme delays. Difficulties also arise in harmonising different opera-tional requirements and delivery schedules leading to compromise solutions. The case for collaboration will be further supported by major producer groups of managers and trade unions seeking new lucrative and long-term contracts in protected markets. These groups will be supported by the scientific lobby with its desire to expand the frontiers of scientific knowledge at the taxpayer's expense. Overall, pressure from various interest groups will result in excessive government bureaucracy and duplicate procurement organisations.

Collaboration inefficiencies are not restricted to the procurement arrangements and also arise on the supply side of the programme. Efficiency criteria suggest that a single prime contractor with contractual and financial responsibility for the programme might be the most efficient form of industrial organisation and management. Instead, the partner nations in a collaboration will prefer an international industrial consortium of their major producers. The partner nations will impose inefficient work-sharing rules under which each partner demands a 'fair share' of the work comprising high technology and production work where work share is based on 'political-equity' criteria rather than comparative advantage and competitiveness. On aerospace collaboration, the result is duplication of flight test centres and final assembly lines based in each partner nation. Further sources of industrial inefficiency in collaboration arise from differences in managerial philosophy and practices amongst firms in the partner nations. This is most obvious where a collaboration involves privately-owned and state-owned firms where private firms are subject to capital market constraints and state firms are not subject to hard budget constraints.

Modelling collaboration also offers opportunities for applying bargaining and game playing behaviour within political markets. Bargaining predominates as each partner nation in the form of its government, bureaucracies, producers and scientists will demand that their operational requirements be enforced, that their national champions be selected as project leaders and that each nation is awarded the most exciting technical advances. The early stages of negotiations will be dominated by each national interest group submitting its claims, using its bargaining power and skills and threats to withdraw from the programme. At this stage, games of bluff, chicken and brinksmanship will be deployed. Nations might exaggerate their planned orders to gain work share advantages. Inevitably, the resulting international agreement will be a compromise between the maximum bids of each partner and their minimum bid required to persuade them to join and remain in the club. Compromises will reflect bargaining behaviour rather than efficiency criteria: the final agreement will be based on 'fairness and equity' rather than the competitiveness of each partner nation's aerospace industries. Indeed, in some collaborations, one of the partners might be a new entrant to the industry where its membership is conditional on receiving an appropriate share of high technology work. As a result, the partner nations will have to bear and share the costs for the new entrant (e.g. Spain and its membership of the Eurofighter Typhoon project).

Once started, collaborative programmes are difficult to stop. They create a major interest group of bureaucracies, contractors, unions and scientists in each partner nation. Such international groups of experts will be influential in persuading vote-seeking governments of the technology, military and wider economic benefits of continuing with a collaborative project. These groups will support optimistic cost, time and performance estimates for the project where the costs of optimism are spread across each partner nation's numerous taxpayers. Exit from a collaborative project might be costly for any one partner nation requiring compensation payments to the remaining partners: hence, the view that it is difficult to cancel collaborative projects. The outcome of political bargaining is a government-created, protected and regulated market forming an international cartel of each nation's national champions. A country will join and remain a member of a collaborative programme so long as it offers a range of economic and non-economic benefits which are believed to be superior to alternatives such as national independence. Public choice models predict that multinational programmes will be inefficient with work allocated between partner nations on the basis of political and equity criteria (fair shares or *juste retour*) rather than on economic criteria of efficiency, comparative advantage and competitiveness. The various international interest groups in collaborations are not subject to competition or bankruptcy, nor are they motivated by efficiency and profitability criteria. As a result, it is not surprising that international collaboration is characterised by inefficiency. How large are such inefficiencies?

Estimating Inefficiencies

Estimates of collaboration inefficiencies are usually based on comparisons with national programmes. But national comparators are difficult to find: the fact of collaboration means that nations have chosen collaboration over a national venture. Also, national comparisons are often based on hypothetical and perfect national projects which are assumed to be 'problem free' (e.g. encountering no cost overruns or delays in delivery). Nor should anecdotal evidence be the basis of serious criticism of multinational collaboration: such evidence needs to be treated with care, caution and critical appraisal.

Two rules can be used to assess the magnitude of collaboration inefficiencies. First, *the square root rule* applies to development costs. It suggests that the development costs on a collaborative project can be estimated by applying the square root of the number of partner nations. For example, with four equal partner nations, the project's development costs might be twice the costs for a national project. Similarly, for a two nation collaboration the project's development costs might be some 140 per cent of the costs of a national project whereas with a seven nation collaboration (e.g. A400M) development costs might be 2.65 times the costs of a similar national project. However, these additional costs are shared between the partners so that each nation has lower development costs compared with a national venture, but the cost savings are lower than predicted for the perfect case scenario.[4] An alternative rule of thumb

---

[4] Consider an example where development costs are 100 for a national project. In the perfect case scenario, a four nation collaboration would also have total development costs of 100 with each nation paying only 25. The square root rule suggests development costs on a four nation venture would be 200 with each nation paying 50: more than under the perfect case scenario but still less than for a national project.

suggests that collaboration increases development costs by some 50 per cent for each partner nation beyond the first (Pugh, 2007). Table 12.4 shows examples of development costs for comparable national and collaborative aerospace programmes. The table suggests collaboration development costs rising with the number of partner nations ranging from some 40 per cent for two nations to 60 per cent to 80 per cent for three nations and about 100 per cent for four nations.

Table 12.4   *Development costs for comparable national and collaborative aerospace projects*

Project	National Alternative	Number of Partners	Total Development costs as % of National Development cost
Eurofighter	P120	4	196
Tornado	National development of airframe and engine	3	161
Merlin Mark 1	UK national programme	2	143

Source: HCP 300 (2001).

Second, a similar rule of thumb applies to development time-scales. It suggests that compared with a national project, delays on collaborative programmes can be estimated by applying *the cube root* of the number of nations involved. For example, a two nation collaboration might take some 26 per cent longer; a four nation collaboration might take some 60 per cent longer than a similar national project; and an eight nation collaboration might take twice as long as a national venture. UK estimates show that collaborative programmes might slip by an average of 28 months with some 11 months attributed to co-operative factors (HCP 300, 2001). Within the collaboration delays, the most significant cause of delay was attributed to the industrial organisation, especially where joint venture companies were formed for the project. Such specially formed joint companies have no separate commercial logic behind them and lack a successful prime contractor capable of clear leadership (HCP 300, 2001, p20).

Inefficiencies also arise in collaborative production. In the perfect case scenario, a doubling of output is expected to result in a reduction in unit production costs of up to 10 per cent; but this assumes efficient production. Actual collaboration involves production inefficiencies, especially through the establishment of duplicate final assembly lines. As a result, the scale economies achieved on collaborative production programmes are about half those on national programmes (HCP 300, 2001).

Figure 12.2 illustrates the inefficiencies in collaborative development and production programmes. Figure 12.2(a) shows that with a two nation collaboration, inefficiencies in development work might raise total R&D costs by some 40 per cent compared with the perfect case collaboration. Similarly, Figure 12.2(b) shows that production inefficiencies might lead to a higher unit production cost curve (upc_1) so that unit costs do not fall by as much as for perfect collaboration (compare Figures 12.1 and 12.2).

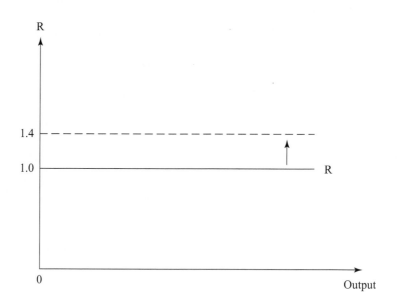

Figure 12.2a   Research and development

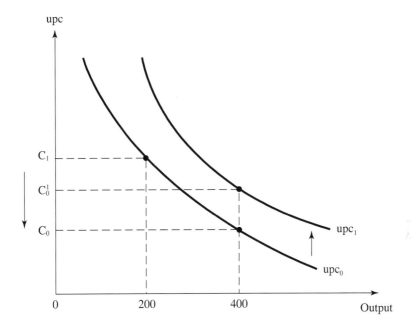

Figure 12.2b Production

CONCLUSION

Any economic evaluation of international collaboration on aerospace programmes requires evidence on the performance of multinational projects. Which have been successful; which have failed; and why? Is success or failure related to the number of partner nations with more successful projects associated with few partners; or is success based on the creation of a single joint company rather than a project-specific consortium; or is success related to the extent of technical advance in the programme with high technology projects more likely to be unsuccessful? These issues are addressed in Chapter 13.

REFERENCES

Augustine, N. (1987). *Augustine's Laws*, Penguin Books, London.
Hartley, K. (2012). *White Elephants? The Political Economy of Multi-National Defence Projects*, New Direction, Brussels.

Hayward, K. (1986). *International Collaboration in Civil Aerospace*, Francis Pinter, London.

HCP 300 (2001). *Maximising the benefits of defence equipment co-operation*, National Audit Office, TSO, London.

Heuninckx, B. (2008). A primer to collaborative defence procurement in Europe: Troubles, achievements and prospects, *Public Procurement Law Review*, 3, 123–145.

Pugh, P. (2007). *Source Book of Defence Equipment Costs*, Dandy Books, London.

Williamson, O.E. (ed.) (1999). *The Economics of Transaction Costs*, Edward Elgar Critical Writings Reader, Cheltenham, UK and Northampton, MA, USA.

13. International collaboration: the reality

INTRODUCTION[1]

Collaboration has been a distinctive feature of European defence industrial policy. Other components of this policy embrace the Single European Market and the European Defence and Technological Industrial Base (EDTIB). This chapter adopts a project case study approach to analyse international collaboration. Three military aircraft projects are analysed, namely, the collaborative Typhoon which is compared with two European national programmes consisting of the Swedish Gripen and the French Rafale. Comparisons are also made with rival US combat aircraft and with the collaborative civil aerospace projects of the Airbus Group (formerly EADS).

METHODOLOGY

The three aircraft case studies reflect different procurement options embracing international collaboration and national independence. Other procurement policy options include the import of foreign equipment and the licensed production of a foreign-designed aircraft. Each procurement option involves different costs and benefits (see Chapters 11 and 12). Overall, the various procurement options can be viewed as choices about military requirements and work shares. A national project can be designed to meet a nation's specific military requirements whilst appearing to offer some 100 per cent of the work to the national defence industry. In contrast, importing means accepting a foreign-designed aircraft where the foreign supplier obtains all the work share. The

---

[1]   Nick Owen, Europe Economics, kindly commented on parts of this chapter and the usual disclaimers apply.

remaining procurement options offer combinations of work share and equipment designed to meet national military requirements (Hartley, 2012).

The three aircraft case studies are analysed using a cost–benefit approach. Costs include acquisition and operational costs over the project's life-cycle. Benefits include the contribution of the equipment to national defence as reflected in security, protection, deterrence and peace. But defence output is difficult to measure and typically, it is assumed that output equals input, which is a far from satisfactory measure of defence output. In addition, military aircraft contribute to wider economic and industrial benefits reflected in jobs, technology, spin-offs and exports. Ideally, these wider economic benefits need to be included in any economic evaluation of new defence equipment and its alternatives. In this chapter, the alternatives are restricted to rival combat aircraft (European and US). The economic evaluation of alternative combat aircraft, and hence procurement choices, will occur at the initial project approval stage where decision-makers face considerable uncertainties about the costs and benefits of each aircraft (e.g. comparisons between an aircraft which does not exist and one which is available 'off-the-shelf').

Within any cost–benefit analysis, costs are more easily identified and measured in money terms. Benefits are usually more difficult to identify, measure and value. For example, even if employment benefits can be identified and quantified (e.g. including supply chain employment impacts), there arises the task of placing a money valuation on the total numbers of additional jobs supported by a new aircraft project. There are also questions as to whether labour markets are failing to work properly and whether jobs are the proper concern of national defence policy. Other benefits are more intangible such as the valuation of national independence and military standardisation. The valuation which policy-makers place on these benefits will differ between nations, especially for partner nations in multinational collaborations. Whilst cost–benefit analysis has its problems, it nonetheless provides an analytical framework for project appraisal (i.e. it is better than relying on hunches and personal biases). It also provides a general check on any project choice by requiring policy-makers to assess its costs and benefits asking whether its benefits are likely to exceed its costs: if an aircraft costs Euros X billion, are its expected benefits at least equal to Euros X billion? These issues are addressed using experience from three European project case studies comprising Typhoon, Gripen and Rafale.

CASE STUDY I: TYPHOON

PROJECT DESCRIPTION

Eurofighter Typhoon is a single seat, twin-engine, delta-wing, multi-role combat aircraft. Unlike Gripen and Rafale which are national projects, Typhoon is an *international collaboration* involving four European nations comprising Germany, Italy, Spain and the UK. It is developed and produced by an international company known as Eurofighter, based in Munich, Germany. Project management is the responsibility of the NATO Eurofighter and Tornado Management Agency (NETMA) which acts as the prime customer.

Initially, in 1979 France, Germany and the UK explored the possible joint development of a European Combat Aircraft. This project collapsed in 1981 over different operational requirements, a French insistence on design leadership and British preference for a Rolls-Royce engine and French preference for their Snecma engine. By August 1985, after further collaboration plans, West Germany, Italy and the UK announced their decision to proceed with the Eurofighter programme. Spain joined the programme in September 1985 but France withdrew to pursue a national project which became the Dassault Rafale.

At the start, the planned Eurofighter procurement was for the UK and Germany to acquire 250 aircraft each, Italy 165 aircraft and Spain 100 aircraft giving a total for the four partner nations of 765 aircraft. Initially, work shares were based on planned production with British Aerospace (UK) and DASA (Germany) awarded 33 per cent shares, Aeritalia (Italy) a 21 per cent share and CASA (Spain) a 13 per cent share. The Munich-based Eurofighter company was established in 1986 to manage development of the project. A similar company named Eurojet was created to manage development of the EJ200 engine with work shared between Rolls-Royce, MTU Aero Engines, Fiat Avio (now Avio) and ITP. Other European industrial consortia were created for major parts of Typhoon (e.g. Euroradar CAPTOR comprising Selex Galileo (Italy), Airbus Defence and Space (Germany and Spain) and INDRA (Spain); and EuroFirst for the airborne tracking equipment system developed by Selex Galileo, Thales and Tecnobit (Spain)).

Delays to the programme occurred in 1991 due to the costs of German reunification and a German desire to cancel the project; but the cancellation costs were unacceptable to Germany and the project continued. First flight was achieved in March 1994 and the first production contract was signed in January 1998 involving Eurofighter, Eurojet and NETMA.

At this stage, the four partners planned to buy a reduced total of 620 aircraft with the UK planned buy of 232 aircraft, Germany 180 aircraft, Italy 121 aircraft and Spain 87 aircraft. Work shares were based on planned procurement with British Aerospace awarded a 37.5 per cent share, DASA a 29 per cent share, Alenia a 19.5 per cent share and CASA a 14 per cent share (EADS Germany and EADS CASA became Cassidian which is now Airbus Defence and Space).

Typhoon entered operational service in August 2003. Typhoon work shares are based on specialisation for parts of the aircraft with each nation building the same parts for all the aircraft but with each nation assembling its own aircraft resulting in four final assembly lines. On this basis, EADS Germany builds the main centre fuselage, BAE Systems builds the front fuselage, canopy and the rear fuselage section, EADS CASA builds the right wing and Alenia the left wing. Work shares are also designed so that no money crosses national borders. At early 2014, the planned purchase of Typhoon by the four partner nations was 160 aircraft for the UK, 143 aircraft for Germany, 96 aircraft for Italy and 73 aircraft for Spain, giving a total buy for the four nations of 472 aircraft plus exports of 99 Typhoons to Saudi Arabia, Austria and Oman (see Table 13.1). Further delays to the programme occurred in 2010 when the partners agreed to slow down production rates to retain industrial capability.

AN ECONOMIC EVALUATION

Costs and Output of Typhoon

The UK National Audit Office has published detailed costs for the UK component of the Typhoon programme (NAO, 2013; 2011). The UK costs are 37 per cent of Typhoon total costs for all four partner nations. The contracts for the UK airframe and engine were non-competitive. For the UK Typhoon, total development costs are estimated at Euros 8.2 billion and total production costs at Euros 16.6 billion giving total programme costs of Euros 24.85 billion and unit production costs at Euros 90 million (UK costs only: 2012 prices and exchange rates). Total *life-cycle* costs for the UK Typhoons are estimated at Euros 46 billion with equipment acquisition accounting for 61 per cent of this total. UK employment on Typhoon at BAE Systems, Rolls-Royce and Selex Galileo (UK site) is estimated at 8,600 jobs; but this number is for three UK companies only, excluding other UK firms and their supply chain employment. Broadly, some 40 per cent of Typhoon production costs are allocated to the airframe, 40 per cent for equipment and 20 per cent for the engine.

Table 13.1   Major features of Typhoon multinational combat aircraft

Contractors	Aircraft Performance
Prime: Eurofighter	Speed: Mach 2
Major Suppliers:	Combat radius: 860 mls
Eurojet	Single seat
Euroradar	Twin engine
Time-scales	**Dates**
Start of funded development work	May 1983
Programme approved	August 1985
First flight	March 1994
Entry to service	August 2003
Development time-scales	**Total Months**
Total time from start to first flight	130
Time from programme approval to first flight	103
Time from start to service entry	243
Time from approval to service entry	216
Output	**Units**
UK	160
Germany	143
Italy	96
Spain	73
Saudi Arabia	72
Austria	15
Oman	12
Total	*571*

Notes:
1. Funded development work led to the BAe Experimental Aircraft programme (EAP).
2. Output is based on sales and orders at July 2014. All output and export sales are liable to change reflecting cancellation and new orders.
3. Where no exact dates are available, the relevant date was assumed to be the middle of the month.

The UK costs can be 'grossed-up' to provide an estimate of Typhoon's total development and production costs *for all four partner nations* (assuming UK costs are representative for all four partner nations). On this basis, total development costs for Typhoon are estimated at Euros

22.2 billion; total production costs at Euros 44.9 billion; and aggregate acquisition costs at Euros 67.1 billion (2012 prices).

For the UK, total programme costs are estimated to have increased by +20 per cent (over fewer aircraft). Of the Euros 4.3 billion cost increase, some Euros 2.7 billion (63 per cent) were due to inefficient collaboration arrangements, obligations to international partners and to project technical complexity. Delays on the UK Typhoon totalled 54 months with 32 months of this delay due to technical factors and 22 months (41 per cent) due to international collaboration.

The Costs of Collaboration

Typhoon has been criticised for inefficiencies in both development and production, reflected in its industrial organisation, work-sharing arrangements and programme management. The programme lacks a single prime contractor, comprising an international consortium of national firms (Eurofighter) established to deliver one product, namely, Typhoon. Programme management lacks a single customer with the partner governments vulnerable to different and changing requirements, national budget pressures and exit costs (national projects are also subject to such pressures and cancellation costs).[2]

Critics have highlighted the inefficient work-sharing on both development and production. For development, there have been duplicate flight testing centres and major problems with the flight control system. Whilst British companies had demonstrated their competence to undertake work on the flight control system, other companies became involved who were either 'not up to the job' or whose involvement made arrangements 'unduly cumbersome'. As a result, it was concluded that 'the industrial arrangements for the flight control system had all the characteristics of an accident waiting to happen' (HCP 222, 1994, pxiv).

Production inefficiencies have also been criticised due to duplicate final assembly lines in each partner nation. However, such criticisms are misleading since single source production leading to scale and learning economies accounts for over 95 per cent of unit production costs. The duplication of four final assembly lines departing from single source production account for less than 5 per cent of unit production costs: hence, compared with a single final assembly line, there are duplication costs and a loss of learning in Typhoon final assembly. There are also

---

[2] Estimates suggest that the minimum economic production quantity for Typhoon would be 400–450 aircraft including exports. On this basis, Typhoon could have survived the withdrawal of two nations (HCP 299, 1992, pxxviii).

some offsetting benefits from Typhoon's four final assembly lines through technology transfer, security of supply and in-service support for the aircraft (Hartley, 2008; 2012). Interestingly, it has also been shown that the current unit production costs of Typhoon are similar to comparable types of aircraft (NAO, 2011, p7).

Official studies have concluded that the collaborative arrangements for Typhoon and the complexity of its technology have increased costs. Collaborative decision-making has been found to be inefficient and slow. For example, key decisions require consensus from all four partner nations with some decisions requiring seven years to reach agreement and some decisions were taken on an over-optimistic basis. As a result, the UK National Audit Office concluded that the UK has not yet secured value for money from its investment in Typhoon (NAO, 2011, p9).

Compared with Gripen and Rafale, Eurofighter Typhoon had much longer development times for each phase of development and entered operational service much later (August 2003 compared with June 2001 for Rafale and September 1997 for Gripen). Collaboration leads to cost penalties and delays in development and production. Typical guidelines suggest that compared with a national project, collaboration *development* costs can be estimated by the 'square root' of the number of partner nations and programme *delays* are represented by the 'cube root' of the number of partner nations. On this basis, a four nation project such as Typhoon can be expected to have development costs which are twice those of a similar national programme and its development time-scale might be some 60 per cent longer than a similar national project. Similar cost inefficiencies on collaborative *production* work means that unit cost reductions are about half those on national programmes.

There is some support for these 'rules of thumb'. A UK study compared the estimated development costs of Typhoon with a national alternative finding that Typhoon development costs were 1.96 times the costs of developing a national alternative which is consistent with the square root rule (NAO, 2001). However, total development costs for the collaborative Typhoon compared with the national Rafale project suggests that whilst Typhoon was costlier, it was less than 10 per cent costlier than Rafale, which is considerably less than predicted by the square root rule. On time-scales and compared with both Gripen and Rafale, the Typhoon took some 10 per cent to 40 per cent longer to develop, which is less than suggested by the cube root rule.

Output levels indicate the achievement of scale and learning economies whilst exports are an indicator of international competitiveness. Compared with Gripen and Rafale, the Typhoon has achieved the greatest scale of output but inefficiencies in collaborative production mean that its scale economies are only 50 per cent of those for a national project: hence, it needs to produce twice the national volume to be equally competitive. For exports, Typhoon has sold less than Rafale and Gripen (99 units for Typhoon; 126 units for Rafale and 102 units for Gripen); and Typhoon has only exported 17 per cent of its output compared with some 37 per cent to 40 per cent for Gripen and Rafale. In terms of unit procurement prices and operational costs, Typhoon is costlier than Rafale and Gripen (see Table 13.6). On this basis, Sweden and France show that some European nations can develop and produce advanced combat aircraft in the form of the Gripen and Rafale, which are competitive with multinational programmes such as Typhoon. Of course, all defence equipment projects create wider economic and industrial benefits and these need to be included in any economic evaluation of Typhoon.

WIDER ECONOMIC BENEFITS

Identification and listing of the wider economic benefits of Typhoon is useful but not sufficient for a comprehensive economic evaluation. The potential benefits have to be identified, quantified and expressed in monetary terms; and ideally, such estimations are needed at the start of the project where there are considerable uncertainties about programme benefits and costs. And the economists' opportunity cost question cannot be avoided: would the resources used on the Typhoon project make a greater contribution to national output if they were used elsewhere in the economy? Ideally, such opportunity cost questions need to be asked about Typhoon, its rival combat aircraft projects and alternative civil public expenditure programmes. For example, alternative civil state spending on, say, roads, bridges and housing might create and support more jobs, but these might be low-skilled and low wage jobs which will not provide the higher living standards expected by society. Some broad estimates are available of the wider economic benefits from Typhoon.

Employment

Typhoon supports large numbers of highly skilled, highly paid and high value-added jobs throughout the four partner nations. Estimates showed that in 2006, development and production work on the Typhoon project supported some 100,000 to 105,000 personnel employed both directly and indirectly in over 400 companies throughout Europe (indirect employment comprises jobs in the supply chain). These jobs were distributed between the partner nations giving 20,000 personnel in each of Germany and Italy, 25,000 personnel in Spain and 40,000 personnel in the UK. Total employment numbers included employment in the final assembly plants located in each partner nation (i.e. four final assembly plants). Learning curves for Typhoon production are estimated at 85 per cent with a 90 per cent learning curve for combined labour and other operations. Breaks in production lead to the loss of learning experience: for example, a break of one year in Typhoon production is equivalent to returning to unit one in production (i.e. learning has to re-start: Hartley, 2008).

Technology Contribution

Typhoon is an advanced, high technology combat aircraft which has contributed to technical knowledge, some of which has provided technical spin-offs to other sectors. Typhoon requires special skills in aerodynamics, flight control systems, structures, avionics and systems integration. Typhoon has resulted in an impressive list of examples of technology benefits. Some of these technology benefits have created and supported world class firms. Examples of technology benefits and spin-offs include carbon fibre technology with further applications to civil aircraft and racing cars; super plastic forming and fusion bonding; aero-engine technology with spin-offs to other aircraft engines and to power generation engines; and spin-offs to firms in the supply chain (e.g. introduction of new technology and modern business practices).

There is no shortage of examples of technology benefits and spin-offs from Typhoon; but a list of examples is no substitute for data on the market valuation of such technology benefits. Problems also arise in identifying the counter-factual of what would have happened to technology and spin-offs in the absence of Typhoon? Also, it has to be recognised that the long lead times for Typhoon development work means substantial lags before new ideas are spun-off to other sectors. Further problems arise once it is recognised that the technology benefits and spin-offs from Typhoon are a 'free gift' from the development of a combat aircraft whose main objective is the provision of national defence.

Some broad generalisations can be made about the relative technology contributions of Typhoon compared with Gripen and Rafale. All three aircraft are likely to have resulted in similar qualitative technology benefits but Typhoon and Rafale are more advanced combat aircraft than Gripen (and used a new engine) so that their technology benefits are likely to be greater per unit of expenditure compared with Gripen. Similarly, Typhoon and Rafale are more likely to have resulted in greater national technology spin-offs since they involved greater spending *within* their national economies than Gripen (hence, fewer leakages of spending).

The market value of Typhoon technology spin-offs can be estimated by using other studies. Eliasson (2010) estimated that Gripen resulted in spill-overs valued at 1.8 to 2.3 times the value of the investment in Gripen. Assume that this multiplier applied to Typhoon development costs only. On this basis, the value of spin-offs from Typhoon might be some Euros 40 billion to Euros 51 billion. Another study of the Netherlands planned purchase of US F-35 aircraft estimated technology spin-offs valued at 13.2 per cent of the total Netherlands development and production expenditure on its purchase of F-35 aircraft (De Vijver, pp75, 82 and Vos, 2006). Applied to Typhoon such a percentage share would lead to spin-offs valued at Euros 8.9 billion; and Typhoon spin-offs are likely to be considerably larger than the value of spin-offs to the Netherlands on its F-35 purchase. Overall, these two studies suggest spin-offs on Typhoon valued within a range of Euros 9 billion to Euros 51 billion. These estimates of the market value of Typhoon spin-offs are based on other aircraft and show considerable variation. There remains scope for a proper economic study of the market value of Typhoon spin-offs.

Tax Revenues

Some analysts argue that tax revenues need to be included in any economic evaluation of Typhoon (and other combat aircraft). Often, national treasuries take a different view and do not include tax revenues since they are transfer payments and all economic activity generates tax revenues (similarly for induced employment estimates). Nevertheless, estimates for Typhoon show that for Germany, 60 per cent to 70 per cent of its costs accrued to the national treasury through taxes and similar dues giving a net cost of some 30 per cent to 40 per cent of the total cost. In comparison, for Germany, a similar purchase of US F-18 aircraft provides a return to the national treasury of 14 per cent so raising its net cost to 86 per cent of the total; alternatively, the licensed production in Germany of US F-18 aircraft leads to taxes and dues of 35 per cent and a net cost of 65 per cent of the total cost.

Exports and Import-savings

Wider economic benefits include both exports and import-savings. Exports provide additional employment, they maintain a national defence industrial base without major additional costs to the national economy and they provide a future stream of economic benefits from the sales of spares, training and mid-life updates. Estimates suggest that the value of this life-cycle business might be an extra 50 per cent to 100 per cent of the initial price over 35 years. Additional balance of payments benefits from Typhoon include import-savings (i.e. savings on imports which would be needed if Typhoon were not available). However, not all exports represent net gains since there might be offset and technology transfer requirements (e.g. 200 per cent offsets for the sale of Typhoons to Austria), the waiving of any R&D levy and generous financial terms on foreign sales. Nor are imports as attractive as they appear. They involve additional costs through adverse impacts on a national defence industrial base, a loss of bargaining power, problems of supply in a conflict, equipment which is not designed for national military require-ments and the reluctance of the exporter (e.g. USA) to transfer advanced technology (especially to nations lacking a competitive defence industrial base with the ability to develop rival technologies). Further costs arise where foreign suppliers become monopolists and charge monopoly prices for their spares (e.g. the initial equipment is cheap but you pay for the spares).

Typhoon's contribution to the balance of payments of the partner nations can be estimated. By July 2014, total Typhoon exports were 99 units. Assuming each aircraft sold at the UK unit production price of Euros 90 million gives a total revenue of Euros 8.9 billion, which might support some 16,000 jobs. There are additional sales revenues over the aircraft life-cycle estimated at 50 per cent to 100 per cent of the initial acquisition price over 35 years. On this basis, aggregate sales revenue from Typhoon exports might total Euros 13.4 billion to Euros 17.8 billion, which might support an aggregate total of some 24,000 to 32,000 jobs (based on export sales at July 2014).

In addition, Typhoon contributes to import-savings: these are the savings on imports of combat aircraft which would be needed in the absence of Typhoon. Here, various estimates are possible, each sensitive to the assumptions made about the costs of Typhoon and its possible rival aircraft. First, it might be assumed that Typhoon represents the least-cost solution so that all its costs can be counted as import-savings (i.e. both development and production). On this 'optimistic, best case' scenario, the import-savings from Typhoon totalled Euros 67.1 billion (total develop-ment and production costs for all partner nations, excluding support costs). Second, the unit costs of alternative and rival combat aircraft can be compared with Typhoon costs to determine whether there are lower-cost alternatives. Identifying such lower-cost alternatives is complicated by the need to obtain reliable and accurate unit price data and by the need to compare differences in the operational capabilities of rival aircraft. For example, assuming that the four partner nations would have purchased 620 aircraft comprising a mix of US F-15 and F-18 aircraft results in import-savings of Euros 39.3 billion.[3] On these assumptions, the total balance of payments contribution of Typhoon is some Euros 52.7 billion to Euros 84.9 billion (2012 prices).[4]

Industrial Benefits

Industrial benefits arise in the form of the contribution of Typhoon to maintaining an independent European aerospace industry as an internationally competitive industry and a rival to the US industry. It also ensures independence and security of supply and re-supply in conflict. Further industrial benefits take the form of demonstrating the ability to develop a modern complex combat aircraft and to manage a four nation multinational collaboration. Society has to reach some judgement of the valuation it places on these industrial benefits.

A Market Failure Perspective

There are more general economic concerns about wider economic benefits from Typhoon or any other combat aircraft. Economists approach wider economic benefits by seeking to identify major market failures which would justify state intervention in the economy. Wider economic benefits concerned with jobs, technology and exports suggests a focus on labour, R&D and foreign exchange markets. Typically, labour and foreign exchange markets work reasonably well but R&D markets might fail to work properly due to externalities associated with spin-offs. However, even where market failures are identified, it does not follow that major defence equipment projects such as Typhoon, Gripen and Rafale are the most efficient solution to such market failure. The wider economic and industrial benefits of Typhoon are summarised in Table 13.2.

---

[3]   It was assumed that the 620 aircraft would comprise 200 F-15s and 420 F-18s at unit prices of $99.6 million and $68.7 million, respectively.

[4]   The estimates are based on the lower-bound of export sales (including support sales) of Euros 13.4bn plus the costs of the US purchases of Euros 39.3bn and the upper-bound estimates of export sales of Euros 17.8bn and the 'optimistic' scenario of Typhoon import-savings of Euros 67.1bn.

Table 13.2   Wider economic and industrial benefits of Typhoon

Wider Economic and Industrial Benefits

Employment	Technology and spin-offs	Exports and Import-savings	Others
100,000 jobs. High wage/ high skill jobs	*Examples:* Carbon fibre technology; aero-engine technology. Possibly valued at Euros 9bn to 51bn	Exports valued at Euros 13.4bn to 17.8bn. Import-savings valued at Euros 39.3bn to 67.1bn. Total balance of payments contribution of Euros 52.7bn to 84.9bn	European independence and security of supply; demonstration of ability to integrate complex systems and manage a multinational collaboration

Conclusion

The net economic benefit of Typhoon for the four partner nations can be estimated by considering its income from exports minus the costs of developing and producing Typhoon minus the costs of creating exports plus the costs of importing from overseas. Using this approach, the net economic benefit of Typhoon needs to be positive. Export values might be Euros 17.8bn (which might increase with future exports); Typhoon costs are Euros 67.1bn (these are acquisition costs only); and the costs of importing alternative aircraft are estimated at Euros 39.3bn (there are no data on the costs of creating Typhoon exports). Using these estimates, the net economic benefits of Typhoon are *minus* Euros 10bn for the four partner nations (i.e. a net economic cost). However, Typhoon is designed to meet European military requirements compared with imported equipment; it has also provided technology spin-offs; and there are other industrial and military benefits. If these wider economic and industrial benefits are valued at Euros 10bn, or more by the partner nations, then Typhoon produces a net economic benefit.

CASE STUDY II: GRIPEN

PROJECT DESCRIPTION

The JAS 39 Gripen is a Swedish multi-role affordable lightweight fighter aircraft where *J* represents fighter, *A* represents attack and *S* is for surveillance. Gripen was designed to replace the Swedish Saab Draken and Saab Viggen. It is a single seat and single engine multi-purpose combat aircraft whose initial development work started in June 1980. The initial Swedish air force contract for five prototypes and 30 production aircraft with options for the next 110 aircraft was awarded in June 1982. Gripen was designed to be a small and relatively cheap multi-purpose aircraft with half the weight of the previous third generation Viggen with greater operational capability at only 60 per cent to 65 per cent of the life-time cost of the Viggen (Eliasson, 2010).

The Gripen was designed, developed and manufactured by the IG JAS consortium. The initial consortium comprised Saab (66 per cent project share and 20 per cent ownership share), Volvo Flygmotor (later Volvo Aero with a 14 per cent project share and 20 per cent ownership share), Ericsson (project share of 11 per cent and ownership share of 40 per cent) plus SRA (later acquired by Philips) and FFV Aerotech (later acquired by Celsius). Later, Saab acquired Celsius and the IG JAS consortium is now owned 80 per cent by Saab and 20 per cent by Volvo Aero. A further change to the industrial organisational arrangements occurred in 1995 when Saab and British Aerospace (BAe) formed a joint venture company, namely, Saab–BAe Gripen to manufacture and sell Gripen world-wide. However, this joint venture arrangement ended in 2004 when BAE Systems sold a large part of its shares with a final disposal of its remaining shareholding in 2011.

The contract for the Gripen specified its performance characteristics, costs and delivery schedules with the consortium partners guaranteeing the contract. The contract was for a fixed price with variation of price clauses (with the Swedish procurement agency accepting the foreign exchange risk). Previously, Swedish defence contracts were cost-plus contracts with separately negotiated charges for modifications. Saab was the prime contractor and systems integrator for the Gripen which involved the company in substantial risk-taking: some of these technical and financial risks were shifted to its subcontractors. The major subcontractors included Volvo Aero for the engine; Ericsson for the radar and flight control system; BAE Systems for the fuselage and wing; Martin Baker (UK) for the ejector seat; and other French, UK and US firms also

Table 13.3   Major features of Gripen multi-role fighter aircraft

Contractors	Aircraft Performance
Prime: Saab	Speed: Mach 2
Major Suppliers:	Combat radius: 497 miles
Volvo Aero	Single seat
Ericsson	Single engine
Time-scales	**Dates**
Start of funded development work	June 1980
Programme approved	6 May 1982
Initial contract for 5 prototypes	June 1982
First flight	9 December 1988
Initial operating capability (IOC)	September 1997
Development time-scales	**Total Months**
Total time from start to first flight	102
Time from programme approval to first flight	79
Time from start to IOC	207
Time from approval to IOC	184
Output	**Number of units**
Sweden	204
Brazil	36
South Africa	26
Thailand	12
Hungary (lease)	14
Czech Republic (lease)	14
Total	*278*

Notes:
1. Next Generation Gripen was ordered in early 2013. It involves the modification of existing Gripen aircraft operated by the Swedish air force. Leased aircraft were leased from Sweden: hence, their numbers are deducted from the Sweden total and reflected in the aggregate total and counted as exports.
2. Output figures include orders and are at July 2014. The order for Brazil awaits confirmation at July 2014. The Swiss order for 22 aircraft was cancelled in May 2014.

acted as subcontractors (many Swedish subcontractors were reluctant to accept the risks of the project: Eliasson, 2010). Sweden ordered a total of 204 Gripen aircraft with the final aircraft delivered in late November

2008.⁵ In relation to the contract, Gripen was delivered ahead of time and at a lower cost than calculated (such performance was unusual for major defence projects which are usually characterised by substantial cost overruns and delays in delivery). In addition to sales to Sweden, Gripen has been exported to Brazil, South Africa, Czech Republic, Hungary and Thailand. Table 13.3 presents some of the features of the Gripen programme.

AN ECONOMIC EVALUATION

Costs and Output of Gripen

Published data on development and production costs for combat aircraft are often unreliable. Gripen is no exception. Various estimates suggest its development costs ranged from Euros 2.3 billion to Euros 4.4 billion to Euros 8–10 billion with unit production costs varying between Euros 35.5 million to Euros 67.5 million (2012 prices). In terms of opportunity costs, Gripen at the peak of the programme employed 6,000 engineers. However, Eliasson (2010) claims that its spill-overs were so large that society did not suffer: in fact, it is claimed that society benefited from the Gripen development (via its spill-overs).

Gripen was developed as a relatively cheap multi-role combat aircraft. It was designed for the specific operational requirements for the Swedish air force (e.g. short take-off and landing; simple maintenance requirements; rapid turn-around between missions, multi-role, etc.). At the time of the original procurement choice for Gripen, how did its unit costs compare with the next-best alternative combat aircraft? Possible options were the US F-18E/F and the French Rafale which were either similar or higher on unit acquisition prices but both were costlier to operate (Table 13.4).

As an illustrative example, consider a Swedish acquisition of the French Rafale. Assume that Sweden purchased 204 Rafale aircraft. As a result, Sweden would have saved some Euros 2.3 to 10 billion on the development costs for Gripen: assume a mid-point estimate of development costs for Gripen at Euros 4.4 billion. However, Sweden would have paid an extra Euros 2.6 million on each Rafale purchased (assuming

---

⁵ In 2004, Sweden operated 200+ Gripen. After 2008, the Swedish air force operated 100 Gripen and reports suggest that in future, it will operate with some 60 Gripen Next Generation (NG).

Table 13.4   Gripen and rival aircraft unit prices

Aircraft	Unit Production Cost (Euros millions, 2012 prices)	Operational Costs (Euros per flying hour, 2012 prices)
Gripen	60.6	3,620
Rafale	63.2	12,705
Typhoon	87.5	13,860
F-16	26.9	5,390
F-18E/F	61.2	8,470 to 18,480
F-35	147.3	23,870

Sources: Hartley (2012); Janes (2012).

France did not require an R&D levy) giving a total additional acquisition cost for Rafale of Euros 530 million. But, the Rafale is much costlier to operate at an extra Euros 9,085 per flying hour. Assuming each aircraft flies 200 hours per year results in Rafale costing an extra Euros 371 million per year. Next, assuming that the fleet of 204 Rafale for Sweden would have an operating life of 25 years results in a total additional operating cost for Rafale of an extra Euros 9.3 billion. On this basis, a Swedish purchase of Rafale might have cost Sweden an additional Euros 5.4 billion[6] compared with the Gripen. On a purely cost basis, the Swedish Gripen was a lower-cost purchase than the Rafale. However, the US F-16 is considerably cheaper than Gripen on acquisition costs and the lower acquisition costs more than offset the higher operating costs. In comparing the Gripen with Rafale and the F-16, the issue of operational performance in relation to military requirements was not considered.

Gripen also provided all the wider military, strategic and economic benefits of buying from Sweden which accrued to Sweden, including the retention of the Swedish aerospace industry. For Gripen, some 67 per cent of the aircraft was sourced in Sweden and Europe and 33 per cent from the US: hence, a substantial part of the economic benefits from Gripen accrued to Sweden. Such economic and other benefits would have been 'lost' with the acquisition of a foreign aircraft. Additional economic

---

[6]   The final figure is a broad order of magnitude. It was estimated by taking the extra operational costs of Euros 9.3bn plus the extra acquisition costs of Euros 533 million minus the saving of development costs on Gripen of Euros 4.4bn. The lack of data on the time distribution of spending also means that the estimates are not expressed in present value terms.

benefits have been derived from the export sales of Gripen with a total of 102 Gripen exported (including leased aircraft).

The Technology Contribution

The technology contribution of Gripen is well-documented reflected in three generalisations (Eliasson, 2010). First, Sweden's aircraft industry acts as a technical university providing research, education and training services free of charge to other firms and related industries. It is claimed that these technology transfers are of a kind which are closer to operations than the more theoretically inclined technical university is capable of developing and providing. Second, examples of spill-overs from Gripen include critical software engineering; general engineering technologies; systems integration; the development of lightweight structures; and medical spin-offs. Third, it has been argued that the capacity to develop a complete military aircraft combat system and the associated systems is an extremely scarce industrial competence which is only available in possibly six nations (France; UK; Russia; USA; possibly China and Sweden: Eliasson, 2010).

Estimates of Gripen's spill-over effects have shown a spill-over multiplier ranging from 1.8 to 2.3 times the actual investment generated in the Swedish economy. The Gripen spill-over multipliers are additional returns to society of a particular military investment over and above the value of the product being developed as a multiple of the original investment (in constant prices and present value terms). The spill-overs from Gripen are estimated at Euros 20.3 billion to Euros 37.2 billion based on a total programme cost for Gripen of Euros 13.4 billion (2007 prices: Eliasson, 2010). It has been claimed that 'It is difficult, probably impossible, to find another industry in the markets for public goods and services that rivals military aircraft in generating spillovers' (Eliasson, 2010, p36).

CASE STUDY III: RAFALE

PROJECT DESCRIPTION

The Rafale is a French twin-engine, delta-wing, multi-role combat aircraft manufactured by Dassault Aviation. There are single seat and two seat variants for the French air force (Rafale A and B models) and a carrier-based variant for the French navy (Rafale M and N models). It is claimed to differ from other current European combat aircraft in that it is built almost entirely by one country involving most of France's major defence contractors such as Dassault, Thales and Safran.

About 50 per cent of the Rafale is produced by Dassault and the other 50 per cent is divided between the two major partners, namely, Thales and Safran. Avionics account for a substantial part of the cost of the aircraft (i.e. radar, electronic communications and self-protection equipment). Thales supplies the radar, electronic warfare system, sensory targeting and reconnaissance pods and is involved in a joint venture with MBDA providing the defensive-aids system and with SAGEM-OSF providing the search and track system. Safran supplies the Snecma M88 engine; Crouzet provides the direct voice input system; Air Liquide supplies the on-board oxygen generating system; Nexter (formerly GIAT) provides the cannon; and Martin Baker (UK) provides the ejector seats. There is a network of 500 subcontractors. Estimates suggest that the programme employs 7,000 workers although this appears a low figure and might apply to employment at Dassault only.[7] There is an annual production rate of 11 aircraft; and each aircraft takes 24 months to build. An approximation of the cost distribution shows the airframe accounting for 58 per cent of the unit cost, engines accounting for 23 per cent and avionics for 19 per cent.

Rafale was planned to replace the Jaguar, Crusader, Mirage, Etendard and Super Etentard operated by the French Armed Forces. Initially, in 1979, Dassault joined the UK-German European Combat Aircraft project which developed into the five nation Future European Fighter Aircraft project (with Italy and Spain). By 1985, France had withdrawn from the project to pursue its own national programme. The French withdrawal was due to differences in operational requirements, including its requirement for a carrier-capable version and its demand for a leading role in project management. Next, in October 1982, Dassault was awarded a contract to build a technology demonstrator which became the Rafale A, which first flew in July 1986. In April 1988, the French government awarded Dassault a contract for four Rafale prototypes. At the time, there was a planned requirement for 330 Rafales and the aircraft was expected to enter service in 1996. The end of the Cold War, reductions in the French defence budget together with political and economic uncertainties resulted in considerable delays to the Rafale's development time (work on the Rafale programme

---

[7] This employment estimate is low compared with Typhoon employment. Also, total employment at Dassault in 2012 was 11,472 employees comprising all activities (Rafale and civil aircraft production).

was suspended between 1995 and 1997 with French government demand-ing cost reductions). The prototype Rafale C model flew in May 1991 and the first squadron of Rafale M for the navy was formed in May 2001 (Rafales for the French air force were delivered several years later in 2006). At December 2011, a total of 180 Rafale aircraft had been ordered for the French air force and navy (there are reports that the total order for the French Armed Forces might be 225 aircraft).

Costs and Output

Total programme cost in 2011 was Euros 43.6 billion for 286 aircraft giving a unit total cost of Euros 154.9 million in 2012 prices. Various estimates of unit procurement costs in 2012 prices range from Euros 57.1 million (Rafale C version) to Euros 62.4 million (Rafale M version) to Euros 105.3 million (Rafale F3 version). In 2012, Rafale was awarded an export contract to India for 126 aircraft comprising 18 aircraft supplied by Dassault with the remaining 108 aircraft manufactured in India. The total value of the Indian contract was Euros 8 billion giving a unit cost of Euros 63.5 million (2012 prices). The main features of the Rafale programme are summarised in Table 13.5.

AN ECONOMIC EVALUATION

Both Rafale and Gripen demonstrate that France and Sweden are capable of the independent national development of a modern combat aircraft. In contrast, Eurofighter Typhoon was a four nation collaborative programme involving Germany, Italy, Spain and the UK. Compared with the Swedish Gripen, the French Rafale started later and was in service much later. Rafale achieved shorter development times to its first flight but required longer from start to service entry. Of course, development time-scales based on specific points in the development cycle need to be interpreted with caution since aircraft can differ in their operational status at first flight and at service entry (e.g. at first flight, the aircraft might lack its avionics and its design engine).

Compared with Gripen, the Rafale is more expensive on unit acquisi-tion price and operational costs (see Table 13.4). In terms of international competitiveness, both Rafale and Gripen have achieved similar export sales.

Table 13.5 Major features of Rafale multi-role combat aircraft

Contractors	Aircraft Performance
Prime: Dassault Aviation	Speed: Mach 1.8
Major Suppliers:	Combat radius: 655–1,093mls
Safran/SNECMA	Single/two seat
Thales	Twin engine
Time-scales	**Dates**
Start of technology demonstrator	October 1982
Contract for 4 prototypes	April 1988
First flight Rafale C	May 1991
Entry to service (IOC: Navy version)	June 2001
Development time-scales	**Total Months**
Total time from start to first flight	103
Time from contract to first flight	37
Time from start to service entry	224
Time from contract to service entry	158
Output	**Numbers**
France	225
India	126
Total	*351*

Note: Output and export data at July 2014. The Indian order awaits confirmation in July 2014.

The Technology Contribution

Like many other studies in this field, there is an impressive list of technologies and spin-offs from Rafale. Examples include complex software, data fusion; cryptology; sensor technology; materials sciences; man-machine interfaces; engine design; and spin-offs to the automobile, civil aerospace, engineering, petroleum, shipbuilding and steel industries. Compared with Gripen, the higher proportion of French inputs on Rafale should result in greater national technical developments and spin-offs per unit of expenditure.

Conclusion

Rafale supports the general industry finding that the aerospace industry is a source of high technology knowledge and associated spin-offs. But these findings simply provide a list of examples with an absence of two aspects. First, there are no monetary valuations for these technical benefits; and second, little is known about whether other industries generate similar or 'better' technology benefits and spin-offs compared with the aerospace industry.

OVERALL EVALUATION: THE THREE CASE STUDIES AND RIVAL US AIRCRAFT

Competitiveness

Prices and delivery dates are an indicator of international competitiveness. Table 13.6 shows data on unit total costs comprising both development and production costs. Data are also shown on the dates of first flight and service entry. These data suggest two conclusions. First, Typhoon is costlier than its European rivals and some of its US rivals (see also Table 13.4); but the European aircraft are cheaper than the US F-22 and F-35 aircraft. Second, the first flight and service entry of the US F-15, F-16 and F-18E/F aircraft were generally earlier and ahead of the three European aircraft with these US aircraft requiring some four years between first flight and service entry. This suggests that the US has a competitive advantage in development time-scales.

Exports are a further indicator of international competitiveness. At July 2014, the nationally developed Gripen and Rafale had the best export performance of the three European combat aircraft reflected in export numbers and shares of total output.

Life-cycle Costs

Table 13.7 shows estimates of life-cycle costs for European and US combat aircraft. The Swedish Gripen and the US F-16 are the least-cost aircraft in the sample. Also, Gripen and Rafale are competitive with the US F-18E/F. In contrast, the US F-35 is the costliest aircraft in the sample.

Combat Effectiveness

Competitiveness indicators need to be adjusted for aircraft quality in terms of operational performance (are we comparing like with like?). Table 13.8 presents some published indicators ranking the rival European

Table 13.6   Unit costs and delivery dates

Aircraft Type	Unit Total Cost (Euros, million, 2012 prices)	Date of first flight	Date of service entry
Gripen JAS-39C	66.4	December 1988	September 1997
Rafale C	118.0	May 1991	June 2001
Typhoon	124.9	March 1994	August 2003
F-15 Eagle	n/a	July 1972	January 1976
F-16	n/a	February 1974	August 1978
F-18E/F Super Hornet	85.1	November 1995	November 1999
F-22 Raptor	302.4	September 1997	December 2005
F-35 JSF	123.8	December 2006	After 2016

Notes:
1. Data based on standard definitions and methodology. Typhoon based on German data. n/a is not available.
2. All prices adjusted to 2012 prices using national inflation rates and exchange rates.

Source: DA (2006).

Table 13.7   Life-cycle costs

Aircraft	Euros millions, 2012 prices			Total Unit costs (Gripen = 100)
	Annual Acquisition costs	Annual Operational costs	Annual Unit costs	
Gripen	4.57	0.72	5.29	100
Rafale	4.71	2.54	7.25	137
Typhoon	6.46	2.77	9.23	174
F-16	2.01	1.08	3.09	58
F-18E/F	4.56	2.70	7.26	137
F-35	10.97	4.77	15.74	298

Note: Annual costs are annualised based on aircraft life of 20 years, 200 operational hours per year and a discount rate of 5 per cent. Annual acquisition costs are production costs only.

and US aircraft. The combat effectiveness ranking confirms the US F-22 Raptor as the world's most advanced combat aircraft with Typhoon ranked above the Rafale and other US combat aircraft.

Table 13.8   Relative combat effectiveness

Aircraft	Combat effectiveness
F-22	0.91
Typhoon	0.82
F-15F	0.60
Rafale	0.50
F-18E/F Super Hornet	0.25
F-16C	0.21
F-18 Hornet	0.21

Note: Combat effectiveness rating of 1.0 means that the aircraft will always win a combat engagement; 0.5 means that it has an even chance and less than 0.5 means that it will usually lose (HCP 299, 1992). The US F-35 was not available when the 1992 study was undertaken.

Output

Scales of output are a further indicator of competitiveness showing the achievement of scale and learning economies. Table 13.9 shows output levels for European and US combat aircraft. US scales of output are considerably greater than those in Europe, resulting in American aerospace firms achieving substantial economies of scale and learning, leading to lower unit production costs. Typical national output levels for US combat aircraft exceed 1,000 units which is considerably greater than typical European output levels. For the European nations to achieve US scales of output requires either export sales and/or international collaboration.

However, care is needed when making international comparisons of unit costs. Nations operate on different unit cost curves so whilst a nation might be producing at a large scale of output, it might be operating on a unit cost curve which is at a higher level than its rivals. As a result, a nation with a smaller scale of output might actually achieve lower unit costs. The position is illustrated in Figure 13.1 where nation A (e.g. France; UK) with small-scale output but operating on a lower unit cost curve (upc_0) achieves lower unit costs than nation B (e.g. USA) with a larger scale of output but operating on a higher unit cost curve (upc_1).

Table 13.9   Output levels

Aircraft	Output Levels (including exports)
Gripen	278
Rafale	351
Typhoon	571
F-15A-D	1,198
F-15 E (Eagle)	814
F-16	4,500+
F-18 Hornet	1,480
F-18E/F Super Hornet	665
F-22	195 (187 operational aircraft)
F-35	3,163

Note: Outputs at July 2014 including planned orders and export sales.

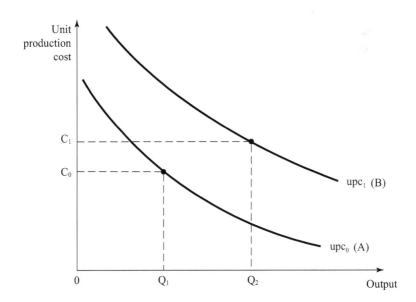

Figure 13.1   Unit production cost and scale of output

Collaboration for the Three European Types

Consider the output implications if the European nations currently producing three different types of combat aircraft had chosen to collaborate. The result would have been one type of combat aircraft produced for the air forces of six European nations. Total orders for the nation's air forces would have been some 900 units (national orders only excluding exports) which is much greater than the scale of national orders for each of the current three types. In addition, there would have been savings in R&D costs since only one R&D bill would have been incurred. For illustrative purposes only, assume that Rafale is selected by all six European nations. Compared with the current three types, the selection of Rafale would lead to possible savings in development costs of Euros 32.2 billion (for Gripen and Typhoon) and possible savings in unit production costs of over 20 per cent. However, some of these cost savings might be reduced if, as seems likely, the six nation programme is characterised by inefficient work-sharing arrangements.

This chapter has focused on three European combat aircraft and their US rivals. A broader question now needs to be considered, namely, which have been the successful collaborative aerospace projects?

SUCCESSFUL AEROSPACE COLLABORATIONS

A successful collaboration requires an assessment of its costs and benefits. Aerospace collaboration has embraced both military and civil projects comprising aircraft, helicopters, missiles and space systems. This section presents some limited indicators for measuring the performance of projects and is meant to be illustrative and suggestive rather than definitive.

Military aerospace projects are assessed in terms of output and exports with comparisons between collaborative and similar national projects. Table 13.10 presents some examples for military aircraft. In terms of output, exports and export shares, it is noticeable that most national projects have achieved better performances than similar collaborative projects.

Airbus as a Successful Collaboration

In the civil aircraft market, Airbus is often regarded as the example of a successful European collaboration. It is a world-class firm forming a

Table 13.10   Identifying successful military aircraft collaborations

Aircraft	Total Output (units)	Exports (units)	Export share of output (%)
Alpha Jet	503	152	30
Hawk	1,000+	797+	80
Jaguar	603	200	33
Mirage 2000	601	315	52
Tornado	992	120	12
F-111	563	24	4
Typhoon	571	99	17
Gripen	278	102	37
Rafale	351	126	36

Note: Alpha Jet was a Franco-German collaboration; its comparator is the BAE Hawk. Jaguar was a France–UK project; its comparator is the Dassault Mirage. Tornado was a Germany–Italy–UK collaboration; its comparator is the General Dynamics F-111.

duopoly with Boeing in the world large jet civil aircraft market. Interestingly, Airbus was a relatively recent new entrant to the US-dominated jet civil aircraft market, entering the market in 1969 and achieving parity with Boeing by 2009. It has achieved US scales of output for its major jet airliners (e.g. output of A320 family of 6,132 units at mid-2014). Airbus demonstrates that European collaboration can be successful in terms of creating a world class rival to Boeing (McIntyre, 1992).

There are, however, differences between Airbus and European military aerospace collaborations. Airbus success has been in civil aircraft markets where there are large numbers of buyers, many being privately-owned profit-seeking airlines. Airbus is also a European company with a permanent existence compared with the usual *ad hoc* consortium for military aerospace collaborations. Furthermore, Airbus has a small number of partner nations (two major partners and a junior partner) which might demonstrate the success of collaborations based on small numbers of partner nations (Hartley and Braddon, 2014).

CONCLUSION

Inefficiencies in military aerospace collaborations need to be addressed. These inefficiencies arise from duplication in procurement and in industrial arrangements, from work shares, from a lack of market incentives and hard budget constraints and from a large number of partner nations. Some proposals for improving efficiency include the appointment of a single prime contractor, allocating work on the basis of competitiveness, awarding fixed price or target cost incentive contracts and restricting the number of partners to two nations (additional partner nations would join as junior partners similar to the F-35 industrial arrangements).

REFERENCES

DA (2006). *Real Cost of Fighter Aircraft*, Defence-Aerospace.com.

Eliasson, G. (2010). *Advanced Public Procurement as Industrial Policy: Aircraft Industry as a Technical University*, Springer Sciences and Business Media, New York.

Hartley, K. (2008). *The Industrial and Economic Benefits of Eurofighter Typhoon*, Eurofighter, Munich.

Hartley, K. (2012). *White Elephants? The Political Economy of Multi-National Defence Projects*, New Direction, The Foundation for European Reform, Brussels, October.

Hartley, K. and Braddon, D. (2014). Collaborative projects and the number of partner nations, *Defence and Peace Economics* (forthcoming).

HCP 222 (1994). *Progress on the Eurofighter 2000 Programme*, Defence Committee, House of Commons, HMSO, London.

HCP 299 (1992). *European Fighter Aircraft*, Defence Committee House of Commons, HMSO, London.

Janes (2012). *All the World's Aircraft*, Janes Information Group, Surrey.

McIntyre, I. (1992). *Dogfight: The TransAtlantic Fight Over Airbus*, Praeger, London.

NAO (2001). *Maximising the Benefits of Defence Equipment Co-operation*, National Audit Office, HCP 300, TSO, London.

NAO (2011). *Management of the Typhoon Project*, National Audit Office, HCP 755, TSO, London.

NAO (2013). *The Major Projects Report 2012*, National Audit Office, HCP 684, TSO, London.

Vijver, M. and Vos, B. (2006). The F-35 Joint Strike Fighter as a Source of Innovation and Employment: Some Interim Results, *Defence and Peace Economics*, 17, 2, 155–159.

14. Future prospects

INTRODUCTION: KEY QUESTIONS

Predicting the future of the aerospace industry and the role of public policy over the next 50 years is fraught with difficulties and is well-nigh impossible. The future is characterised by unknowns and unknowables. At best, speculations rather than predictions can be made about possible general trends and their potential influence on aerospace industries.

No one can predict accurately the future. Austrian economists focus on the role of uncertainty and the impossibility of predicting accurately future changes in demand and supply in domestic and world markets. Consumer preferences are not static and are always changing. In the past, for example, horses and carriages were replaced by motor cars, air travel replaced some surface travel, mobile phones have replaced landline phones and computers have replaced secretaries. Supply side changes are caused by new entrants, lower-cost sources of supply and new technology. Examples include the emergence of new aerospace industries and new firms, the development of international supply chains (globalisation) and technical progress reflected in the introduction of jet engines, UAVs and space exploration. As a result, the comparative advantages and disadvantages of a nation's industries are not fixed in perpetuity. Aerospace is no exception.

Austrians view competition as a rivalrous process with private sector entrepreneurs seeking to outperform each other. With this approach, competition is both innovative and destructive: it is about producers who discover new lower production costs or identify new demand opportunities. Innovative competition involves new products, new technology, new sources of supply and new types of organisation. Entrepreneurs who identify these new opportunities before their rivals are more likely to be rewarded with profits but if their judgements are wrong, then they will incur losses leading to exit from the unsuccessful sector (Boettke, 1994).

However, the Austrian 'story' has limitations when applied to aerospace industries and their future prospects. Aerospace industries continue to be dominated by governments rather than private entrepreneurs. Governments dominate aerospace industries through their military demands, their involvement in state funding of civil aircraft development and through their ownership of firms. As major buyers of defence aerospace equipment, governments can use their buying power to determine the size, structure, conduct, performance and ownership of their national aerospace industry. They also influence the civil aerospace industry through their willingness to fund new civil aircraft and engine programmes and their control over national property rights (e.g. over-flying and landing rights). Governments might also own aerospace firms. Without ownership rights, the manager of a state-owned aerospace enterprise has no incentives to consider consumer demands nor the opportunity cost of scarce resources because neither profits nor losses provide an incentive mechanism for good or poor performance.

Recognition of the role of government suggests that public choice models provide a more appropriate basis for analysing and understanding aerospace industries (Chapter 9). On this view, governments will seek to 'pick the winners' in the form of those firms it believes will be the future successes. Their choices will be strongly influenced by established interest groups of bureaucrats and producers where firms seek revenue from governments in the form of preferential purchasing, protection and subsidies. If government choices are 'wrong', they can be blamed on decisions by the previous government and the taxpayer funds the costs of failure.

Can governments respond to the uncertainties identified by Austrian economists? Governments are not entrepreneurs: they do not have the market knowledge and skills to identify new market opportunities and new forms of industrial organisation. Instead, governments are more likely to protect their national aerospace industries from competition in its innovative and destructive forms. John Stuart Mill famously stated that 'There are some things with which governments ought not to meddle and other things which they ought; but whether right or wrong in itself, the interference must work for ill, if government not understanding the subject which it meddles with, meddles to bring about a result which would be mischievous' (Mill, 1883, p552). Aerospace industries are witness to the mischiefs of governments failing to understand the industry!

This chapter explores the possible future for aerospace industries over the next 50 years. It does not claim to present a comprehensive view of the future (an impossible task guaranteed to be wrong). Instead, it outlines possible trends likely to affect the future industry. Governments and military demands are the obvious starting point.

MILITARY DEMANDS: FUTURE THREATS

History shows that we have yet to achieve a peaceful world where, as Isaiah stated, 'swords are converted into plowshares ... and nations will not learn warfare anymore' (Isaiah, 1976). Instead, the world remains a dangerous place where new threats to peace and security are always emerging. In 2014, there was a lengthy list of threats comprising potential threats in the Ukraine and Crimea, nuclear proliferation, terrorism, continued tensions in the Middle East, civil war in Syria, tensions between North and South Korea, Japan and China and conflicts in Africa. It is not unknown for what appears to be minor events becoming the catalyst for major wars (e.g. origins of World War I).

Over the next 50 years, completely new threats will emerge in different parts of the world, including space. Nonetheless, the basic form of threat will remain unchanged, namely, a threat to the security and protection of a nation's citizens, their property and assets and its national interests. Threats will be reflected in increased defence spending by potential enemies leading to risks of conflict from an arms race; or, in contrast, risks and threats arising from reductions in defence spending making a nation more vulnerable to attack (Hartley, 2011). Conflict will continue to result from the desire of nations to achieve a re-allocation of resources by using military force. Examples include a nation using military force to acquire more territory, more natural resources and population and to acquire 'strategic positions' (e.g. Golan Heights). These continued threats lead to military demands for defence spending some of which will be in the form of aerospace equipment required by air, land and sea forces.

The military demands for aerospace equipment will be subject to technical change. New technologies will emerge and armed forces will demand such 'state of the art' equipment. Historical examples include the original introduction of manned aircraft, the impact of the jet engine, the emergence of missiles, rockets and UAVs. Some of these new technologies had major substitution effects on armed forces. Missiles replaced manned combat aircraft, attack helicopters replaced tanks, maritime patrol aircraft replaced surface warships and nuclear forces replaced large-scale conventional forces. The immediate future will see a focus on the role of UAVs and their substitution for manned aircraft and ground troops (e.g. in long-endurance surveillance roles; drone attacks on foreign terrorist bases). Some substitution effects have implications for the traditional monopoly property rights of each of the armed forces. For example, ground-based air defence missiles and attack helicopters operated by armies and cruise missiles operated by navies might replace manned combat aircraft operated by air forces. Future threats from terrorism will mean greater emphasis on acquiring information and knowledge and on policing mass transit systems (e.g. underground and surface rail travel). There will be new demands for surveillance systems which will favour the electronics industry. As a result of these possible changes, questions will arise about the future viability of an independent air force.

Economics will also determine the future of a nation's armed forces and its aerospace industry. Three factors will be crucial, namely, the size of national defence budgets, its allocation between each of the armed forces and cost trends for military aerospace equipment. Wars and the threat of conflict will lead to higher defence spending but peace will result in lower defence spending and national preferences for social welfare spending (e.g. education, health, care for the elderly and disadvantaged). Air forces are not cheap: they demand equipment which is costly and whose unit costs continue to rise. Norman Augustine famously forecast that by 2054, the US would only be able to afford a single combat aircraft which would have to be shared by the air force and navy except for a leap year when it would be available to the marines for the extra day! Advocates of helicopters suggest that a single helicopter solution would be reached in 2064. The UK was expected to reach the single aircraft solution by 2052 (Augustine, 1987, pp143–144). Critics point to the limitations of simple extrapolations of past trends in unit costs. However, the general point is that continued rising unit costs will mean smaller production orders for military aircraft and smaller numbers of aerospace equipment operated by the armed forces.

The trend towards smaller production runs for military aircraft will create pressures for international collaboration and incentives to replace nationally produced with imported equipment. There will be attempts to change the historical trend towards rising unit costs. An example is joint procurement where a variety of national requirements are combined into a single national requirement as in the case of the US F-35 aircraft purchased for the Air Force, Navy and Marines. New technology might also represent an opportunity to change the traditional historical trend of rising unit costs. However, the emergence of UAVs is unlikely to be the solution. One view forecasts 'that by the time unmanned aerial vehicles are as capable as their manned counterparts they will have become equally as expensive and, so, just as unaffordable' (Pugh, 2007, p31). Nor has the end of the Cold War made any difference to unit cost escalation: it has continued as before with the unit costs of combat aircraft more than doubling between generations. As a result, the UK and similar sized nations are unlikely to be able to afford a replacement for Typhoon (or

Gripen or Rafale): a successor to Typhoon would be at least four times its unit cost (Pugh, 2007, p29). On this basis, some commentators have forecast the end of manned combat aircraft. Already, some of the world's air forces are unable to afford fast jets and have abandoned a fast jet fleet (e.g. New Zealand).

Space is a further dimension which cannot be ignored. Military satellites are the basis for international communications and surveillance. The Outer Space Treaty prohibits the use of nuclear weapons and other weapons of mass destruction in space and limits the military use of the moon and other planets. The Treaty establishes space as a common property resource. However, the Treaty lacks an effective monitoring and policing agency. For the future, it is possible that a nation or nations will regard space warfare as offering 'first mover' advantages: it provides an opportunity to destroy a nation's satellite system and its communications and surveillance capability. Space warfare might involve ground to space and space on space conflict which will create demands for completely new space vehicles and missiles. Hollywood has provided visions of space warfare!

Certainly the future will be different from the present. Military procurement numbers for national aerospace industries will continue to decline. Questions arise about whether future new projects might be funded privately? Private funding for costly new military aircraft projects is unlikely. The high costs and risks of such projects means that private firms will be reluctant to risk a firm's assets on projects which rely on one customer and have no alternative-use value. Also, governments usually impose barriers to new entrants so restricting the opportunities for new ideas. However, private funding might be available for relatively cheap demonstrator programmes to assess new technologies, especially where such technologies have value in other uses and where the demonstrator costs might be recouped from future government sales.[1] Declining military sales will also persuade aerospace firms to seek alternative civil markets, leading to more diversified firms.

---

[1] In 2014, there is an example of a new privately funded military aircraft initiative. A joint venture between Cessna and a new entrant, namely, Textron AirLand is developing a light attack fighter known as the Scorpion. This is the first US fighter developed independently of US government support since the Northrop F-20 Tiger-shark. It is seeking a launch customer (Flight, 2014).

CIVIL AEROSPACE DEMANDS: NEW HORIZONS

Generally, technical change proceeds on an evolutionary basis, occasionally subject to revolutionary change. The jet engine was a revolutionary change and since its introduction, technical change in civil aircraft has been evolutionary. Since the first jet airliners were introduced in 1952, they have developed into larger, faster and longer-range aircraft. These trends are reflected in the examples shown in Table 14.1 which compare the first generation jet airliner with those of today. Modern jet airliners fly faster and further with more passengers, fewer crew and fewer engines; but in current prices, they are much costlier. High costs and rising unit costs mean that civil jet airliners are subject to the Augustine problem identified for military aircraft. But civil markets are different in that the demand for civil aircraft depends on the income and wealth of large numbers of private consumers and their preferences for air travel.

Table 14.1   Technical progress in jet airliners, 1952 to 2014

Features	DH Comet	Boeing 787 Dreamliner	Airbus A380
In-service date	1952	2011	2007
Number of passengers	36–44	280–323	525–853
Cruising speed	460mph	567mph	587mph
Range	1,500mls	9,030mls	9,755mls
Number of crew	4	2	2
Number of engines	4	2	4
Unit price ($ million)	0.89 (1952)	212–289 (2013)	404 (2013)

Note: Figures in brackets show date of unit prices – e.g. Comet prices are in 1952 prices.

Jet airliners have shown evolutionary technical progress. A good example is the Boeing 737 which entered service in 1968 and by 2014 was the world's best-selling jet airliner which has been subject to modifications, upgrades, fuselage extensions and new engines. Evolutionary developments include the use of new and lighter materials, improved flight control systems and greater safety.

Over time, jet engines have become more fuel-efficient and more powerful leading to large, long-range twin jets replacing three and four-engine airliners. The future jet engine will be more fuel-efficient, more powerful, more reliable, quieter and more environmentally friendly. A focus on higher speeds means a return to supersonic travel (cf. Concorde) which will have to be more efficient and more environmentally friendly. New engine technology will be the key to future developments in civil airliners and might revolutionise jet airliners (e.g. rocket engine technology).

Large jet airliners and their engines will need financing. Traditionally, governments have been involved in providing such finance but WTO decisions might limit the future availability of state funds. If so, prime contractors will seek new methods of raising private sector funds. Examples include the greater use of risk-sharing partnerships with global suppliers and their subcontractors and the possibility of profit-sharing arrangements on specific projects (e.g. Airbus A350; Boeing 787).

Elsewhere, other civil aircraft sectors offer new market opportunities, especially where there are extensive opportunities for new entrants. Examples include space travel, helicopters and light aircraft, all of which are potential fields for private funding. Space represents a completely new civil market, available for private travellers willing and able to pay the required price. Helicopters might also be a market awaiting a new technical breakthrough providing higher speeds, greater passenger loads, greater range, quieter machines and much improved reliability and safety. For light aviation (e.g. pleasure flying), there are opportunities for developing relatively cheap jet aircraft. Changes in both military and civil markets will affect the future aerospace firm.

THE FUTURE AEROSPACE FIRM

The future aerospace firm will be different from the firms of today. For instance, compare the aerospace firms of the early 1900s with those of 1945 and today. Today's giant aerospace firms did not exist in the early 1900s and many of the firms which existed in 1945 have since disappeared either through acquisitions and mergers or through exits (e.g. Supermarine company which manufactured the Spitfire no longer exists). In fact, the long-run trend appears to be towards a smaller number of larger aerospace firms.

Currently, there are two broad types of private-enterprise aerospace firm. First, there is the defence specialist supplying military aerospace equipment together with a range of other land, sea and defence electronics equipment (e.g. BAE Systems; Lockheed Martin; Northrop Grumman). Second, there is the specialist aerospace firm supplying a range of military and civil aircraft (e.g. Airbus; Boeing). None of these firms existed in the early 1900s; few existed in 1945 and even fewer will exist in 50 years' time.

Under private ownership, new forms of industrial organisation will emerge reflecting the search for lower transaction costs resulting in different combinations of making in-house versus buying-in specialist tasks from global suppliers. For example, the future aerospace firm might be a systems house undertaking some specialist R&D with all production activities based overseas in an international supply chain (e.g. final assembly lines). The Internet provides access to world-wide suppliers, including specialist design firms. The future aerospace firms will be able to 'buy-in' specialist design services so that they no longer need to retain large in-house design and development teams, especially during troughs in development work. There will be continued industrial re-structuring with further mergers, especially amongst suppliers and new opportunities for international mergers (e.g. trans-Atlantic aerospace firms). Continued pressures on defence budgets and rising unit costs will lead to incentives to make greater use of civil firms, their technologies and their expertise. As a result, there will be opportunities for mergers and acquisitions between aerospace and non-aerospace firms where large diversified firms provide insurance against the risks and instabilities of aerospace defence markets. Mergers with large electronics firms are one possibility.

Governments will determine the extent of future industry rationalisation and consolidation through their commitment to maintaining competition in domestic military aerospace markets and their willingness to allow national and international mergers. There are, of course, alternative policies for retaining competition in national military aerospace markets. Examples include the use of competing technology demonstrators or a willingness to buy aerospace equipment from foreign suppliers. Or, governments might have to accept that it is no longer possible to maintain competition within national defence markets. In the absence of domestic competition, governments will have to develop rules for regulating privately-owned national monopolies, including the determination of prices and profitability whilst providing efficiency incentives for non-competitive contracts. The alternative model is to transfer ownership from the private sector to the state sector. Whatever the form of ownership, a trend towards larger aerospace firms will create powerful producer groups seeking to influence defence aerospace and civil aerospace policy (e.g. defence procurement policy; contract awards; funding for new civil aircraft and engines).

There is also the challenge of maintaining 'key' national aerospace defence industrial capabilities during gaps in development and production. Here, policy options include support for national aerospace research teams through technology demonstrator programmes, the award of small-scale production orders to retain industrial capability and the option of 'mothballing' key physical capital (e.g. retaining empty plants; storing jigs and tools). Each policy has its costs and benefits which need to be addressed. For example, the 'mothballing' option appears cheap but it ignores the costs of retaining the 'mothballed' facility and the costs and time required to regenerate a skilled labour force (this process is not like turning on a cold water tap!).

Finding ways of sustaining key aerospace skills for national defence demands will be challenging for all nations. These key skills need to be identified. Military aircraft design and production requires some unique skills which are not found in the civil aircraft sector and once lost, they are difficult and costly to rebuild (Arena et al., 2013).

Governments will have a central role in determining the future of their national aerospace defence industrial capability. They will have to determine which sectors are to be retained, how, at what cost and their willingness to pay. Here, there might be benefits from international collective action. Groups of nations might agree to pool and share their aerospace defence industrial capabilities. Examples include the bilateral defence co-operation agreement between France and the UK or the development of a European Defence and Technological Industrial Base (EDTIB: Hartley, 2011). The European solution would require the development of a genuinely competitive Single European Equipment Procurement Market. In principle, the EU is committed to both the EDTIB and the Single Market but their achievement probably requires a significant 'external shock' to compel Member States to recognise that independent national solutions are too costly and no longer affordable (e.g. national aerospace defence industries).

There is the further concern that a European solution would require agreement on the sharing of costs for retaining 'key' aerospace defence industrial capabilities (which will raise burden-sharing debates). Nor can it be assumed that a European aerospace industrial solution would be based on economic principles of efficiency and comparative advantage: instead, the focus will be on *'juste retour'* principles with nations seeking their 'fair shares' of work and industrial capabilities (cf. Common Agricultural Policy applied to European aerospace defence industries). A European solution would also require trust between Member States: each state would have to be confident that its needs for re-supply in a conflict would be met.

CONCLUSION

In considering the future of the aerospace industry, two final questions need to be raised. First, does the aerospace firm have a future; and what might be the future role for government?

The aerospace firm has a future and will exist in 50 years' time. There will be a substantial civil aerospace business as well as a military business. Unless there is a sudden, unexpected and sustained outbreak of world peace, there will continue to be a demand for military aerospace equipment which requires aerospace defence firms. But the future aerospace firm of 2065 will be radically different. It will be even larger with a mixture of military and civil aerospace business together with civil non-aerospace business providing insurance against downturns in defence markets as well as access to dual-use technologies, products, management and business practices.

Governments will continue to dominate the industry. They remain major buyers in aerospace defence markets with their buying power to influence the ownership, size, structure, conduct and performance of the industry. Government funding determines new technology; it provides finance for the development of new civil aircraft and engines; and it funds entry into new aerospace markets (e.g. space).

These are some of the many major challenges affecting the future of the aerospace industry. There is no doubt that the industry will survive but to survive and prosper, it will have to change quite radically. This is an industry facing exciting times offering new opportunities for 'those magnificent men and women in their flying machines'.

REFERENCES

Arena, M.V., Graser, J.C. and DeLuca, P. (2013). *Implications of an Air Force Budget Downturn on the Aircraft Industrial Base*, Research Report, Rand, Santa Monica.
Augustine, N.R. (1987). *Augustine's Laws*, Penguin Books, London.
Boettke, P.J. (ed.) (1994). *Austrian Economics*, Elgar Companion, Edward Elgar Publishing, Cheltenham, UK and Northampton, MA, USA.
Flight (2014). Can Scorpion repeat success of the Super Tweet? *Flight International*, 18–24 March, p36, Quadrant House, Surrey.
Hartley, K. (2011). *The Economics of Defence Policy*, Routledge, London.
Isaiah (1976). *Good News Bible*, chapter 2, verse 4, p667, Collins Fontana, London.
Mill, J.S. (1883). *Principles of Political Economy*, Longmans, Green and Co, London.
Pugh, P.G. (2007). Retrospect and Prospect: Trends in cost and their implications for UK Aerospace, *Defence and Peace Economics*, 18, 1, 25–37.

Index